GLAUCO CAMBON

DANTE'S CRAFT
Studies in Language and Style

THE UNIVERSITY OF MINNESOTA PRESS
Minneapolis

FOR AUSTIN WARREN, MY FRIEND

ACKNOWLEDGMENTS

THE essays brought together and revised for inclusion in this volume have appeared in various places, and for permission to reprint them here I am indebted to the editors of the Michigan Academy of Science, Arts, and Letters, *Modern Language Quarterly*, *Italica*, *Books Abroad*, *Dante Studies*, *Aut Aut*, *Sewanee Review*, and V. Bompiani and Company of Milan. Chapter II, originally delivered in 1964 as a lecture at the University of Toronto, was published in *The World of Dante*, edited by S. B. Chandler and J. A. Molinaro, in 1966 and is reprinted by permission of the University of Toronto Press. Chapter IV appeared in *A Dante Symposium*, edited by Gino Rizzo and William De Sua, in 1965 and is reprinted by permission of the University of North Carolina Press. Special thanks are due the Johns Hopkins Press for permission to reprint my essay "Vico and Dante," which was written for their 1969 publication, *Giambattista Vico: An International Symposium*, edited by Giorgio Tagliacozzo, co-editor, Hayden V. White.

My textual quotations from Dante are from *Le opere di Dante* (second edition, Florence, 1960), published by the Dante Society of Italy, and are used with the society's permission. The English translations are of course my own.

I am grateful to the Research Council of Rutgers University, to Professor Remigio Pane of the Romance Languages Department at Rutgers, to the Fulbright program of scholarly exchange, and to Professor Agostino Lombardo of Rome University for enabling me to attend to this and other projects in Italy. My wife, Marlis Zeller Cambon, is entitled to more gratitude than words can express for her unabated assistance and encouragement.

G. C.

1967–68

TABLE OF CONTENTS

Dante's Craft

DANTE'S PROPHETIC VISION

IF THESE essays of mine, which are nothing but a drop in the flood of Dante studies, need any explanation, I can only say that for me there was an impulse to obey. The impulse came from a lifelong affection for the stark, rich poetry of the formidable master, from a realization of his relevance to what is strongest in modern literature, and finally from a personal disregard of scholarly monopolies. All roads led me to Dante. Eugenio Montale's germane Italian voice, Thomas Mann's *Kulturkritik*, the apocalyptic utterances of Herman Melville, T. S. Eliot, Ezra Pound, W. B. Yeats, and Robert Lowell were all inducements to reopen my Dante volume, again and again. In this way my loosely-knit booklet insinuated itself on me as the inevitable outgrowth of several aspects and phases of my critical work on the moderns.

Dante's viability for modern literature springs from the depth and latitude of his own probing into the tangled darkness and light of human existence; and, as some of the essays here collected attempt to show, I have come to believe that Dante can give invaluable clues to the reader of contemporary poetry, whether in its expression of derangement in a new Dark Wood or in its rare glimpses of felicity and wholeness. The point has been eloquently made by Theophil Spoerri, and, in a different way, by Allen Tate and Francis Fergusson, not to speak of T. S. Eliot, whose earlier testimonial on Dante's "classic" status was corroborated by assiduous exercise of poetry along lines of despair, experiment, and belief which the medieval poet himself would not have disowned.

Dante's use of his background, rather than his conditioning by it, has been my focus of interest; which is like saying that at all times the *Comedy* has appealed to me as the adventure of poetry, the very making of it, apart from its doctrinal assumptions. I found a counterpart to such an experimental approach in the statements of Gianfranco Contini,[1] whose 1965 essay on the *Comedy* was published by a Florentine review long after I had delivered my lecture on Dante's drama of language, here represented as a duly footnoted chapter. Needless to say, I was happy to see my own emphasis on Dante's stylistic and linguistic versatility so authoritatively confirmed. And generally speaking, after Spitzer and Auerbach, my attention to the phenomena of style, particularly as exemplified in the chapter on the episode of Paolo and Francesca, should require no defense.

The above considerations bring me to Croce. Croce's iconoclastic reading, the scandal of orthodox Dantists, has long been replaced by the organic and integral (or structural) interpretation we owe to such scholars and critics as Charles Singleton, who insists on the necessity of reading Dante against the background of his theological culture, mainly lost to us modern skeptics. It took some temerity, therefore, to vindicate what was vital in Croce's unfashionable approach (in Croce's, and in his master Francesco De Sanctis'). That temerity, witness Chapter IV, was only a calculated risk. I appreciate the work of careful readers like Singleton, and I am the first to admit that Dante's high points should not be wrenched out of context, because I believe in the intrinsic relevance of the total structure to the texture of Dante's poetry, as my chapter on "Patterns of Movement" tries to prove.

I do, however, fear that by now the shift of emphasis to doctrinal and structural exegesis may have entailed serious losses on the side of poetical immediacy. Granted that we should keep in mind Dante's historical background — namely, what nurtured him and thereby afforded him the subject matter of his imaginative grasp — are we then to conceive of him as so historically conditioned that he cannot speak to us at all without philological intermediaries? What comes first, the history (and that includes the "ideology" or philosophy) or the poetry? We know what Croce's answer was, and it does not take his extremism to realize that something in the approach of doctrinal structuralism may make for warping interpretations. As a consequence, I take my stand somewhat to the left of the theological structuralists because I cannot subordinate each episode's insight to the overall scheme of the great poem if that should mean obliterating the unpredictable. Brunetto Latini is not the perfect sodomite, nor is Farinata the darkest heretic, and, as to Ulysses, he retains his heroic stature within the circumscribing context. Dante clearly could have used worse felons than Ugolino to embody the sin of compound treachery if that had been his dominant purpose rather than a complex portrayal of human nature which somehow can survive its own perversion.

The unity of Dante's poem should be thought of not as monolithic, but as elastic. There is a resilience in his moral imagination which allows him to honor the damned without disowning his God's judgment. How much more tragic this attitude is than that of a one-sided, pious moralist who would go through Hell merely to collect an instructive catalogue of sins, as if what burns, rots, or freezes there were not a part of himself. Thus, contrary to the prevalent opinion, I do think that Croce's radical mistake is more useful to us now than any theological correctness, because it provokes us into revising interpretive categories that may otherwise harden into deathly scaffoldings. Who cares for "unity" if that unity is no living one?

The problem of unity versus individual focus parallels another problem I encountered, that of history versus immediacy. Certain of my essays take a phenomenological approach, for they bracket any preconceived notion of what should be found in or behind the poetry, in order to discover that poetry in its immediacy. Other essays (notably Chapter II) on the contrary insist that a knowledge of Dante the thinker (above all in matters of linguistics and style) is essential to a fuller understanding of Dante the poet. This way a circle of poetry and poetics arises, as an expansion of the original focus on style. Rather than create a contradiction, it should show that while Dante's poetry mainly speaks to us with the clarity of an unclouded language, the poetry itself stimulates us to enlarge our scope by looking into what is not so immediately accessible. In other words, Dante's poetry is "contemporary" to the extent that we favor sharpness, economy, and versatility of style; but his philosophy is anachronistic on many counts, as Santayana well knew. It is the poetry that leads us back to the philosophy, not vice versa; Dante's Middle Ages interest us above all because they *became* Dante in Dante's experience, culminating in his work, though nothing prevents us from taking the reverse path: only let us remember that the latter alternative involves a passage from the specific, concrete, individualized reality of Dante's poetry to the general reality of those facts, ideas, and institutions which existed before and outside his unique poetical experience. From the viewpoint of literature, this would be a regression, not a progress — a dissolution of poetry into its hypothetical chemical components, not a scanning of its live physiognomy.

Yet even this needs qualification; the eschatological element of Dante's medieval Christianity is not lost on our age, beset by a different eschatology; the requirement of ethical choice, Dante's own drama, is to a large extent our own drama, though we are worse equipped than he for solving it. If his poem embodies a quest for truth, so does our best literature, and the idea that man is responsible for himself and can make or unmake himself by his own choice within a cosmic system of values, the idea that Love is the root of all good and all evil in us, likewise appeals to the modern reader as an appropriate myth for a culture engaged in demythologizing itself. A Freudian, an existentialist might spell out the same insight in different and possibly poorer terms.

Along with the circle of poetry and poetics, then, we come to perceive a circle of interaction between Dante's poetry and Dante's philosophy (which includes his historical background), and if at times the nexus between philosophy and poetry can be grasped immediately, it may turn out to remain elusive at other times. A happy example of that immediate nexus, brought about by the overpowering force of poetry, is discernible in the way the key words "Amore" ("Love") and "Muovere" ("Move") innervate the organism of the *Comedy* microcosmically while also governing it on the macrocosmic scale as archetypal ideas. Style and structure here feed on each other, and I hope that my study of Francesca's *Inferno* episode bears it out. Another attempt at descrying the compenetration of structure and style, the mutual enhancement of the macrocosmic and the microcosmic perspective, is represented by my chapter on "Patterns of Movement."

To possess the great poem — a never-ending enterprise — means to keep surveying it at close range and from a distance. It means inhabiting it, and the difficulties of checking the maps with our experiential findings will persist. This did not discourage me from venturing into the Dark Wood. I felt I could not dispense with this bewilderment, and with the attendant exhilaration which is the lot of Dante's reader. Were we but equal to the test, Dante could be to us what Virgil was to him. Dante's voice is ever present as poetry finally is, and not time-bound. If in a way he is remote from our post-Christian age, he is also the first modern voice, the first assertor of the individual self as center of an epic action — a literary arrogance inspired precisely by that Christian philosophy which shaped our Western destiny, down to our apostasies.

Dante's status is that of a classic, and the definition carries overtones of marmoreal finality; but Dante's intervention in the live tangle of his own cultural situation was revolutionary, and he became the father of his language, and by the same token the sponsor of all European vernaculars. While modern experimenters can look up to him for an example of radical innovation (one need only read Dante's Latin eclogues to Giovanni del Virgilio, along with Giovanni's side of the poetical correspondence, to see how truly radical that was), they must feel hopelessly unequal to the model, who came at the right historical juncture to found a culture they have tried so hard to revitalize. The anachronistic aspects of Dante's thought are more than counterbalanced by the historical timeliness, and perennial exemplariness, of his poetry and of his approach to language — since for him too "in the beginning was the Word," whether the word of Virgil, or the word of Christ, or the humble word spoken by Italian gossips in so many alleys and market squares he visited in the course of his pilgrimage. Perhaps, too, profound thought combined with comprehensive poetical utterance is anachronistic in itself; either too much in advance of the times, or too far behind, Dante's dream of unity, justice, and happiness, anchored to Pope Gregory the Great's *respublica christiana* and to Charlemagne's anachronistic Empire, was no exception.

Precisely because he is so anachronistic, so medieval and Ptolemaic, Dante remains so timely, and he can really be all things to all men, so that we can legitimately study him not only in himself (not just his work as a self-contained entity), but also "beyond," "outside" himself, in the writers he has variously affected. The life of a poem, of a man, of an idea, is larger than that poem, that man, that idea. This accounts for my inclusion of the last three chapters in the present collection. Their purpose is to show how an ideal dialogue between Dante and his creative modern readers can be conceived without violating the sense of his, and their, uniqueness. If Dante can speak to us from his remote station in time, what shall we answer? If we are Eliot, or Montale, or Pound, the answer will take the shape of a poem as mysteriously lucid in its way, as ruthlessly critical of the age, as Dante's work was. To a considerable extent, his poetics has become ours, in several respects. Ossip Mandelstam testified to that from the prison camps of Siberia in the nineteen thirties. Dante's prophetic vision, whether in its secular or in its transcendent aspects, has likewise acquired the value of an interpretive archetype for the writer grappling with the modern predicament. Magic Mountain, unappealable Court, labyrinthic Castle, Waste Land, No-exit Hell: these and other myths of the modern imagination have Dantean ancestry; and who but Dante should teach us how to face the resurgent nightmares?

PART ONE *The Example*

CHAPTER I

DANTE'S *CONVIVIO*
THE DIALECTIC OF VALUE

I F W E take at face value Dante's own statements on the genesis of the *Convivio*, we shall be tempted to reduce this work to an act of politically motivated self-defense, as some modern scholars have done.[1] In *Conv.* i, ii, 15–17, he mentions fear of infamy, along with the desire to convey a doctrine nobody else could, as his main reason for undertaking the learned commentary on his own misread poems, and a passage in *Conv.* iii, i, 11,[2] clearly confirms this. Allegory as a strategy of self-defense can be a very devious thing,[3] and when Dante insists that the *donna gentile* who temporarily usurped Beatrice's place in his heart and in his verse was no creature of flesh and blood, but Lady Philosophy,[4] one might conceivably suspect this maneuver of being nothing more than a clever rationalization. Dante would not be the only undependable self-explicator in literary history.

Yet, difficult as it is to disentangle the possibly rationalizing superstructure from the straightforward part of his amazing prose, one cannot dismiss its recurrent tone of deep commitment, or the poetical imagery which informs the unfinished treatise.[5] The motivation itself, as given by Dante, is mixed and credible: he wants to clear his name from any belittling or immoral implications that biased critics may have read into his poetical work, but at the same time he is obeying the urge to explain himself to a wider public, to communicate his world view, to establish a method of literary interpretation valid for any poetry and not just his own. Thus in the process of self-explanation we can see the writer outgrowing his initial impulse, the occasion that sparked the fire of thought: as he has it, when you are looking for silver you may very well come across gold. And if in our exploration of the *Convivio* we give up the silver of factual biography for the gold of self-transcending revelation, we shall have bypassed a cumbersome obstacle on our way to the understanding of the book.

It is both confession and theory, and the theory sometimes obscures the confession by introducing extraneous material; yet this much at least is clear, that the theorizing impulse leads the reader beyond and above the merely private facts of the author's life, while endeavoring to reach the haven of self-knowledge through a stormy period of existence. Dante wants to be considered an *exemplum*, not just a *casus*; and in this light even the machinery of the fourfold method of allegorical interpretation, which he mounts at the very beginning of the second trattato and painstakingly applies to the first two canzones, acquires a plausible physiognomy for the modern reader who is unwilling to appropriate that peculiar *forma mentis* of the Middle Ages. The allegory of the *Convivio* is much more contrived than that of the *Comedy*, where it mostly coincides with spontaneous symbolization; yet even in the *Convivio* we can penetrate its scaffoldings, and what we see there is basically a force that points away from petty individualism in the direction of universal values. This in itself is not devious, when we think that the effort to be known, to know himself, and to know the ultimate — heterogeneous as it appears here — will finally result in the successfully fused discourse of the *Comedy*, where theory and confession, poetry and explication, are simultaneous in the creative act of the mind. In the *Convivio* Dante is groping toward the certainties he will reach only in the great poem by discarding self-justification for self-accusation as an initial posture; and this means that the earlier, more awkward book is chiefly viable to us as a quest for value, for the enduring significance of personal events, struggles, and ideas.

Such is the overall direction of the commentary, as can be seen from many striking details; nobody, for instance, will fail to respond to Dante's telling choice of scriptural poetry as an adequate sample text for allegorical illustration: Psalm 114, both in the *Convivio*'s second trattato and in the Epistle to Can Grande, not to mention its focal quotation in *Purgatorio* II, 46, "*In exitu Israel de Aegypto* . . ." The Florentine exile dreamed of transforming his banishment into deliverance, but Florence was both his Egypt and his Promised Land. Like the two Latin treatises and the Italian epic for the sake of which he left the *Convivio* unfinished, the latter transitional work is to be more deeply understood from the situation of exile, which provided Dante with the existential motivation for his philosophical and literary quest.

This motivation will enable us to see the autobiographical element itself in a universal light; inner biography will then supersede factual biography, and the nexus between the personal element on the one hand, and linguistics, aesthetics, politics, history, epistemology, and cosmology on the other, will become clearer. A man wronged by ruthless enemy factions and uprooted from his home would naturally cling to whatever image rose in his mind with the promise of enduring compensation; if he could no longer retain his local roots on earth, he would have to put forth new ones in the heaven of mind and being. Love was a god of hunger, and love prompted the wanderer to speak of his book in terms of wheat and bread, the *Panis angelorum* of a Platonic banquet to which he invited mankind, or at least the Latin part of it, in an infinite gesture of self-giving. Love was a god of doubt, and evoked in his mind competing images — Beatrice beckoning from the higher spheres of memory and the *donna gentile*, perhaps Lady Philosophy, perhaps a more terrestrial goddess, claiming the allegiance of his soul:

> Tu non se' morta, ma se' ismarrita,
> anima nostra, che sì ti lamenti . . .
>
> You are not dead, but just bewildered,
> o soul of ours who is lamenting so . . .

Love, as a god of curiosity, took the guise of study to become an *amor dei intellectualis* . . . The Latin etymology of *studio* was not consciously grasped by our poet when he thus tried to make his passion plausible, but of course *studium* originally meant zest, and Dante was reviving the secret history of a word in his apparently arbitrary equation; Boethius had sought consolation in philosophy, and if that exalted lady had been enough to light the darkness of jail for the Roman senator, she could certainly serve the Tuscan pilgrim. Even with Dante's elucidation, we don't know exactly how to take the canzone of the warring ladies, except that like Poe's *Ulalume* it bears abundant witness to a mental drama. To complicate matters, Beatrice's powerful rival, Lady Philosophy, who seems to install herself as a victor in Dante's mind after a certain point (second canzone and third trattato) and to provide fulfillment in the form of godlike or God-enlightened speculation, takes on more and more of Beatrice's own traits: she tames pride, she inspires humility, she receives and imparts a divine power (*virtù divina*), she overpowers the human mind with the radiance of her smile and darts flames of love. Compare especially the fourth stanza of the canzone beginning with the line "Amor che ne la mente mi ragiona" with the *Vita Nuova*'s canzone "Donne ch'avete intelletto d'amore," fourth stanza, and you will wonder if Dante himself was aware of the ambiguity. Is the new lady a usurper, or merely another aspect of Beatrice? Be that as it may, the conflict of images expresses a crucial stage in Dante's groping for the meaning of existence. Possibly realizing the difficulty, he eventually dropped the subject to pass on to the issue of nobility in the third canzone ("Le dolci rime d'amor ch'io solia") and the appended fourth trattato — which moreover states how this last part of the work refrains from allegory with a view to presenting as plainly as possible a very direct problem rooted in history. The nonallegorical canzone also tells us how Her Philosophical Highness had behaved haughtily to our poet; and this may mean that after finding his highest value in an intellectual approach Dante was dissatisfied with it and temporarily abandoned the dangerous ground of abstract speculation to revert to the safer area of history.

Thus redescending to earth from a rarefied atmosphere, the fourth chapter of the *Convivio* is symmetrical with respect to the first in its straightforwardness. This discussion of nobility stems, of course, from Guinizelli's canzone "Al cor gentil ripara sempre Amore" as well as from other sources, like Guido delle Colonne and Thomas Aquinas.[6] The central idea — that nobility does not reside in riches and cannot be inherited because it is an attainment of the individual, an accomplishment of the heart and mind — is a logical development of the whole *stil nuovo* orientation and historically interests us for the antifeudal stand it represents. Value here is felt and portrayed very concretely as a goal within human reach, as the direction and result of human development; status is an individual responsibility, not a guaranteed heritage. The Renaissance is clearly in sight. We have an emergent, as against an inertial, conception of value, a polemic against dynasty. Time is thus understood as the neutral possibility of value, not as its security. The confrontation of nobility and time is the essence, or better, the sense of human history; but on the other hand human life and words themselves must follow the harmonious rhythm of development which inheres in the nature of time, for "tutte le nostre brighe . . . procedono quasi dal non conoscere l'uso del tempo" ("all our troubles . . . seem to derive from our not knowing the use of time," *Conv.* iv, ii, 10). Of course, this is no merely academic discussion on the part of the exile who had to bide his time, and of the poet who devoted a lifetime to the responsible use of words. Words are like seeds (*Conv.* iv, ii, 8), and they must bide their time to come to fruition; thus they will have a chance to manifest the "valore" ("value") or "gentilezza" ("gentility") or "bontade" ("goodness") or "potenza di natura" ("natural power") inherent in them as well as in the mind that utters or receives them (*Conv.* iv, ii, 11–12).

This imaginative use of an Aristotelian cue brings us very close to the center of the book, because it reviews for us most of the synonyms employed throughout for the idea of value, but even more because it concentrates on language itself as a repository or carrier of value in time. Spurred by such vital suggestion, the modern reader eagerly returns to the nonallegorical prologue (Trattato i), which discusses Dante's choice of the Italian vernacular instead of the customary Latin for the scholarly work at hand. It is here that Dante speaks most convincingly to us through the filmed-over interval of so many centuries. His fiery temper, which breaks out in invectives against the detractors of the native language, makes him so intensely present in the work that for the sake of this introductory chapter we are willing to accept everything else in the book. Here the cobwebs of scholastic argument are no impediment, and, if anything, they take on a quality of passion that enables them to innervate the prose — or else to be burned in the process.

Language, for Dante, is much more than a vehicle of value; it is a value in itself and a living entity. What else could be closer to the roots of his individual being, and to his universal concerns? One follows the growing momentum of thought from the initial formal homage to the authority of Latin to the passionate reversal of valuation in the end, where Dante declares his flaming love for the vernacular, and this emerges as the real motivation of his epoch-making choice. Latin, in *Conv.* i, v, 7–10, is exalted above the vernacular in such a way as to perplex us. It is said to be much more noble because of its perpetuity and immunity from corruption, whereas the vernacular is extremely changeable, even within the range of a lifetime, and therefore, being so eminently corruptible, should not make the nobler language subservient to itself in a commentary. Italian and not Latin should properly be used to comment on Italian verse, if we do not want to invert the rightful hierarchy of value — the more so as Latin has much more specific *virtù* or conceptual efficiency (*Conv.* i, v, 11–12) as well as beauty (*ibid.*, 13). As the lord it is, Latin would not have qualified for the job of a "servant," for it could not be "obedient" as Italian can, and besides, Latin does not "know" the vernacular in its diversification, that is, its individuality.

As the argument proceeds, we sense how this involved dialectic really aims at removing His Majesty the Latin Language into a more comfortable sphere, where it will be a dormant god in its transcendent immutability, for the poet has chosen the humble, "corruptible," living language, and he wants to defend his choice with all the apparatus of diplomacy. The tactful debate bears witness to the birth of a literary culture. In throwing in his lot with Italian, Dante has staked everything on the living reality of history as against the mythologically suprahistorical, that is, fixed and dead Latin medium. The choice will be decisive for the *Comedy* and for the whole of Italian literature.

And what moving resourcefulness is displayed in Dante's plea for his beloved vernacular! A reason that is far from perfunctory is given in *Conv.*

1, viii, 1–18, and 1, ix: "pronta liberalitate mi fece questo eleggere e l'altro lasciare" ("its exceedingly liberal nature convinced me to choose this [language] and leave the other"). Italian is "liberal" because it gives to many, being available to a much wider circle of readers than Latin; because it is useful, being more readily communicable; and finally because it makes a spontaneous gift of itself. Usefulness is goodness and value, and this attaches to the vernacular, which is used by the majority of people. Value is here understood in a very concrete, pragmatic, historical way, contrary to the initial argument of nobility as the theoretical mark of Latin. From now on (x through xiii) the poet drops the mask of the lawyer, and speaks as a lover. He has been motivated by a "naturale amore della propria loquela" ("natural love of [his] own speech"), and to love he adds jealousy, the hyperbole of concern. This love, he says, arose from proximity, for nothing is closer to a man than his native vernacular, and it also has to do with his very existence, the native language having been the agent of his parents' meeting, as fire and hammer concur in producing the knife. The reality of his love for the language is not be questioned: he contends it is to be seen as "fire in a burning house"! Language really was the "house" of the exile, in Heidegger's sense of the word; it was the reality and value in which he could find shelter.

The simile has a weird relevance; and if in the last lines of the chapter Dante envisions himself as a Christlike dispenser of the bread of life (Italian literature) to the future generations, he is rightfully prophetic. The availability of language, this most intimate and public of activities, is identified with the infinite availability of the poet, and a generous imagination transcends all the subtleties of rhetoric and casuistry. We get here the "house," and the "supper table," instead of the "ship," which is such a frequent image in roaming Dante.[7] He had become aware of his only opportunity of permanence in an unreliable world, and paradoxically enough he had found it by espousing the cause of change, the promise and risk of history as embodied in the growing *lingua volgare*. The consuming fire of love would refine, not destroy, its object and medium; Dante, in his never-abandoned quest, was soon going to traverse "il foco che gli affina."

The problem of allegory in Dante's lyrical poetry and didactic prose (of which the *Convivio* is a paramount example) is closely connected with the problem of heretical interpretations that have been advanced by various critics. This being a topic strictly for specialists, I did not want to go into it when the preceding essay was first published nine years ago, apart from listing in a footnote some of the relevant sources. I also had another reason to avoid the issue, namely my focus of interest on style and language. But it does seem to me that the question of a possible heretical phase in Dante's development from the *Vita Nuova* to the *Convivio* should not be hastily dismissed, even if no external proof has been produced for the tempting hypothesis. In fact I notice that the issue has been taken up lately in France, to judge from Paul Renucci's contribution to the 1965 Convegno di Studi Danteschi in Florence.[8] The hypothesis may have suffered from the punctilious extremism of Cesare Valli, its most clamorous propounder in our century, since he made short work of the poetry in order to prove his theory of Dante's *dolce stil nuovo* circle as an Albigensian sect interested only in exchanging coded messages of a religious, antipapal import, under cover of courtly love conventions.

Against this one-sidedness, critics like Ulrich Leo have every reason to vindicate the lyrical quality of Dante's first work, and there is no need to remind the reader of Contini's work on Dante's *Rime* and on the poets of the thirteenth century. A classic essay on the *Vita Nuova*, likewise refusing or ignoring the heretical approach, remains Charles Singleton's terse book of 1958, while among more recent contributions along this line I would recommend P. Boyde's elegant essay, "Dante's Lyric Poetry."[9] These and other studies confirm that poetry was of the essence in the literary activity of the *Stilnovisti*.

Yet I am not entirely satisfied with Ulrich Leo's denial of any allegorical dimension in the *Vita Nuova*, and not even Charles Singleton's perceptive interpretation of that book manages to clarify certain obscure points for me. Why, for instance, does Dante say more than once in Chapter XIII and in the sonnet "Tutti li miei penser parlan d'Amore," which forms the text discussed therein, that "madonna Pietade," my lady Pity (and/or Piety), is his enemy? Why does he say, in Chapter xiv, that the person leading him to a wedding banquet, where he unexpectedly will see Beatrice, is worthy of trust because he had "led a friend to the extreme pass of life" ("fidandomi ne la persona la quale uno suo amico a l'estremitade de la vita condotto avea")? Is Dante's ensuing seizure at the sight of Beatrice, which he describes as a "transfiguration," entirely understandable in terms of youthful love, or does it hint at a mystical experience, as Valli believes? Why is "Pietate" personified again in the sonnet "Con l'altre donne mia vista gabbate" (Chapter xiv) as the enemy of Love? Elsewhere he remarks that the "donne gentili" ("gentle women") belonging to the court of love "non sono pur femmine" (are "no mere" females, or maybe, not females at all).

At the beginning (Chapter ii) he asserts that the "glorious lady of [his] mind" was "called Beatrice by many who did not know how to call her," and this statement threatens to invalidate the theory, still accepted by Leo, that the Beatrice of the *Vita Nuova* should be equated with the historical Beatrice Portinari. Later on in the book (Chapter xxviii) he explains why he refuses to deal in detail with Beatrice's death: the fourth (and most cryptical) reason is that it would not be suitable to do so because this would involve "self-praise," a most blameworthy thing. But if we compare this passage with others where Beatrice is said to be one and the same thing as Love (Chapter xxiv) or as the sacred number Nine (Chapter xxix), then the suspicion that she may be just a "donna della mente," a lady of the mind, a projection of mystical rapture, gains some ground. Significantly enough, Dante takes pains, in Chapter xxv, to "demystify" the poetical personification of Love by saying it is an accident and no substance; that is, in Aristotelian terms, not an independent reality but a mere modification of one, like, for instance, a state of mind; and he produces a number of examples from the classical poets to defend the poetical license of personifying abstract forces of the mind. If so, the rhetoric threatens to undercut his own book as a whole, unless it is a covert warning to read it "in code," beyond the literal level.

Add to this the surprising revelation in the *Convivio* that the *donna gentile* who, in the *Vita Nuova* and in some of the canzones explicated by the later treatise, seems to have temporarily taken over Beatrice's sovereign place in her poet's heart, was no real woman but just Lady Philosophy. Since in the *Vita Nuova* the *donna gentile* is given as much localized concreteness as that elusive work can afford, and certainly more, not less, than Beatrice herself, the allegorical interpretation so firmly set forth by Dante in the *Convivio* reverberates not just on herself, but also on her august rival Beatrice. The deviousness I was hinting at in 1960 may have had a much more serious reason than the alleged one; with the frank love poems Dante wrote to or about several girls ("pargolette") or "stony" ladies (Madonna Petra), he didn't have to stake so much moral zest on clearing himself from the accusation of having betrayed his deceased lady Beatrice for the *donna gentile*; conversely if the *donna gentile* was Lady Philosophy — that is, not a person but a personification of the highest values that the rational use of the mind can attain — then Beatrice herself, whether she had had a feminine counterpart in the flesh or not, must have embodied those mystical values that reason alone, in the earlier and later opinion of Dante, could not reach or explain. She must have been more personification than person.

I find it hard to believe in the merely private import of Dante's vicissitudes with Beatrice, when I read in Chapter xxx of the *Vita Nuova* that "after she departed from this life, the whole city . . . remained as a widow stripped of any dignity" and that he consequently "wrote a great deal to the princes of this world about its [the desolate city's] condition, taking [his] cue from that verse of Jeremiah that says '*Quomodo sedet sola civitas*' ('how desolate sits the city')." Love can lead to many hyperboles, and the convention of courtly love as inherited from the Provençal troubadours may have accounted for the exclusiveness, the secrecy, the *trobar clus* or coded writing so conspicuous in the *Stilnovisti* and in the young Dante. If so, the "real" Beatrice became only a pretext for the focusing of an ineffable sum of mental experiences which Dante had to share with his initiated friends because much more was at stake than amorous idylls. The extant conventions, in this case, lent themselves very well to serving as safe vehicles for conveying the troublesome experience of a hypostatized Love which called in question the system of accepted ideas. The process from erotic hyperbole to metaphysical hypostasis has occurred again in Western literature and independently of Dante or his *dolce stil nuovo* friends: one impressive example is John Donne's poetical mourning of Elizabeth Drury, the thirteen-year-old girl whose death he equates with the loss of the world's soul because he needs an "occasion" to release his deep-seated intellectual and existential concerns.

In the case of Dante, however, the existence of a circle of initiates, the "Fedeli d'Amore" ("Devotees of Love") as he calls them, having a hierarchy of their own that prevents his giving too many explanations about the poems and their inspiring object, and the attendant use of a rather exclusive style which is a kind of *trobar clus*, posits the problem of spontaneity versus convention. While Valli rejects any spontaneity or even poetry, treating as he does the whole *dolce stil nuovo* literature as religious and political communication in code with no literary aim except protective mystification, I see in the experimental use of literary convention, as expounded in Chapter xxv of the *Vita Nuova* and again in Treatise ii of the *Convivio* (where allegory is discussed), Dante's need to sharpen his expressive instrument in view of the upsetting and exhilarating quality of the experience he had to clarify for himself and his connoisseur friends. Ideas as such were experiences to them, and the erotic charge of reformer-mystics like Gioachino da Fiore was in the air. A double vision thus became possible, in which Beatrice and Giovanna could be themselves and yet really "donne dello schermo" ("decoy ladies") for the much larger intellectual realities they were symbolizing. In this way I see the possibility of rescuing the heretical approach from artistic insensitiveness and the literary approach from dogmatic restrictiveness.

An overpowering experience for which analogies were sought in the career of his friends and predecessors spurred Dante to find suitable language to express and communicate it, and this language had to resort to the available conventions of a privileged group, while progressively reshaping and eventually expanding them to the point where the *Comedy*'s epos could be the only satisfactory result. Without a mastery of the inherited conventions, and the motivating intensity of his own fierce *Erlebnis*, the masterpiece would not have arisen. Thus I equate the polarity "convention-spontaneity" (or "coded message–love poetry," to put it in terms of the two warring schools) with the formula "experiment-experience," experiment as such leading to further, that is, literary, experience, and experience in turn feeding on literary experiment, in an endless circle. This already intimates how close to the modern literary temper Dante must be, despite the huge historical gap.

In this perspective, it no longer matters whether Dante and his friends would have qualified for the dangerous definition of heretics; they probably did not. What counts is that they must have shared a radical experience. The Beatrice of the *Vita Nuova* is a subverter of received values, of plausible appearances; there are intimations of a Second Coming about her. A rigorous scholar like Ernst Curtius has noticed her Gnostic aura, if I may refer for a moment to that philological monument, *Europäische Literatur und Lateinisches Mittelalter*. With this in mind, we should reread Dante's postexilic sonnet against Philip le Beau and Pope Clement V, enemies of justice, where he laments that they have instilled freezing fear in the hearts of the faithful ("de' tuo' fedei," the devotees of the God who is Love and Justice, probably the "Fedeli d'Amore" themselves). Or let us peruse the letter to the Marquess Moroello Malaspina, where Dante reports the lightning-like apparition of a beautiful lady near the Arno, which caused him to fall again under the total sway of "formidable and imperious Love" after a period of "suspect" and "assiduous meditations." That letter bears memorable witness to the dramatic nature of Dante's intellectual experiences. They certainly made a stalwart dissenter of him.

In particular, the letter to Malaspina sends us back to Canzone CXVI and to the sonnets exchanged between Dante and his friend Cino da Pistoia during the time of Dante's exile. Despite the talk of love in the customary sense between them, one senses the deeper implications, and, as to the canzone, it can only have a political and religious import, since the powerful Love he sings of calls into question even his will to return to Florence. A hypostasis of intellectual commitments is again the real subject, and the inner struggle between the claims of different allegiances gives the canzone its nerve and the letter its interest. In the letter, by saying that fierce Love took entire possession of him once again after the interval of "suspect" and "assiduous meditations" on "terrestrial and celestial things," he is probably telling his noble friend and patron that the phase of the *Convivio*'s philosophical rationalism is over, for "Beatrice" has gained the upper hand again over her rival. Mystical experience, and along with it a philosophical orientation that discounts the merely rational for the ineffable, is the new phase.

We now see an alternating pattern from work to work and from phase to phase of Dante's life, in that the allegiance shifts from Beatrice to the *donna gentile* when the claims of independent reason assert themselves over the claims of a unique revelation that has changed Dante forever, only to make way for Beatrice again when Dante the thinker feels defeated in his attempt to understand reality apart from that special revelation. Everything is in tension, and his entire intellectual career is at stake; the resulting "drama of the mind" (as Francis Fergusson has called the *Comedy*) will find its catharsis only when our poet recognizes that his special revelation, Beatrice, has come to confirm the faith shared with so many humble millions, because to renew is to reassert, and that there is no irreconcilable rivalry between faith and reason since Virgil will be needed to lead him to Beatrice. In fact, by now she will have incorporated the rational sphere.

Apart from the importance of recognizing that Dante's examination by St. John and St. Peter in the *Paradiso* seals the final vindication of his own orthodoxy as a believer in the Church qua critic of the Church's political errors, it pays to grasp the pattern of tensions governing Dante's development as poet of faith and reason. It was all prefigured in the *Vita Nuova*, but it had to grow far beyond its compass. There was an original experience of religious and social values to understand, and he spent his whole life doing just that; if poetry sprang from this, it was no wonder, since poetry was itself an act of understanding, indeed, a gnosis, invested from the start with prophetic overtones. Dante keeps writing poetry on his peculiar experience, and commentaries on the poetry, then poetry again to incorporate the explication, in a spiraling progress of vision and analysis which finds its proper goal in the *Comedy*. To say this is to say that the tension between convention and spontaneity, or experiment and experience, is only a form of the tension between the ineffable and the rational, between faith and reason. Dante staked all of himself on the issue, whose violent repercussions in his mind could only be absorbed by the ever-renewed engagement of poetry. At one end of the scale the ineffable was the idiosyncratic, the demoniac, Plutus, Nimrod, the perversion of language. At the other end it was the divine; and Beatrice, his original subverter, the angel of ecstasy and anxiety, was also his Muse, the transcendent spirit of poetry which alone could heal the lacerating contrasts that beset him. The "heresy" of poetry had become, on the threshold of death, the consolation of shared faith.

CHAPTER II

DANTE AND THE DRAMA
OF LANGUAGE

AT THE peak of his creative effort, Dante acknowledged crucial difficulties of subject matter — "perch'a risponder la materia è sorda" ("for matter is reluctant to respond," *Par.* I, 129) — and of language:

> ché non è impresa da pigliare a gabbo
> discriver fondo a tutto l'universo,
> né da lingua che chiami mamma o babbo

> for it is no paltry enterprise
> to get to the foundation of the universe
> in portraying it, no task for an infant language
> > (*Inf.* XXXII, 7–9)

> Oh quanto è corto il dire e come fioco
> al mio concetto! e questo, a quel ch'i'vidi,
> è tanto, che non basta a dicer "poco"

> Oh how expression pales, how it falls short
> of my conception! which in turn, compared
> to what I saw, is even less than little
> > (*Par.* XXXIII, 121–23)

To dismiss such an avowed inadequacy of expressive power as merely a rhetorical device is to ignore Dante's lifelong concern with problems of language — a concern which became actual drama and myth, thereby feeding the very work it might have been expected to undermine. Like so many of our representative modern writers all over the West, though for very different reasons, Dante could not take his own language for granted, and a career of ceaseless struggle with the medium was the consequence. Long before Mallarmé or Eliot he knew what it cost to "purify the dialect of the tribe," the more so as this dialect had to be broadened, and to some extent even invented, before it could be purified. If he had worried only about purity, he would never have developed into the powerful epic writer we know. He was not Petrarch.[1]

For Dante, as for the experimental moderns, there was a language to repossess; but in his case it was a language in the making and not a worn-out one to be reactivated by some stylistic iconoclasm. He had a culture to create, we have a culture to save or to reject (depending on how we feel about our massive heritage). In either case, it seems fair to say that the contemporary agony of European culture can find itself mirrored, symmetrically, in the growth crisis of Dante's world. The attendant apocalyptic mood led him to take the posture of a prophet, a posture familiar to such contemporaries of ours as Eliot, Mann, and Yeats, whose bent for Dantean (and biblical) apocalypse is an avowed fact. This helps to explain why Dante's poetry, after an eclipse during the Enlightenment and a Romantic revival which was partly a misinterpretation,[2] has come to sound as close and relevant to our eschatological time as it seemed remote to earlier literary ages. A concurrent reason for this renewed relevance has to be recognized in the present affinity for Dante's conscious craftsmanship and theoretical awareness of linguistic problems. Besides, as Giulio Marzot has so painstakingly shown,[3] the apocalyptic temper has its repercussions on his style; and the same is true of his latter-day brethren.

In talking of Dante's attitude to language, whether in the theoretical or in the creative sphere, I do not forget that in one sense his predicament (the inability to take his medium for granted) is common to all authentic writers at whatever cultural juncture they happen to operate, since every poet will have to transform the given language of his time and place into a personal style. This unavoidable disparity between the given and the created language is what has prompted Luigi Malagoli to discuss "language and poetry in the Divine Comedy,"[4] and Theophil Spoerri to apply De Saussure's binomial concept of *langue et parole* in one of the liveliest among recent interpretations of Dante.[5] But the dynamic ratio of personal style to linguistic convention and heritage is by no means the same in every case, and it will rise to high tension for someone like Dante, who, lacking an established literary language (outside of his poetically uncongenial medieval Latin) for his most ambitious purpose, had to constitute one by founding the tradition of epic poetry in the Italian vernacular.

How dramatic this gesture was in itself, even apart from the dramatic strength of the resultant accomplishment, can be best judged by the development of Dante's own thoughts on the history, nature, and range of the *lingua volgare*. Partly, they come to a head in the polemical Trattato i of the *Convivio*, where he passes from scholastic diplomacy to fiery invective and prophetic metaphors in order to vindicate the worth of his beloved Italian vernacular against learned prejudice and princely snobbery or political neglect. As we have seen in Chapter I, the claim he makes here for the *lingua volgare* is limited to its use as a commentary on poems written in the same tongue. Although in the scholastic part of his argument he makes it sound as if this were a way of putting the upstart vernacular in its place since it would be beneath the dignity of changeless Latin to stoop to such a low scholarly service, the tone is unmistakable. Eloquence supersedes syllogistic diplomacy when it comes to asserting the personal relevance of *lingua volgare* to the author, whose very existence is shown to derive from the operation of that living everyday speech which had been instrumental in bringing together his father and mother, and striking similes begin to sparkle through the texture of rationalizing rhetoric: fire, hammer, and knife to exemplify the generative power, house on fire to allegorize the force of his love for the native language (*Conv.* i, xii, xiii).

By the end of the chapter, when Dante envisages himself as the dispenser of the new (linguistic-literary) bread of life to coming generations, and actually compounds this evangelic metaphor with that of the new sun (the Italian vernacular) which is going to efface the old one (Latin), we see that eloquence in turn is on the verge of transcending itself into poetry.[6] Thus a doctrinal commentary instigated by earlier poetry becomes itself the matrix of further poetry when it focuses on the problem of language — a theme of the utmost aesthetic and existential importance for our roving exile. Nor can we miss, in the underlying movement of imagery, a religious hypostasis: Dante first recognizes his sonship to the vernacular, then takes it in charge as a sacramental food and ministers to it as a priest would to a godhead revealing its own power through the sun. The parallel to the Eucharist ritual is oddly reinforced by a totemic meal analogy; Dante has invested all his values in the native language, as poet, citizen, and thinker, and it in turn grows into much more than a vehicle of thought; it becomes the symbolic epitome of his ideal community and, as such, a living force to be linked with procreation, food, and light. In Catholic terms, we could say that this beloved medium is in fact, to Dante, the element of a sacrament, and even, to some extent, the divine presence inherent therein. The living language, as contrasted to the fixed and dead one, is the aptest medium for a communion that is both ritual and everyday intercourse. Notice also that when he metaphorically officiates as a priest of language, he is offering as food for the hungry congregation a metaphoric equivalent of his own body: his own poetry in the *lingua volgare*:

Così rivolgendo li occhi a dietro, e raccogliendo le ragioni prenotate, puotesi vedere questo pane, col quale si deono mangiare le infrascritte canzoni, essere sufficientemente purgato da le macule, e da l'essere di biado; per che tempo è d'intendere a ministrare le vivande. Questo sarà quello pane orzato del quale si satolleranno migliaia, e a me ne soperchieranno le sporte piene . . .

Thus by casting a backward glance to gather the reasons previously discussed, we can see how this bread with which the canzones that follow must be eaten is clear enough of any flaw and coarse admixture; so that it is time to serve the food. This will be that barley bread which sates people by the thousand, though my own bags will remain full of it to the brim . . .

(*Conv.* I, xiii, 11–12)

Therefore, to recapitulate, he is the son of language, language being identified with his parents. Then he identifies with it to the point where he is almost a sacrificial victim, and finally he becomes its priestly keeper, with fatherly connotations vis-à-vis the future communicants. From sonhood to fatherhood is a normal reversal of role in the course of a life, but it is exceptional where a whole culture is concerned. Only people like Dante become the fathers of their own language after having been its offspring.

In the *Convivio* this reversal is more hinted at than actually formulated, but it counterpoints the dramatic reversal of valuation concerning the respective merits of Latin and of the Italian *volgare*. The former is initially given primacy and described as the absolute lord looking down from the turrets of abstraction on the busy servant, the vernacular; then a crescendo of eloquence actually shifts the whole argument to the latter's side, and carries the day for it, at the ecstatic climax. Nothing in the remaining three chapters of the *Convivio*, despite their doctrinal interest, equals this heightening process, in the course of which Dante's prose ranges through much of the modal gamut his masterpiece will rehearse in the subtler modulations of ripe verse. The chapter begins and ends on a personal note, and in between it touches a variety of keys, from the elaborately discursive to the rhetorical and lyrical, with typical outbursts of political invective subsiding into gentler rapture. Such vehemence of anger and prayer we shall find again in the *Comedy*, and it already stamps this manifesto with the essential form of Dante's spiritual dynamism: a perilous oscillation between the extremes of fury and love which recurrently strains the balance of the wronged man's mind. Remember the swoons of Hell and of Heaven, and how the poet clings to the discipline of strict form as a saving device to protect himself from the centrifugal pulls of savage passion. Here in the first chapter of the *Convivio* a kindred urgency makes the poet's voice overheard throughout, and its vehemence is sparked by the thought of language. For language was the exile's special trust and salvation. It was indeed his ark of the covenant in the ordeal of pilgrimage.

At this point it would seem that my initial argument has reversed itself. I began by speaking of a self-confessed inadequacy in Dante's language at certain climactic points, and I insisted that, since he could not take his language for granted, his poetical career became a lifelong struggle with the medium. The *Convivio* instead, in my interpretation, invests language with a sacramental aura and almost deifies it. If there can be talk of inadequacy here, it could only refer to the poet himself vis-à-vis his medium, and not to the medium as such, which he sees as all but holy. Moreover, if the vernacular, raised by him to epic dignity, was his true shelter in the homeless life he had to lead after the overthrow of his party in Florence, one would assume on Dante's part a trustingly restful, not a struggling, attitude to it. In the *Convivio* he adduces proximity as his first and chief reason for choosing the humble vernacular over the official language of scholarship; and warm intimacy is indeed the quality of his relationship to it in these lively pages. What are we to make of this?

The truth is that Dante's attitude to language was very complex, for it involved emotional, technical, and philosophical factors in constant interaction, and this (along with the progress of personal experience) also made for change. We can follow this change from book to book as he each time rethinks the problems of language which found a formulation first in Chapter xxv of the *Vita Nuova*, then, several years after, in the memorable opening chapter of the *Convivio*, then (after a short interval) in the *De Vulgari Eloquentia*, and finally, as theory which is resolved or infused in the action of poetry, throughout the crowning poem. Whether the change is a process of evolutionary continuity from beginning to end, as an authority like Bruno Nardi believes,[7] or a more dialectical one, is a secondary question which a close reading of the texts in due order may help to decide. But the dramatic complexity of Dante's attitude to language cannot be denied. In the *Convivio* itself, for instance, after the mystical accolade he gives to the vernacular in Trattato I, he complains in Trattato III (iii, 14–15; iv, 1–4) about his own language's inadequacy to the ineffable theme of the *donna gentile* — a statement which clearly anticipates the lines quoted above from *Paradiso* XXXIII.

We could explain this complexity by keeping in mind what language meant to Dante as a man of his city and nation, as a member of Christendom at large, and as the artist he was. As an artist, he felt both the potential and the limits of his native medium; as a Florentine, he cherished in it a personal heritage, the tradition handed down to him by the ancestors who had made him what he was; as an Italian, he saw it as a pledge of national unity, a fledgling language which had to compete with the Latin so many poets and thinkers and saints had canonized; however, as a Christian, he could not help recognizing in Latin the necessary bridge to other thinking men who spoke different vernaculars, and he realized the limitations of any language. Through the vital medium of language he could retain his roots in several communities, from one of which, the closest to him, he had been violently uprooted, while the amplest of them, the community of scholars and Christians which could not disavow him, existed more as an ideal than as a palpable actuality. Thus he was certainly at home in his native speech and felt it as a living thing of intimate concern, something to worship and chide in turn, while at the same time endeavoring to extend its powers into those broader, deeper, and higher areas of experience which had not been claimed for it by his predecessors. His relation to it was intimate, but could hardly be restful or simple, and hardly unchangeable despite his constant fidelity to the language which had nurtured him from the cradle and which he in turn adopted for the highest enterprise a poet could dream of.

There is a demonic impatience in every major artist who is reshaping his medium, and lovers' quarrels will be inevitable. The demonic urge shows in the fiery metaphors at the end of the first chapter of the *Convivio*: when he says that his love for the native language is as obvious as fire would be in a burning house, he is expressing the complex nature of his relation to it, implying that the vernacular is his inalienable shelter, but that he dwells there not in a peaceful, but in a consumingly restless way. He had to educate what had culturally begotten him; but he never forgot the source, as the persistence of homespun vocabulary and imagery, even in the rarefied spheres of the *Paradiso*, clearly proves.

And then we must consider Dante's awareness of the historical nature of language. As Bruno Nardi points out,[8] this linguistic historicism reaches its fullest form in *Paradiso* xxvi, where Adam says to Dante that not Hebrew (as Dante had earlier stated in *De Vulgari Eloquentia*) but a lost speech was the original language of the human race. Thus our language-conscious poet takes the final step to show that not even the sacred language of the Bible could remain totally exempt from historical vicissitudes. Hebrew was still the revered language of the patriarchs, but it could no longer claim the distinction of having been the first language, the prelapsarian speech, the *Ursprache* of mankind:

La lingua ch'io parlai fu tutta spenta
  innanzi che all'ovra inconsummabile
  fosse la gente di Nembròt attenta;

The language I spoke was totally extinct
  even before the unfulfillable task
  claimed the energy and care of Nimrod's people;

                              (*Par.* XXVI, 124–26)

Pria ch'io scendessi a l'infernale ambascia,
  I s'appellava in terra il sommo bene
  onde vien la letizia che mi fascia;
e *El* si chiamò poi; e ciò convene,
  ché l'uso de' mortali è come fronda
  in ramo, che sen va e altra vene.

Before I went down to the anguish of Hell,
  "I" was the name on earth of the Highest Good
  from whom issues the bliss that swathes me;
and afterward he was called "El"; and that is right,
  for the usage of men is like the leaves
  on a branch — one bunch withers and another sprouts.

                              (*Ibid.*, 133–38)

Along with the philosophical implications, one should not miss here the poetical effect. The philosophy points to humanism:

Opera naturale è ch'uom favella;
  ma così o così, natura lascia
  poi fare a voi, secondo che v'abbella.

That man should speak, is nature's very work;
  but as to the manner, Nature then allows
  you to decide as it best pleases you.

                              (*Ibid.*, 130–32)

and this is not the only passage where the theologically minded Dante can be shown to harbor in himself a budding humanist, despite Rudolf Palgen's massive effort to deny it by reducing him to his medieval sources.[9] The poetry feeds on the repeated vegetal imagery that comes to a head in this canto with an intimation of Eden-like happiness, and the distance between the prehistoric state Adam remembers and the late station in history from which Dante is enabled to address him is qualitatively intensified by the idea of a lost Edenic speech. It is a matter of epic perspective enhanced by thoughts of language, and by the direct action of language itself, if we pay due attention to the capital sampling of both the Edenic and the Hebrew word for God in a vernacular context. But perspective is a dominant device in Paradise, the metahistorical realm which affords a bird's-eye-view of history and of the "aiuola che ci fa tanto feroci" ("the small garden that makes us so ferocious"); in this passage linguistic distance compounds with the chronological distance from the beginning of history itself and with the dizzily exhilarating spatial distance from history's earthly scene to achieve an effect of felt transcendence. That effect can only be transcended in turn by the eventual threshold experience in which all perspective is annihilated, the

> . . . punto che mi vinse,
> parendo inchiuso da quel ch'egli inchiude.
>
> . . . point that overwhelmed me,
> seeming encompassed by what it does encompass.
>
> (*Par.* xxx, 11–13)

Thus language in action creates perspective, aesthetic space, in one of the culminating episodes of the *Comedy*, at the point where Dante meets, in Adam, the archetypal earthly father and the father of all language, before the glimpsed visage of the Heavenly Father supersedes all the long progression of earthly ones, from Virgil to Brunetto and Cacciaguida, and makes language renege. For the *Divine Comedy* certainly is, in one central aspect, a long quest for father and mother, and for the source of all fatherhood and motherhood to which all parental images lead. No wonder that, at the last climax of vision, the tried master of language should regressively feel like a babbling baby, since language fails him in the end when confronting in the Creator the supreme fount of love, maternal no less than paternal:

> Omai sarà più corta mia favella,
>   pur a quel ch'io ricordo, che d'un fante
>   che bagni ancor la lingua a la mammella
>
> Henceforth my language will fall shorter

of what I remember, than a baby's talk
who still wets his tongue at mother's breast
                    (*Par.* XXXIII, 106–8)

In the architectural economy of the whole, the final vision of the triune
God offsets the perverted trinity that Lucifer had embodied at the end of
the *Inferno*; and, correspondingly, language here, confronted by the rapture of ecstasy, reaches its own upper threshold in avowed powerlessness,
just as its nether threshold was avowedly touched in the horror of Hell
(*Inf.* XXVIII, 1–6; *ibid.*, XXXII, *cit.*). Such dynamic symmetry between the
two extreme limits of imaginable experience — infernal harshness and paradisiac speechlessness — also finds a counterpart in the structural relation between Adam's quoting of the aboriginal holy word in the lost Edenic language, and Nimrod's unintelligible outburst in the *Inferno* (XXXI, 67):
"Raphèl maỳ amèch zabì almì." Just as three-headed Satan is a parody of
the Holy Trinity, this babelic utterance is a parody of the primal language
Adam and Eve spoke, and the fact that it sounds vaguely like Hebrew
sharpens its effect of weird distortion. As readers, we shall be asked to remember Nimrod's cultural disruptiveness when Adam talks to Dante in a
communicable language to mention the incorrupt language of the world's
dawn:

> La lingua ch'io parlai fu tutta spenta
> innanzi che all'ovra inconsummabile
> fosse la gente di Nembròt attenta;
>
> The language I spoke was totally extinct
> even before the unfulfillable task
> claimed the energy and care of Nimrod's people;
>   (*Par.* XXVI, 124–26)

Whatever the various scholarly attempts at deciphering Nimrod's gibberish may have proved, I here take my stand with the poet himself, who
has Virgil tell us:

> ". . . questi è Nembròt, per lo cui mal coto
> pur un linguaggio nel mondo non s'usa.
> Lasciamlo stare e non parliamo a voto;
> ché così è a lui ciascun linguaggio
> come 'l suo ad altrui, ch'a nullo è noto."

". . . this is Nimrod, thanks to whose ill-conceived idea
one language is no longer used throughout the world.
Let us leave him alone nor speak in vain;
    for any language is to him exactly
    as unknown as his is to anyone else."
                                    (*Inf.* XXXI, 77–81)

I am in no position to demonstrate that there is no occult meaning em-
bedded in the belabored infernal line, but I would not put it past Dante's
wit to have aimed at teasing his commentators by coining something which
sounds as if it might have a meaning and yet has no traceable one; for this
would suit very well the dramatic purpose of the specific context. Nimrod's lost language is unintelligible to Virgil and Dante, and therefore to
us as well, who are supposed to share imaginatively the poet's shock at being threatened by gibberish which apes language but is actually a non-
language. Incommunicability is here enacted by language as the utterly
fallen, indeed demoniac condition. It supplies a linguistic equivalent of the
dull opacity into which matter gathers around the frozen bottom of Hell,
at the physical and metaphysical center of sin, and thus it fits the monstrous
mass of the noisy Giant who stands out as the most heinous monster of the
chained company towering all around the lower edge of Circle VIII because, by building the Tower of Babel, he brought about the confusion of
tongues.

Perversion of language, and disruption of mankind's linguistic unity, is
in Dante's eyes one of the worst offenses against the spiritual order, and he
therefore makes biblical Nimrod a lesser Lucifer who, by his hubris,
dragged busily aspiring humanity into another Fall; Nimrod is appropriately punished by confinement in a realm of brute mass and meaninglessness. Once again I find myself compelled to stress, against Palgen's over-
emphasis on Dante's naïve indebtedness to medieval sources, Dante's poten-
tially humanistic attitude where civilization is at stake. Here, in *Inferno*
XXXI, Dante sets up a mythical hyperbole of what Roman classics would
have called "hominem barbarum atque immanem" as an infernal foil to
what civilization means: the city as a place of active order, the endowment

of speech as the norm of significant intercourse. One can easily see that throughout Hell this implicit image of the city counterpoints the infernal distortion of it, that Hell is indeed the anti-city just as Paradise is "quella Roma onde Cristo è romano," the transfigured city.

City, garden, and court, Dante's Heaven is the place of perfect mutuality in a hierarchy of interrelation, which language repeatedly manifests in choral hymns; Dante's Hell is the negative of that unison, the place of discordant uproar, of frozen passion and self-contained individualism, as Irma Brandeis has shown,[10] and Nimrod's linguistic unrelatedness precipitates all that into an apt image. Babel is the negation of Eden and the caricature of Rome-Jerusalem, but since the very texture of imagery makes Dante's Paradise a synthesis of Holy City and Celestial Garden, Hell is essentially babelic, a combination of anti-garden (the Dark Wood, the Wood of Suicides) and anti-city (the City of Dis), and our transcendental pilgrim's first impression of it is fittingly babelic:

> Diverse lingue, orribili favelle,
>   parole di dolore, accenti d'ira,
>   voci alte e fioche, e suon di man con elle
> facevano un tumulto, il qual s'aggira
>   sempre in quell'aura sanza tempo tinta
>
> Confusion of tongues, horrible forms of speech,
>   pain-ridden words, expressions of anger,
>   loud and dim voices, with clapping of hands,
> made an uproar which forever haunts
>   that air beset with timeless darkness
>
> (*Inf.* III, 25–29)

"Confusion of tongues" (as John Ciardi has chosen to translate the beginning of this passage) [11] signals to Dante's receptive ear the phonic essence of the infernal condition at the very moment of entering Hell, and the rest of the *Inferno* will verify this aural prologue. Dante's imagination was keenly auditory no less than visual, and Eliot, who has given special emphasis to this latter aspect,[12] would have come even closer to descrying the roots of his own elective affinity for the well-traveled Florentine's poetry if he had recognized the part that linguistic awareness plays in it, and for that matter in the initially discontinuous progression of theoretical prose which started as early as the *Vita Nuova* to be finally reabsorbed in the living tissue of the major poem. Against Eliot's Crocean contention that Dante's mind was especially suited to the creation of great poetry because it could not be "violated by ideas," I would bring the evidence of the *Convivio*, where the drama of ideas is unleashed by the author's extant poetry and clearly points to his future poetry, which it helps to kindle. Between Dante the thinker and Dante the poet there was a lifelong cycle of action and reaction which came to its consummation in the *Comedy*, for however much of a "naïve poet" he may have been (in Karl Vossler's Schillerian sense of the word [13]), he contained in himself a restless critic and philosopher who kept challenging the poet to self-transcendence; and nowhere does this come out so markedly as in his writings on language, which throughout his career brought out in him the philosophical theorist along with the craftsman and the mythmaker.

These writings culminate in *De Vulgari Eloquentia*, and their very sequence is a drama.[14] Chapter xxv of the *Vita Nuova* deals with the limits of the historically recent vernacular and with the responsibilities of the poet, who pledges himself to raise it from its literary infancy by making it carry all the suitable burden of meaning within what still seems its only legitimate province — that of the short love lyric. He is conscious of having a young language to grow with, and he vows to supersede his "gross" predecessors in the art of verse by looking up to the normative example of the Latin classics, whose figures of speech were never devoid of significance. Many years later, the *Convivio*, as we have seen, sanctioned the use of the vernacular in learned commentary on vernacular poetry and widened the gap between Latin and the *volgare* to the extent of incommensurability, only to shift the balance in favor of the latter; and the three chapters of textual explication which follow the linguistic manifesto of Trattato i to illustrate its principles in concrete detail, go far beyond the initial assumptions of the *Vita Nuova* because they come to terms with his actual poetic practice since the composition of that treatise. Now we see that poetry in the vernacular is by no means limited to the subject of courtly love, and in fact it may carry the allegorical weight of ethics, cosmology, and theology, or grapple with the issues of politics in a straightforward way.

Then, with the praise of Lady Philosophy at the end of Chapter IV, the *Convivio* stops short of the projected length, since only three canzones have been explicated instead of the intended fourteen; the author is now entirely absorbed by the task of inditing a "booklet" on *volgare eloquenza* which he had announced in the *Convivio* I, v, 10. But his creative urgency has risen to breathtaking pitch and even the pioneering *De Vulgari Eloquentia*, a work important enough in its own right to be considered the first European treatise on historical linguistics, will stop short of completion to make room for the all-encompassing poetical endeavor to which it has served as doctrinal prelude. It will be his special grace, and our good luck, that he just manages to carry out this ultimate project to which the previous two have been sacrificed.

A pentecostal frenzy animates these years around 1305–7, which see enterprise supersede enterprise in a crescendo of work; and we cannot help noticing that it is a climactic meditation on language, the central theme of Dante the thinker, that spurs Dante the poet to his definitive undertaking. How far behind the *De Vulgari Eloquentia* has left the chronologically contiguous and partly overlapping *Convivio*, as regards the philosophy of language, can be appreciated when one considers that the vernacular is now openly called "nobler," not just emotionally closer, than Latin; that it qualifies for the lofty or "tragic" style in verse; and that its proven mutability no longer marks it as inferior to the unchangeable *gramatica*, but simply places it in the historical predicament of life along with the other vernaculars, whereas Latin is now seen as a constructed language of litterateurs.

The vernacular's literary relationship to Latin, which in the *Vita Nuova* was conceived as submissive apprenticeship without prospects of full emancipation, and in the *Convivio* as perfunctory obeisance in actual estrangement, is now dialectically refocused on the principle of open autonomy. Open, and not closed, because after the *Convivio*'s declaration of limited independence, now supplemented by a total one, the vernacular can afford to compete with the vehicle of Latin classics on its own ground, without uneasy admissions of semantic or aesthetic inferiority. Competition implies the acknowledgment of a model to emulate; the model is recognized in the formal achievement of the Latin writers, the "regular" writers ("poet[a]e regulati") who committed their excellence to an artificial medium (the "gramatica") especially devised to universalize their thoughts in geographic space and stabilize them in historic time. Servile imitation is out of the question; the vernacular is the spontaneous, the concrete language of all ("vulgarem locutionem asserimus, quam sine omni regula, nutricem imitantes, accipimus" — "we call vernacular that speech which we learn without any set rules, by just imitating our nurse"), while Latin is an abstract "locutio secundaria" and "potius artificialis" of the learned few (*De Vulg. El.* i, i, *passim*). And yet, when it comes to literary usage, the spontaneous tongue can look to the "grammatical" one for formal guidance — spontaneity and convention being the two poles of linguistic reality for Latin, Greek, and (if we follow Dante's obvious trend of thought) highly literate peoples anywhere. Dante firmly places himself at the pole of spontaneity, and he establishes the ideal as well as the historical priority of the spontaneous language, that, is vernacular speech, over the institutionalized one (*De Vulg. El.* i, viii–ix).

This revolutionary conception, not to be superseded in its essence (as Spoerri has seen), explains why Dante will feed so much earthy idiom into the fabric of his rigorous epic structure, where on the other hand the guiding function that a formalized literary language like Latin can perform for the developing vernacular finds its dramatic embodiment in one aspect of the relation between Virgil and his ward. Even the fact that Virgil eventually proclaims his disciple's emancipation and leaves him to his own devices on top of Mount Purgatory seems to reflect something of the dynamic relation of vernacular to Latin poetry as ultimately outlined in the *De Vulgari Eloquentia*. It must be said that in his treatises Dante apparently confuses the Latin of the classical poets he knew with the Latin of the Schoolmen, which he himself adapted to his purpose in the *De Vulgari Eloquentia* as well as in the *De Monarchia* and in the *Epistole*; the former would have qualified for the guiding function he ascribes to "poet[a]e regulati" in the

De Vulgari Eloquentia, while the latter is more probably what prompted him to assign priority to the vernacular.

But if he shows critical naïveté in this regard, he does exhibit a remarkable problematical awareness of what the vernacular as such is, and he thus accomplishes another qualitative leap beyond the level of understanding already reached in the *Convivio*, where there was no question of defining scope and variations of the *lingua volgare*, but merely of identifying it emotionally to justify its use in a broad philosophical inquiry. The *Convivio* simply assumed the vernacular's identity along with its existence; the *De Vulgari Eloquentia* recognizes its factual existence but inquisitively probes its many-faceted identity in a specifically linguistic perspective which has become emphatically national and European. By narrowing his theme to the problem of the nature, history, and uses of the vernacular tongue, Dante has discovered its complexity, which he materializes in the bestiary-like image of the nationwide wood ("silva") to be ranged in hunting for the elusive "odorous panther" of *volgare illustre* (*De Vulg. El.* I, xi, xiv, xv, xvi).

For he realizes that the vernacular is not one, but many: three main families of vernaculars in Europe, three closely related national vernaculars within the Latin area of the continent, and fourteen regional dialects in the Italian peninsula, with endless municipal variations:

Quapropter, si primas et secundarias et subsecundarias vulgaris Ytalie variationes calculare velimus, et in hoc minimo mundi angulo, non solum ad millenam loquele variationem venire contigerit, sed etiam ad magis ultra.

Therefore, should we want to reckon with the basic, secondary, and tertiary varieties of the Italian vernacular, why, even in this small corner of the world we should find not just one thousand varieties of speech, but many more.   (*De Vulg. El.* I, x, 9)

Such multiplicity becomes intractable to the writer in search of a nationally acceptable medium (*volgare illustre*), and Dante concludes that the latter can be found nowhere and everywhere, that it inheres to some degree in every regional and municipal dialect of Italy as an essence, to be limited to no particular part of the peninsula. Here the linguistic problem becomes the stylistic one, and the standards of elegance and euphony Dante mercilessly applies to the sampled dialects (including his native one) show he has come to take the role of author of his own language; for the *volgare illustre* clearly has to be invented.

Dante's search for his language throughout Italy parallels here what the *Comedy* will dramatize as his search for a haven. Home was nowhere and everywhere for our exile; he was afloat in the wide world:

Nos autem, cui mundus est patria velut piscibus equor, quanquam Sarnum biberimus ante dentes et Florentiam adeo diligamus ut quia dileximus exilium patiamur iniuste . . .

But we, to whom the whole world is home as the sea is to the fish, though we drank of Arno's water from before our teething months and though we love Florence so much that because of this love we have to bear an unjust exile . . .   (*De Vulg. El.* i, vi, 3)

The epic space Dante is going to range in his poem already makes itself felt in the linguistic space he covers here in the Latin treatise, where problematical awareness and empirical perception intertwine with a mythical urge that the *Comedy* is destined to turn to full account. Thus the myth of the Tower of Babel, which we found to be focal to the whole *Inferno* and not only to the one canto of the Giants, already serves to structure the problem of the multiplication of tongues, that is, their historical differentiation, in Chapters vi, vii, and viii of *De Vulgari Eloquentia* i; and Dante's observant eye imagines the details of the original linguistic catastrophe (i, vii, 6–7) with a zest that reminds us of a painting by Brueghel rather than of the absolutely laconic biblical source of this myth.

The man who cared so much for the spiritual and political unity of mankind could not help feeling that the confusion of tongues had been a second Fall for the descendants of Adam; hence his implicit emphasis on the role of the poet as a cultural unifier of his people, to counteract the disruptive effects of the babelic Fall at least within one ethnic area. The bewildering richness of unstable human languages matched the unruly proliferation of strife-ridden local governments, and Dante tended to envisage it as a form of historical entropy to be redressed by creative action. Man was the "mutabilissimum et instabilissimum animal," who had to make the best of his fallen condition. Of course Dante seems to waver between a degenerative and an emergent conception of linguistic history; in *Paradiso* XXVI the passage he puts on Adam's lips does not consider the multiplicity of tongues a sign of corruption, and in the *Convivio* and *De Vulgari Eloquentia* the fervor with which he espouses the vernacular as the pledge of future historical life contrasts with the grim philosophy he has outlined in his myth of Babel.

Whether dialectically resolvable or not, these tensions contribute to make Dante's approach to language a dramatic one; witness the telling instance of the *De Vulgari Eloquentia* I, iv, where Dante reshuffles Genesis a bit to paint his grandiose scene of the first man talking to God in answer to God's question as mediated verbally by the compliant cosmic elements. Apparently disregarding the beginning of the Gospel of John, Dante here says that the word is exclusively human, not divine; and in the two previous chapters he has made language the human endowment par excellence, between the silence of God and Angels on the one hand, and that of demons and brutes on the other.[15] This protohumanist myth can be in itself the key to a deeper understanding of Dante's major poem, which explores the whole spectrum of language from the infrared threshold of demoniac unintelligibility to the ultraviolet threshold of paradisiac inexpressibleness. In between these extremes the whole range of speech unfolds, to create from its own protean resources as many images of man as Heaven and Hell, and the intermediate realm, can contain.

For it is language in action that evokes Francesca. She is pure voice, and she haunts the poet, who conjured her from the dark whirlwind with his "affettuoso grido." She haunts us, a complete presence as nothing visual can ever be. She is a gesture of language. And Farinata posits his essential reality, and his tangled bond to the fellow Florentine, by a dramatic act of speech which is recognition of their common language in the most unlikely of places:

> O Tosco che per la città del foco
>   vivo ten vai così parlando onesto,
>   piacciati di restare in questo loco.
> La tua loquela ti fa manifesto
>   di quella nobil patria natio
>   a la qual forse fui troppo molesto.

> O Tuscan, who through the city of fire
> alive goes, speaking in such neat fashion,
> be so kind as to stop here awhile.
> Your manner of speech clearly shows you
> to be a native of that noble country
> to which perhaps I was too much of a scourge.
>
> (*Inf.* x, 22–27)

Speech is the bond between the living and the restless dead, and between the two inimical exiles. Cavalcante, an apt foil to the contentious Ghibelline giant, is entirely portrayed in his anxiety by the hammering, broken questions he addresses to Dante; and a misinterpreted inflection of his interlocutor's language in the cautious reply — a past tense in the verb referring to Cavalcante's son — is enough to plunge the pathetic man into howling despair, which the pitch of the voice and the panting pauses effectively convey:

> . . . Come
> dicesti? elli ebbe? non viv'elli ancora?
> non fiere li occhi suoi lo dolce lome?
>
> . . . How
> did you say? he *had*? isn't he living any more?
> does the sweet light no longer hit his eyes?
>
> (*Inf.* x, 67–69)

Disembodied Pier delle Vigne exists exclusively in the urgency of his talk, and in the mimetic mannerism of his style; and he takes shape in the excruciating effort of spilled blood to become word:

> Come d'un stizzo verde ch'arso sia
> da l'un de' capi, che da l'altro geme
> e cigola per vento che va via;
> sì de la scheggia rotta usciva inseme
> parole e sangue . . .
>
> As from a green log which is being burned
> at one end, so that from the other end
> it moans and creaks with the escaping air puffs,
> thus from the broken twig there issued forth
> words and blood at one stroke . . .
>
> (*Inf.* xiii, 40–44)

Likewise, Ulysses' struggle with the swathing fire enacts the dramatic birth of language:

> Lo maggior corno de la fiamma antica
>   cominciò a crollarsi mormorando
>   pur come quella cui vento affatica;
> indi la cima qua e là menando,
>   come fosse la lingua che parlasse,
>   gittò voce di fuori . . .

> The higher prong of the ancient forked flame
>   started to shake all over murmuring
>   just like a flame that's harried by the wind;
> then, stirring its tip this way and that
>   as if it were the tongue articulating,
>   it burst out into speech . . .

> (*Inf.* XXVI, 85–90)

He is a tongue of flame, his own torment and catharsis; he is like the odyssean poet from Florence who lived by that which consumed him. He is a Pentecost in Hell; we see him only as a stubborn glow, and we touch him in the muscular movements of his recapitulating voice. That other flame, sinuous Guido da Montefeltro, the reverse of Ulysses in so many ways, also takes shape for us as a pure creation of the inflected word, and lives as a kinetically aural image right from the start, when his fiery pain strives to become language:

> Come 'l bue cicilian che mugghiò prima
> . . . .
> mugghiava con la voce dell'afflitto,
> . . . .
> così, per non aver via né forame
>   dal principio nel foco, in suo linguaggio
>   si convertian le parole grame.

> As the Sicilian bull that bellowed first
> . . . .
> bellowed with the voice of the tormented man,
> . . . .
> thus, since they had no way out

> from their source in the fire, the painful words
> were changed into his kind of language.
>
> (*Inf.* XXVII, 7–15)

Especially in this Bolgia of the Evil Counselors, where language is the agent of damnation, we find the poet, his guide, and his interlocutors very sensitive to linguistic nuances: thus Virgil intercedes for Dante with Ulysses and Diomede to make them speak, for they are Greek and might be inaccessible to Dante's native speech (*Inf.* XXVI, 70–75); and Guido is impelled to address Virgil because he overhears his North Italian cadence (*Inf.* XXVII, 19–21). As elsewhere, Dante the poet is helped by Dante the linguist, and the *De Vulgari Eloquentia* looms once again behind the *Divine Comedy*.

We also remember the poet's own difficulties with his irksome theme, as confessed at the outset of *Inferno* XXVIII and XXXII, when we see him stress Ulysses' and Guido's efforts to overcome their obstructions to break into articulate speech. Above all, we are then aware of Dante's dynamic conception of language, a conception which informs and sustains his creative practice of repeatedly conjuring the human image as an expressive process. And at the bitter end of Hell, where ice freezes that image, gushing anger symbolically overcomes the most infernal obstruction to change it into a cleansing flood:

> Ahi Pisa, vituperio de le genti
>   del bel paese là dove 'l sì suona,
>   poi che i vicini a te punir son lenti,
> muovasi la Capraia e la Gorgona,
>   e faccian siepe ad Arno in su la foce,
>   sì ch'elli annieghi in te ogni persona
>
> Ah Pisa, you dishonor of all the folk
>   of the lovely country where Sì is heard,
>   since your neighbors are slow to punish you,
> may Capraia and Gorgona close in on the shore,
>   and dam the Arno in at its very mouth,
>   so that he drowns you to the last inhabitant
>
> (*Inf.* XXXIII, 79–84)

There could be no more violent catharsis for the desperate patriot than this superhuman fury, so ironically counterpointed by the loving mention of his sweet native speech in that place where wrath is the only force that can reconvert the ultimate image of death into a momentary rush of life. After Ugolino, only the mechanical silence of ogre Lucifer.

That fairy-tale monster, like the Gulliverian giants of Canto XXXI, reminds us of *De Vulgari Eloquentia*, where the qualitative difference of man from demon was posited as the infinite distance between articulateness and muteness. The same distance is here dramatically operative. It helps us to feel the impact of the purging which Dante has undergone in Hell through the ordeal of language, which here touched its lowest ranges along with its greatest passionate intensity. Now it can leave behind the *rime aspre*, and the vulgar and the gory and the excrementitious, as a serpent sheds its skin. In Purgatory the "dead poetry" will celebrate its "resurrection"; Casella's nostalgic music will replace the anal trumpets of the devils and Nimrod's senseless bugle. In Purgatory Arnaut Daniel's Provençal utterance will supersede the babelic "diverse lingue" with a congenial linguistic chord, for here multiplicity is no longer anarchy and Babel's cacophony yields to polyphony.[16] Arnaut's refining fire, a truer Pentecost than Ulysses', will mark the nearly accomplished second catharsis of our pilgrim shortly before he is ready for the effortless voices of Heaven.

Dante's drama is the drama of his language, which he raised from literary adolescence to fullest maturity. By the time he was writing the *Comedy*, the initially narrow limits of his fledgling vernacular had come to coincide with the limits of human language as such. The fact that language never stopped worrying Dante the thinker, the craftsman, and the mythographer finds appropriate expression in the special distinction the *Divine Comedy* enjoys among the great epics of the West: that of insisting on dramatic utterance, and on the becoming of the word, as its central effect. This is why we should not overlook the philosopher of language in Dante when approaching his conclusive poem. The *Comedy* drew on the *De Vulgari Eloquentia*, even though at several points transcending its conceptions, as poetry must finally transcend even the most germane discursive thought. Thus, for instance, in the *De Vulgari Eloquentia* Dante indicates the limited canzone as the only metric pattern for lofty poetry in the vernacular, and in matters of vocabulary he seems to think rather in terms of static purity than of dynamic purging.[17] The *Divine Comedy* will burst those bounds. But in one fundamental point the final poem verifies the preliminary speculation: that of making language the specifically human act. Out of whatever tensions and raptures, over and over again the Dantean characters say to us: *Loquor, ergo sum.*[18]

CHAPTER III

FRANCESCA AND THE TACTICS
OF LANGUAGE

DANTE's deep commitment to the cause of political justice and religious
purity makes itself felt in the overall design of the *Comedy* as well as in

NOTE. Since writing this essay in its original form, I have read Renato Poggioli's essay
"Tragedy or Romance? A Reading of the Paolo and Francesca Episode in Dante's *Inferno*" in *PMLA*, LXXII (June 1957), 313–58. This article convincingly argues some
of the main points I was trying to make — namely, that Dante feels a deep compassion
for the two unhappy Ravenna lovers but does not absolve them, that consequently the
episode is "truly infernal" instead of eccentric to the total design of the *Inferno*, and
that Francesca's implicit self-condemnation includes a poignant critique of dubious
"romantic" literature, as well as of its irresponsible use. There is, according to Poggioli,
a "tension between the ethos of contemplation and the pathos of experience . . . the
artistic achievement lies in the fact that the poem reconciles within itself Dante the
witness of the wretched misery of man, and Dante the beholder of the awful majesty
of God."
   The subsequent publication in book form of Domenico Vittorini's "Francesca da
Rimini and the *Dolce Stil Nuovo*" (in *High Points in the History of Italian Literature*,
New York, 1958), however, encourages me to set forth my ideas in the hope that other
elements of understanding will be added to Poggioli's masterful, but far from exhaustive, treatment. (It will be recalled that Vittorini, resuming an old Romantic position,
sees Francesca as a paradisal figure, in but not of Hell.) And Poggioli's interpretation
itself may bear revision when, in order to refute the current view of Francesca's style
as *dolce stil nuovo*, he maintains that she "speaks not in verse but in prose" and sees
her speech as "rhetorical stylization." I feel he is overstating his case here for the sake
of a sane polemic, and I am also uneasy about his denial of a tragic status to Francesca
in the *Divine Comedy*. It is the whole poem as such that progresses beyond tragedy,
while Paolo and Francesca are locked in it as examples of fallen nobility.

several of its most dramatic episodes. But the massiveness of his conception should not obscure the subtlety of its modulations, which are, of course, a matter of style — language in action. It is through this resourcefulness that the poet manages to individualize his creatures. He thus knows them in themselves, as human characters of much greater richness than what would be evoked by a mere catalogue of sins. He knows them by eliciting self-revelation in the gestures of speech, so that we can talk of something like the tactics of language. The scene of Paolo and Francesca in *Inferno* v, which has aroused some controversy among critics, is one of the paramount examples of such tactics. Language and discovery here are one and the same thing; style modulates Being, as it were, to the point where the uniqueness of Francesca's own character matters much more than the question whether she does or does not belong in Hell. She does belong, but in her unique way. The poet has singled her out from the crowd of famous fornicators and illicit lovers, and it is when she appears and begins to speak that the catalogue of names makes way for a focal action of cognition and recognition.

It will be noted that Francesca's account may be divided into two parts, spaced by Dante's moved silence and the attendant exchange with Virgil; and both times she begins to speak at the express request of the poet — a trait of modesty which shows her to be a born gentlewoman (Pier delle Vigne, Farinata, and other rugged males do not have to be solicited to speak). The same breeding shows in her oblique mention of the murderous husband, who appears in her discourse anonymously, and only once — when evoked by the word "morte":

> Amor condusse noi ad una morte:
> Caina attende chi a vita ci spense.

> Love led the two of us to a shared death:
> Caina awaits the extinguisher of our lives.
>
> (*Inf.* v, 106–7) [1]

This could be termed a poetical execution. The lady refers to Gianciotto in the quickest possible way, as if to avoid touching a repulsive object, and she makes it explicitly clear that he indeed finds himself in the lowest pit of Hell, as indicated by the tenor of the vocabulary used (the constellation of deathly references — morte-Caina-spense). By refusing to name him, or even to qualify his relationship to herself, she preserves her feminine modesty and shows how really remote from her thoughts he is. Paolo is her man, not this legal husband who married her almost by proxy and for political reasons; and Paolo arose first in her speech, in connection with love. Even him she refrains from naming directly; he is referred to as "costui." Modesty again, intensified by love; but note how qualitatively different that gestural pronoun is from the frozen impersonality of "chi."

It is indeed fitting that Gianciotto Malatesta, the cruel avenger who did not hesitate to inflict on his carefully spied-upon relations the fate Hamlet once would have liked to mete out to another kind of kinsman, should end up in ice. Whatever the wrong suffered by him, or rather by the divine sacrament of marriage, he is more sinning than sinned against; he represents abstract legality and death. For this, and for not having given her a chance to save her soul, and Paolo's, she resents him as a sneaking murderer: "e 'l modo ancor m'offende" ("and the way it was done still offends me"). She refuses to give him even a semblance of life in her narrative — which accounts for her using the passive form the first time she mentions her death ("della bella persona/ che mi fu tolta," "of the beautiful body/ that was taken away from me"), rather than introducing him as an agent. Indeed, when she has to acknowledge his existence at all, she does so by making him a passive object of action in the formal convention of discourse — a verbal stratagem of retribution.

Once the references to death enter her account, however, the story is told, and her own silence, unlike her listener's, has a deathlike finality. She has given him a concentrated biography, from the alpha of birthplace to the omega of murder. It is now Dante the man, the fool and hero of love, who cannot accept such headstone finality; accordingly, he will now put a direct question to her, as he had not done the first time:

> Ma dimmi: al tempo de' dolci sospiri
> a che e come concedette amore
> che conosceste i dubbiosi disiri?
>
> But tell me: at the time of those sweet sighs

in what manner or terms did love allow you
to recognize each other's doubtful desires?

This way the elicited answer will conclude the interview on the note of
love — another tribute of Dante to the conjured victim, in the form of a
symbolic reaffirmation of love in the face of death. He has carefully chosen
his question. He wants to know how the fateful love was mutually revealed: namely, the turning point of the two interlocked lives, marking the
climax of happiness and the beginning of doom. He narrows the focus of
dialogue to grasp in a flash his interlocutor's essential reality, just as the face
of destiny — sinful love — was an instant's revelation for the two lovers:

Per più fiate li occhi ci sospinse
quella lettura, e scolorocci il viso;
ma solo un punto fu quel che ci vinse.

Several times did that reading impel
our eyes on, and discolor our faces;
but one point only overwhelmed us finally.

It is toward this "punto" that the enveloping tactics of language have
been moving all along, and on it pivots Francesca's harrowed memory. This
was the moment of decision, the kiss of fate:

questi, che mai da me non fia diviso,
la bocca mi baciò tutto tremante . . .

this man, who will never be parted from me,
kissed my mouth, trembling all over . . .

We are now at the center of the whirlwind with Dante and Francesca; the
absolute focus has been reached through firm graduality, from an initial
confused perception of wails, yells, and forms turning around in darkness
to a recognition of their state, to an occasional identification of some of the
fleeting crowd's members, to the choice of two of them for personal colloquy. And the colloquy itself has passed from the general exposition of its
first part to the completely intimate revelation of the second part; from an
account of the birth, growth, and workings of love in the distended arc of
time to its sudden breakthrough in the perpendicular of an irrevocable moment. This reaches the highest poetical intensity by concentrating everything — love, sin, death, damnation — in the ideal projection of a kiss:

Galeotto fu il libro e chi lo scrisse:
quel giorno più non vi leggemmo avante.

Gallehault [a pander] was the book and he who wrote it:
that day we read from it no longer.

In her story Francesca has moved from sequential, historical time to the pivotal instant, and this in turn becomes her eternity, the revolving time-lessness of damnation. She sums herself up in her last words by telescoping everything she and Paolo were, and did, and are, in one final gesture of reticence. In the act of disappearing, like so many Dantean figures, she is realized; and we must be careful not to interpret her concluding line too narrowly. She is thinking primarily of the embrace that followed that kiss and sealed the sinful couple's fate; "quel giorno" is the first day of fulfilled love (deceptive though such fulfillment may be in terms of Dante's ethics) and not, chronologically speaking, the day of physical death. Gianciotto is by now safely removed from her thought, having been disposed of in the way we saw; but she puts it as if time had stood still, and this expresses both her natural desire to prolong the climactic instant forever and the nemesis visited upon it. Thus the implication of violent death is also contained in the blindingly simple line, but only in a secondary way: it is unconscious on Francesca's part, or at least subliminal, and fully present to her listener, with whom every reader is here identified. This makes for an accumulative effect at the end, following the dynamic pattern of rising pitch that is varied throughout the *Divine Comedy*, notably in *Purgatorio* v and xxvi and in *Paradiso* i, iii, xxvi, and xxxiii. Orchestrally, such a solution is the reverse of a crescendo; the tempo of the verse accelerates while the volume (usu-ally) diminishes, with the ever-shrinking phrase gaining more and more momentum until it tends to release the purified essence of the whole canto.

Here, however, this development does not take place in linear progres-sion, as it can be said to do, for instance, in *Purgatorio* v or xxvi. The focus has been sharpened throughout by the gradation of discourse, which began in an intentional "looseness" of stage setting to become more and more pointed; but with each tone shift there has been a corresponding recoil in theme or mode or attitude, something like a new start. Thus Dante, im-mediately before each address to the select sinners, is gripped by "pietà":

see lines 72, 109–11, and finally the conclusion (139–42), when Francesca's sorrow, fully shared, gets to be too much for him, and he breaks down, unable to comment any more, to think, or even to retain his senses. Between the two complementary parts of her narration, his charged silence creates an interval analogous to the pause in the storm mentioned by the passionate lady at line 96: "mentre che 'l vento, come fa, ci tace."[2]

Each time, Virgil has to tide him over the growing wave of compassion, so that he may speak to the grieved spirits, until it gets the better of him and puts an end to expression, conversation, and episode. Francesca both times begins by acknowledging Dante's kindness (lines 88–93, 121–26) in such a way as to prepare the climax of his final involvement. And she keeps reverting to her central concern, the fiery dawn of love: each of her posthumous speeches is a rehearsing of the tragedy she will never be able to transcend, and each points to an endless repetition of the single memory she keeps turning in her mind, so that her very discourse constitutes a mimesis of the whirl in which she is eternally caught. Dante in his turn rehearses this rehearsed vortex of despair, as a further internalization of the pictorial image given at the start.

The scenography has been completely absorbed by the thinking and suffering mind in the dominant spiral pattern that emerges from this progression-through-recoil; and we now see why this structure occurs in Hell rather than in Purgatory or Paradise, where, as has been remarked above, the heightening effect follows a more linear movement. Eternity as untranscended Eros, as ceaseless repetition, in the whirlwind of unenlightened passion: this much divides Paolo and Francesca, despite their intensely noble humanity, from the liberated souls like Pia, Daniel, or Piccarda. Translated as it is into pure dynamic design, the cosmological fiction leaves no mechanical residue here and rises to absolute poetry.

On the same showing, the whole movement of this canto implicitly describes the painful birth of poetry from the blind chaos of passion, through inchoate recognition, naming, liberating cry, articulated vision, dramatic speech, and engulfing silence. From howling darkness to the muteness of swoon, the Word has a hard time being born and achieving itself; it is also, like civilization as a whole, repeatedly threatened by the speechless passion which is its matrix. Since the canto is, in its salient position, an epitome of the whole poetical itinerary from the perspective of Hell, we are not forcing adventitious literary interpretations on it by reading it in such a broadened horizon of meaning; for Dante's pilgrimage through the Beyond (or through Existence itself, if we discard his theological assumptions) can achieve the intended salvation or purification only by heeding the liberating word of poetry.

True poetry, or good literature in general, is a deliverer, not a seducer, as Francesca herself seems to imply when she deprecates her weakness and Paolo's in surrendering to the temptation of *Lancelot du Lac* — a love story that pandered to passion instead of sobering it: "Galeotto fu il libro e chi lo scrisse." Her insistence on the verb "leggere" ("to read") and derivatives in the second part of her speech (four times in twelve lines!), her knowing reference to Virgil as "dottore" (Dante's teacher and mentor), and the fact, unknown to her but not to her audience, that she is talking to a writer, seem to clinch the point in this regard. Dante had written Chapter xxv of the *Vita Nuova* and the entire *Convivio* as a plea for responsible art; the clear example of it, Virgil, is present in this scene in such a way that a telling comparison of his *Aeneid* with the meretricious story *Lancelot du Lac* is inevitable. And we may add that the *Comedy* itself, as a poem in the making, exemplifies the good use of literature in its relation to the Latin epic.

Francesca and Paolo succumbed to romantic literature and duplicated its seductive image in their lives; Dante lets the lesson sink in. (Don Quixote will be a later, and comic, version of the same predicament, except that his romanticism, by placing Dulcinea in the sphere of unattainable fantasy, will escape, if not the confusion of reality and fiction to which the Ravenna couple fall prey, at least their ultimate catastrophe.) Virgil's discretion in the whole scene adds to his stature; he lets Dante do all the talking and never intrudes except to prod his overwhelmed disciple on to further questioning after Francesca's first declaration:

> china' il viso, e tanto il tenni basso,
> fin che 'l poeta mi disse: "Che pense?"
>
> I bent my head, and kept it down so long
> that finally my poet said: "What are you thinking?"

This is the Virgil who stands to Dante, in the latter's poem, as wisdom to youth, as teacher to pupil; the guide who, in *Purgatorio* xvii–xviii, will clarify the problems of love, which can err through a wrong choice of object or through excess or lack of strength. The retrospective focus on Francesca's canto is obvious, and so is the reason why Virgil, while respecting Dante's compassion, tactfully urges him to draw Francesca out. Thus it seems to me that the ethical point of the canto, dramatically and not didactically made, does not exclude the tragic dignity of Francesca herself, as Poggioli seems to believe.

At any rate, if De Sanctis, Croce, Maud Bodkin,[3] and Domenico Vittorini had seen the episode as something more than just episodic, by relating it to the overall drama of Dante's education, their several contributions would be less misleading than they actually are, despite their respective degrees of brilliancy. Because they find the episode poetically self-contained (which is true of several others in the *Comedy*, but only to some extent), or because they are uneasy about the relegation of great love to Hell, they have to make it totally eccentric to the general pattern; and it escapes them that this eccentricity, if it exists, is not the one of a comet, but springs from the inner circles of the system and ultimately rejoins a stable orbit. Powerful centrifugal forces are at work in Dante's soul as he undertakes his journey, but he knows that they must be counteracted by a centripetal pull:

> . . . e io sol uno
> m'apparecchiava a sostener la guerra
> sì del cammino e sì della pietate,
> che ritrarrà la mente che non erra.

> . . . and I, alone of living men,
> braced myself to bear the brunt of struggling
> both with the journey's and with pity's hardship,
> which an unerring memory will portray.

> (*Inf.* ii, 3–6)

The ordeal of compassion in the first stage of the trip through Hell and the ordeal of terror, hatred, and disgust in the subsequent ones are prerequisites of the Aristotelian tragic catharsis that will make a new man out of the bewildered pilgrim, who is the poetic focus of the action, not just its mechanical pretext. We can forget that Dante is not Lawrence or Byron or even Goethe, and we can condemn his condemnations, or try to catch him napping and riven inwardly between theological judgment and human sympathy. But all this is a necessary tension in the poem; it is objectified as Dante's "bewildered"[4] condition that necessitates the intervention of Beatrice and Virgil. Without the objective system (which is not of itself the structure of the poetry, but which makes it possible) there would be no *Divine Comedy*, and even the individual episodes we justly admire for their dramatic surprise would lack the resilience that represents the degree of freedom paradoxically arising within a tight pattern of absolute norms.

This is not to say that the single episodes are to be seen as simple functions of the total pattern or as pedagogical exemplifications of the underlying doctrine. There is in every case the emergent thrust of poetry, its *principium individuationis* which both demonstrates and transcends the overall idea. Paolo and Francesca, at the passionate call of Dante, provisionally leave their orbit to reenter it in a short while; actually, they have not pulled free from it, but have only varied and widened it for the benefit of poetry's prying eye. Likewise, their whole episode is not tangential to the *Inferno* or to the solar system of the *Comedy*, whose complex harmony results from the elasticity of thrust and counterthrust.

As a consequence, Vittorini's interpretation of this canto as a *dolce stil nuovo* achievement, to be viewed entirely in the light of the *Vita Nuova*, and his definition of the murdered heroine of love as a sister of Beatrice, need careful reexamination. Much of what has been said before would already suffice to question it; but the best way to follow that to its logical completion is to venture into the labyrinth of language, keeping in mind the results thus obtained by Auerbach and Spitzer.[5] One further reason to try the experiment would be to broaden Poggioli's somewhat drastic reductions as mentioned above, although I feel closer to his viewpoint than to most others.

To begin with, when Vittorini links Francesca with Beatrice, he implies only an affinity, based on the atmosphere of gentleness created by Dante's sympathy, by expressions like "Amor, ch'al cor gentil ratto s'apprende" ("Love, that is quick to seize a gentle heart") or "ch'amor di nostra vita dipartille" ("for love made them part with this our life"),[6] and by the very insistence of the word "love." Actually, Dante is instructed by Francesca in love, as he will be later on by Beatrice — but how differently, and how important it is to realize that the couple Paolo-Francesca is what the other couple, Dante-Beatrice, might have become had they yielded to expediency!

This oppositional parallelism, covering the dangers and uses of passion, corresponds to the other antipodal similarity which bears out, in the episode, the possibilities implicit in the use of literature: Francesca–*Lancelot du Lac* versus Dante-Virgil. Francesca and Beatrice are related to each other like the two faces of the moon, and the antithesis is so subtle that a glimpsed ray of lost Paradise illumines Francesca's visage, while a deadly power inheres, before Dante is ready for it, in Beatrice's radiance. Francesca is a victim, self-defeated despite all the extenuating circumstances Dante knows, and Beatrice a victor; the former shows him love as despair, the latter introduces him to heavenly joy. Both tests can be too much for the mortal mind, and Dante in both situations struggles to regain control, only to lose it, finally, in a swoon which represents the zero point of experience. In Hell its counterpart only culminates the "war of compassion," but still it makes memorable punctuation. This pattern is one of the double-star systems that could be added to those von Richthofen descries in the poem with his philological telescope.[7]

The matrix of the Francesca-Beatrice antithesis is to be found in the first poem of the *Vita Nuova*, the sonnet Dante addressed to Cavalcanti and other connoisseurs of love in the hope of obtaining an acceptable explanation of his troubling dream. Fear, even horror in memory, issued from the godlike youth who in mirth fed the dreamer's heart to the cloaked girl he held in his arms and then vanished in tears. At the time, young Dante could not know that what he asked his friends to do in connection with the cryptic poem was to decipher the main problem of his future career. As Charles Singleton[8] and Maurice Valency[9] have said in their studies, the *Vita Nuova* came to crown and transform a medieval tradition of long standing, centering on the ritual of Love, who could be both a ravenous wolf and a nourishing inspiration. The Provençals, cherished by Dante, had known it, and Denis de Rougemont [10] thinks Catharist Manicheism had much to do with it; Singleton interprets the *Vita Nuova* as an imaginative endeavor to domesticate the wild god, retracing a whole culture's steps from Eros to Charity.

In the *Comedy* the dangerous ambiguity of the unruly god is overcome by a strategy of diffraction, which separates the two faces of this double-headed figure — Francesca and Beatrice. Thus in the Francesca episode, after the intellectualizing maneuver of the *Convivio*, a whole stream of European poetry, including the *langue d'oïl* legends of Chrestien de Troyes, the Breton cycle, and so forth, is tapped. The infinite that a more naïve or earthly romanticism had been trying to grasp in love is now hunted for in another way; but Dante could not have done this unless he had brought to full fruition, in the moving poetry of this canto, the earlier tendency. That is why this thorough critique of medieval romanticism is at the same time its imaginative peak; and, the acme of the vision having been attained in the *Comedy* with Beatrice, it is no wonder that European poetry after Dante found it wise not to repeat the attempt. Petrarch, not Dante, was to be the universal model of love poetry; and in the great writers who grappled with Dante's problem after him, the image of Beatrice would be split into Dulcinea and Gretchen. As for Wagner, he would revert to Tristram and Iseult — the beginning of the tradition.

We cannot, therefore, reduce the Francesca episode to its *dolce stil nuovo* antecedents if we recognize the nature of its filiation from them. It is, after all, a matter of style; the similarity is offset by the far more complex treatment of language, rhythm, and speech, which by comparison makes Dante's earlier love poetry sound stiff and naïve. Here he has reached maturity: he conducts a richer, suppler orchestra, and his approach is firmer. Tonal words are placed in sensitive spots in such a way as to differentiate Francesca from Beatrice, and at the same time the latter's climate is not made totally foreign to this subterranean sky. Few polarities are so effective in literature. Hawthorne's Miriam-Hilda binomial is too abstract; Melville's Isabel-Lucy ambiguity, in *Pierre*, has rare moments, but does not compare with this Dantean constellation, to which he keeps referring in that unevenly beautiful grotesque of a novel.

To be sure, the word "Amor" dominates the episode from beginning to end, and a hint of his unearthly power is given by the threefold repetition in Francesca's closely packed autobiography:

> Amor, ch'al cor gentil ratto s'apprende,
>   prese costui della bella persona
>   che mi fu tolta; e 'l modo ancor m'offende.
> Amor, ch'a nullo amato amar perdona,
>   mi prese del costui piacer sì forte,
>   che, come vedi, ancor non m'abbandona.
> Amor condusse noi ad una morte:
>   Caina attende chi a vita ci spense.

> Love, that is quick to seize a gentle heart,
>   possessed this man for the beautiful body
>   which was taken from me so unforgivably.
> Love, that exempts no loved one from returning love,
>   seized me of pleasing him so strongly
>   that, as you see, it still retains its grip.
> Love led the two of us to a shared death:
>   Caina awaits the extinguisher of our lives.

The number three is never without a symbolic meaning in the *Divine Comedy*, whether analogy of the Trinity (as is vaguely implied here) or its parody (as in Lucifer's case); but in these transfixing lines the threefold pattern fulfills a heightening function. Love is here the destructive god untrammeled by ritual; the swift pace of the verse, telescoping a whole life into a few lines, expresses the weird rapidity of the unresistible destroyer. By placing the noun, raised to name status, at the beginning of the first line of each of the three tercets, and using it each time as the grammatical agent, Francesca shows of what god she was a votary, and how the whole drama was enacted this side of reason. This god was a tyrant; the qualification she eventually adds upon Dante's request as to her margin of free will contributes truth and perspective to this unforgettable first account.

The absolute power of Love is here manifested also by the horizontal refraction of the vertical threefold iterative pattern in "Amor, ch'a nullo amato amar perdona": this perpendicular intersection on the page, and in the voice, shows Love as an insistent presence through time (vertical sequence) and in space, spreading from person to fated person. Controlled as it is by rigorous form (but here really engendering it), the repetition raises intensity of feeling to the breaking point — it is hard to see how Poggioli could have read this as "prose" and not "verse." Other traits of the passage contribute to this grand effect, notably the downward movement from "cor gentil" to "morte," and the fact that the beginning of love is described as a fire quickly catching ("ratto s'apprende"), whereas at the end life itself is extinguished ("a vita ci spense"). Love's torch begets a consuming fire which leaves only ashes — and as for the cruel self-avenger, he will be stuck in ice ("Caina").

We have already seen how Love's fiery dominion over the initially captured gentle heart is syntactically stated by Francesca in the dominant, active position she gives to the word "Amor." But if we now look at the verbs it governs, we shall descry a further tyrannical posture to which the lovers passively succumb, for these verbs all express imperious action: "prese" ("seized"), twice repeated and combining with the initial "s'apprende" into a phonetic and etymological trinity; "non m'abbandona" ("does not leave me"); "condusse" ("led"). Against this background, the waiting posture of Hell's deepest circle, icy Caina ("attende") gains in sinister intensity, further enhanced by the faint echo of "apprende" which expressed the start of trouble. Hell itself, in that name Caina, thus becomes a character in the drama, a vulture-like witness who is to wreak vengeance on the slave of revenge and will finally clear the field.

A spontaneous rhetoric in Francesca's talk makes both her and Paolo mere passive objects (even syntactically) of Love's actions, while in her second confession the two lovers appear both as passive objects and agents: her first account gives the subjective phenomenology of love, and her second probes into its crucial groping and occasion.[11] First, we get a picture of Love as an absolute, as a ravenous cosmic force not unlike the Greek Moira or, better, Hindu Shiva; then, at the indirect suggestion of rational Virgil, this picture is questioned and replaced by a more plausible one which admits relativity and resistance and intelligible secondary causes — and without weakening the power of Eros Turannos, who is said to have "clutched" ("strinse") Lancelot. But by the mere device of letting herself and Paolo appear in her discourse as grammatical agents, Francesca has this time implicitly admitted the existence of responsibility; she and her lover are at least the source of their own actions and not just playthings of fate. It has been seen how this device, instead of creating an anticlimax, sets up a subtler dramatic development in the whole.

One sees the resemblance of Francesca's first image of love to the omnipotent "amor che move il sole e l'altre stelle" at the end of the *Paradiso*, except that hers is an inverted image, in the mirror of death and despair, so that we get also a linguistic inverted image throughout the episode. The last line of the *Paradiso*, just quoted, celebrates Love as moving the sun and the other stars, and thereby resumes and completes the first line of that canticle: "La gloria di Colui che tutto move." The source of universal movement, which Dante poetically envisages as the ideal goal of his trip through the spheres and as the theme of the whole *Comedy*, is, of course, the Christian God of love seen through the philosophical eyes of Aristotle-Aquinas as the Unmoved Mover; so that when — through the intercession of Beatrice, St. Bernard, and the Virgin — he has attained unison with this Original Impulse, words fail him, and the poem reaches its perfect consummation:

> All'alta fantasia qui mancò possa;
>   ma già volgeva il mio disio, e 'l velle,
>   sì come rota ch'igualmente è mossa,
> l'amor che move il sole e l'altre stelle.

> My high imagination here lost power;
>   but my desire and will already obeyed,
>   like a wheel kept in steady motion,
> the love that moves the sun and the other stars.
>
>   (*Par.* XXXIII, 142–45)

Movement, of the vital, oriented kind centered on God, is here emphasized on both the moral-psychological and the cosmic level; Dante's "desire" and "will" are now entirely motivated by Divine Love, which is to say that they gravitate toward it as do the heavenly bodies. The verb "muovere" ("to move") carries, therefore, such a weight that we shall find it only in strategic positions from beginning to end, often coupled with

"Amor" as its natural emanation; and the intimacy of this nexus is enhanced by the syllabic echo a*mor*-*mo*ve. Thus, at the outset of the dramatic action, Beatrice's "Prologue in Limbo" to helpful Virgil (as reported by him) goes:

> I' son Beatrice che ti faccio andare;
> vegno del loco ove tornar disio;
> amor mi mosse, che mi fa parlare.

> I am Beatrice who bids you go;
> I come from where I am longing to return;
> love moved me, love that makes me speak.

> > (*Inf.* II, 70–72)

She has received her motivating impulse from Divine Love, and she is communicating it to the Roman poet, who, in his turn, will relay the movement that marks the beginning of salvation to his pupil and ward: "Allor si mosse, e io li tenni retro" (*Inf.* I, 136). Although Virgil's "movement" is severed from direct contact with its divine source, both linguistically and theologically, it is enough to get Dante started on the way to deliverance:

> Così li dissi; e poi che mosso fue,
> intrai per lo cammino alto e silvestro.

> Thus I spoke to him; and when he started moving,
> I entered on the steep and forest-ridden path.

> > (*Inf.* II, 141–42)

The significant constellation amor-muovere appears again and again, particularly in *Paradiso* XXIV, where Dante recites his credo to St. Peter:

> . . . Io credo in uno Dio
> solo ed etterno, che tutto il ciel move,
> non moto, con amore e con disio.

> . . . I believe in one God
> alone and eternal, who moves the whole heaven,
> Himself unmoved, with love and desire.

> > (*Par.* XXIV, 130–32)

It reappears in Canto XXVI, where the tourist of Heaven satisfies St. John on the orthodoxy of his views on Love-Caritas:

> più che in altra convien che si mova
>   la mente, amando, di ciascun che cerne
>   il vero . . .
>
> . . . [to this]
> more than toward any other [essence] must move
>   the mind, by loving, of whoever descries
>   the truth . . .
>
> (Par. XXVI, 34–36)

Later on in the same canto, the intercession of Beatrice with Virgil is appropriately commemorated by Adam with the topical verb, "quindi onde mosse tua donna Virgilio" ("There whence your lady moved Virgil," *Par.* XXVI, 118), where the multivalent intensity of "muovere" could not be improved on. It reminds us of the second canzone in the *Convivio*:

> Amor che ne la mente mi ragiona
>   de la mia donna disiosamente,
>   move cose di lei meco sovente . . .
>
> Love that in the mind keeps holding forth
>   on my lady in desirous fashion,
>   often moves me to such feelings about her . . .

and the attendant commentary in Trattato III, ii, 11–12, which equates "to move" with "to feel" as one of the three basic powers of the soul discussed by Aristotle in *De Anima*. Certainly, in order to "move" Virgil physically, Beatrice had to "move" him psychologically by appealing to his reason and heart; the pun is no mere wordplay. As is to be expected, St. Bernard will talk about Beatrice's command to him in the same terms:

> . . . A terminar lo tuo disiro
> mosse Beatrice me del loco mio . . .
>
> . . . To crown your desire
> Beatrice moved me from my allotted place . . .
>
> (Par. XXXI, 65–66)

and he will refer to St. Lucy's initial intercession with Beatrice with the same powerful verb:

> siede Lucia, che mosse la tua donna,
> quando chinavi, a ruinar, le ciglia.

there sits Lucia, who moved your lady,
when you were lowering your brows toward utter ruin

(Par. XXXII, 137–38)

But in the Paolo and Francesca episode, although "Amor" is abundantly quoted, the joining echo will be with "morte": "A*mor* condusse noi ad una *mor*te." This is what can be called an inverted linguistic image of heavenly love as presented in the *Paradiso*; and the image will be complete if we observe the nearly total absence, in this canto of love, of the privileged verb "muovere" and its derivatives. (It appears only once, to denote Dante's compassionate action in calling the two tragic lovers to an interview: "*mossi* la voce," "I *moved* my voice." Dante of course is still redeemable; they are past salvation.) For "muovere," as focused by Dante in the light of his Thomistic philosophy, expresses only purposive movement, and as such it appears only as a direct or indirect emanation of Divine Love; but the kind of movement to be found in the *Inferno*'s circle of lustful love is mad, disorderly, and obsessively repetitious, like the whirl of passion itself. Consequently, its proper verbal predicate will be "menare" ("to drive," "to drag," "to carry away"), a distorted phonetic echo of "Amor" and "muovere":

> . . . e tu allor li priega
> per quello amor che i mena, ed ei verranno.
>
> . . . and then do beg them
> for the sake of their *driving* love, and they will come.[12]

The phrase, in Virgil's advice to Dante about securing an interview with the Ravenna lovers, aptly describes their mad gyrations in the wind of undirected passion. No expediency of rhyme or rhythm compelled Dante to use "mena" here instead of, say, "move" or even a less specific verb like "porta"; he meant what he wrote with his usual clarity and preciseness. The nature of the action conveyed by "menare" ("chaotic" or "compulsive movement") is unmistakably emphasized at the beginning of the episode:

> La bufera infernal, che mai non resta,
> mena li spirti con la sua rapina:
> voltando e percotendo li molesta . . .
>
> The infernal whirlwind, which never pauses,

> drives the souls on in its relentless fury:
> by turning and smiting it harries them . . .

and shortly after: "di qua, di là, di giù, di su lì mena . . ." ("drives them here and there, up and down . . ."). The fourth time this focal verb appears in the episode, it will have a much less erratic connotation, for Dante has been careful to stress the human dignity of the two unhappy lovers:

> quanti dolci pensier, quanto disio
> menò costoro al doloroso passo!

> how many sweet thoughts, how much desire
> drove these two on to their dolorous passage!

The verb here sounds like "condusse" ("led") in "Amor condusse noi ad una morte"; yet if the action seems more rationally oriented and less chaotic than before, it is defined by its term ("doloroso passo," "mournful passage") as a negative force.

Another key word, "disio" ("desire"), though in itself ostensibly unaltered, changes connotation according to whether it is used in an infernal or in a heavenly context; and it appears frequently indeed. It represents the subjective pull of Love, which, if thwarted, distorted, or unfulfilled as in Hell, engenders misery, and if aimed at the one object of desire, "l'amor che move il sole e l'altre stelle," becomes the needle of happiness in the compass of the soul; thus Dante uses "disio" and "velle" at the conclusion of the *Paradiso*, as quoted above. Beatrice says of herself to Virgil, "vegno del loco ove tornar disio" ("I come from where I am longing to return"), and Virgil describes his allotted unhappiness as desire without hope, "sanza speme vivemo in disio" (*Inf.* IV, 42), which is a fitting definition of wisdom without fulfillment (that is, God). Divine justice is manifested in the souls of the damned in a perversion of desire; they yearn to reach their place of torment "sì che la tema si volve in disio" ("so that fear is changed into desire," *Inf.* III, 126). But in Canto I of the *Paradiso*, the word connotes fulfillment, not deprivation or masochism:

> perchè, appressando sè al suo disire,
> nostro intelletto si profonda tanto,
> che dietro la memoria non può ire.

> for, approaching the goal of its desire,
>   our intellect reaches out into such depths
>   that memory cannot keep up with it.
>
> *(Par. I, 7–9)*

One of Plato's most famous myths, as told in the *Symposium*, has it that Eros (Love) is the child of Poros (Affluence) and Penia (Poverty). Such dialectic of desire we find in Dante, so that we might well consider in a favorable light his recommendation of "Poema Sacro" to Can Grande as a guide to happiness, if by happiness we mean spiritual fulfillment — for that is the great theme of the *Comedy*. Notice, too, that the first time the word "desire" appears in the *Paradiso* (see the above quotation) it shows a paramount semantic change: it no longer means the simple tension of desire toward its object, but the object of desire itself, and thus signalizes our entrance into the realm of Fulfillment.

Here in Francesca's Circle, "disio" is tragically unfulfilled, just as with Virgil it is an expression of quiet, resigned unfulfillment. It acts funereally, by driving the lovers to the "doloroso passo"; it glows with nostalgia — without hope — in the superb simile of the doves:

> Quali colombe, dal disio chiamate,
>   con l'ali alzate e ferme al dolce nido
>   vegnon per l'aere dal voler portate . . .

> Such as the doves at the call of desire
>   with wings spread out and steady toward their sweet nest
>   come through the air, carried by imperious will . . .

The doves are the birds of love, and here they introduce a ray of Paradise, but only as a foil to the two lovers' distress; there will be no "sweet nest" for the latter! On the other hand, two bird similes have been used before in the canto to denote the hopelessness of the souls carried around by the gale; the sureness of instinct, as manifested in bird migrations, emerges here as unavertible doom. The contrapuntal play finds its climax in Francesca's use of the word "pace" ("peace"), twice applied to other subjects than herself: that is, to Dante:

> se fosse amico il re dell'universo
>   noi pregheremmo lui della tua pace . . .

> were the king of the universe our friend
> we would pray him to grant you peace . . .

and to the Po River seeking peace in the Adriatic Sea, near her birthplace:

> Siede la terra dove nata fui
> su la marina dove 'l Po discende
> per aver pace co' seguaci sui.

> The land where I was born sits on the seaside
> where the Po River finally descends
> along with its followers, to find peace.

Peace is what Dante and the river will have, and what Francesca can never have; that she says it by implication is another proof of her "gentility" and gentleness, but also of Dante's mastery, which shines out in even greater power when we reflect how focally he introduces the word "peace" in the *Paradiso*: "E'n la sua volontade è nostra pace" ("and in his will is our peace," *Par.* III, 85).

Peace is not inertia, but the transparency of mind and soul fulfilled in the contemplation of God and forever activated by His love "sì come ruota ch'igualmente è mossa" ("like a wheel kept in steady motion"); therefore, the word "pace" complements, in Dante's verbal universe, "moto" and "muovere," "amore" and "disio," to indicate what the nature of fulfillment is. And just as he contrapuntally inserts "pace" in Canto v of the *Inferno* to deepen Francesca's despair, he also uses the verb "muovere" there, but only with regard to himself, and as a foil to the lovers' driven unrest:

> . . . "e tu allor li priega
> per quello amor che i *mena*, ed ei verranno."
> Sì tosto come il vento a noi li piega,
>   *mossi* la voce: "O anime affannate,
>   venite a noi parlar, s'altri nol niega!"

> . . . "and then do beg them
> for the sake of their *driving* love, and they will come."
> As soon as the whirlwind turns them toward us,
>   I *moved* my voice: "O anguished souls,
>   come speak to us, if it is not forbidden!"

The simple fact that Dante can "move" his voice shows he is connected with Beatrice, whom Love moved to speak, and that he will be capable of salvation. Not so the "anime affannate"!

The master of language, just because he knows his words thoroughly and can focus them like nobody else, succeeds in translating the Penia-Poros, Tristram-Francis, Francesca-Beatrice contrast into one of the tersest, most compact, and unresistible verbal counterpoints to be heard in Western literature. Knowing that true civilization could be founded only on an accurate definition of the wild god of Love, he set out to face the sphinx and tamed it, but at the cost of total risk for himself. Francesca, Virgil, Ugolino were voices in his soul; and here in Canto v of the *Inferno* the clash of philosophies becomes a lucidly faced tempest of the heart. Reason or free passion? The alternative was not an academic problem, but the core of his quest and the perpetual impasse of Western civilization down to Romanticism and beyond. In the terms of his theological symbols, he saw that passion is a dangerous, if fascinating, animal and that reason alone is not enough; so, leaving Francesca and Virgil himself behind (after internalizing them), he tried to progress with Beatrice beyond pure reason, yet with reason. Peace and Movement, the Unmoved Mover: neither stasis nor perpetual unrest; he knew this all along, from the moment he dwelt with Francesca in that deceptive Elysium of a moment which was really the eye of the cyclone.

CHAPTER IV

DANTE'S NOBLE SINNERS · ABSTRACT
EXAMPLES OR LIVING CHARACTERS?

How to approach the *Divine Comedy* today: girt in the knightly armor of scholarship, or with the unarmed candor, say, of an Ike McCaslin vis-à-vis his bear-god of the wilderness? In Faulkner's story, the youth desiring to meet the forest's tutelary numen incarnate must first discard all weapons and man-made instruments; Dante's Dark Wood may, or may not be, another matter. Our trouble seems to be that neither the paraphernalia of "armed vision" by itself nor what Geoffrey Hartman would call "unmediated vision" alone can ensure proper access to the formidable poem. Overcommented as it is, and intricate in its own right, Dante's work discourages subjective ventures. But unless I, as reader, can have a personal meeting with the spirit of poetry that inhabits the *Comedy*, scholarship will not help, whatever its usefulness in defining the aesthetic revelation I shall have had to wrest from the poem itself in the teeth of history's reluctance. Thus I accept the risk involved in making scholarship secondary, that is, accessory to the primary experience of meeting the poem on my own terms. Ike McCaslin has to surrender to the elusive Old Ben before the ritual killing can be enacted.

For it is well to remember, in the face of the dominant structural-theological reading of recent decades, that theological or historical scholarship, beyond a certain point, may overgrow and stifle the poetry. The poetry as such, on the other hand, rescues its own cultural assumptions and makes them good in the texture of language. So much of the *Comedy* is available as given, in the staging of its dramatic action and in the very action of words and rhythms, that boldness can be justified in taking "texture" for a starting point rather than the structure per se and its cultural substructure. This much holds even for one who rejects Croce's aesthetic atomism and appreciates the structural defenders of the poem's unity for having vindicated the protagonist's role as that of an objectified dramatis persona centrally relevant to the manifold epic, which would otherwise fall apart into discrete episodes of the Crocean kind.

But I cannot follow certain dogmatic inferences occasionally drawn from the structural-theological position to the detriment of the poetry. A dedicated, well-informed, and generally cogent scholar like Rocco Montano,[1] for example, develops such a certainty about Dante's preliminary certainties that, with all due respect for his labor of love, I am afraid he tends to become *plus royaliste que le roi* when confronting the interpretive problem of the *Inferno*. His reductive argument goes that Francesca — like Farinata, Pier delle Vigne, Brunetto Latini, and Ulysses — is a sinner *tout court* rather than a noble sinner, and that whatever sympathy or admiration Dante the pilgrim may show for Hell's denizens is conditioned by the pilgrim's temporary obfuscation: the latter is on the way to salvation, but still dangerously close to the passions of the damned, and one must not confuse him, the dramatis persona, with the author of the poem at the time of writing it. Montano concludes that all infernal figures are there only to exemplify how bad vice can be, and he would deny them any final dignity: witness Brunetto Latini's hasty leave-taking at the end of Canto xv, or Farinata's wrangling with Dante, which renews the earthbound factional strifes of Florence and is out of place in the final perspective of salvation.

The argument is so logical that it sounds unanswerable; in fact, it is just a puritanical reversal of De Sanctis' position, which saw only the glory and not the murkiness of Hell's inmates, since De Sanctis wanted to free them from their theological dungeon and thus make the *Inferno* safe for democratic humanism. But poetry is intangibly alive, and it refuses to be strait-jacketed by reductive logic or enlisted in ideological disputes. Even if one admits that Dante's theology was so Manichean as to demand the moral annihilation of all sinners in his poetical world, can we not assume that the poet in him occasionally knew better than the theologian? that achieved vision overcame the dogmatic intentions and thereby, far from destroying the structural unity of the poem, made it subtler? Monolithic conformity only manages to stiffen or fossilize the work of art, whose life I see in an interplay of tensions and correspondences, as described, for instance, by Theophil Spoerri.[2]

To rob Farinata of tragic nobility [3] means to follow Virgil's warning against corruptive pity so literally that all we have left is an oversimplified abstraction instead of a crucial encounter and recognition in the pilgrim's progress of Dante's persona; even Irma Brandeis, for all her sensitiveness to the indwelling spirit of words, tends to see in the unreconstructed Ghibelline only the heretic.[4] He is much more than that. True, Farinata and the others are embodiments of earthbound passion and thus of what limits Dante must overcome if he wants to attain God-given peace. Dante will leave them behind in his striving for harmony and completeness, but they are living figures, not one-dimensional, abstract examples of their respective sins, and as dramatic creations they transcend the ethico-theological scheme the poet used to bring them out.

How can we believe that the dispute between Dante and Farinata is utter vanity, when it concerns, beyond their factional antagonism, precisely that object of so much reiterated anger and love throughout the tripartite poem: Florence, the city, civilization, the focus of our destinies; the burning care of Sordello and Marco Lombardo and Cacciaguida? Neither the climbing of Purgatory nor the flight into Heaven can divest Dante of this care.

> "Ma fui io sol colà, dove sofferto
>   fu per ciascun di torre via Fiorenza,
>   colui che la difese a viso aperto."

"But I was the only one, where all the others

> already agreed to Florence's destruction,
> to stand up for her and defend her openly."

To have stood, alone among one's congregated allies and partisans, for mercy to Florence; to have saved Florence in the hour of Ghibelline victory, and thus to have risen above one's fiery partisanship; to have acknowledged the communal bond, at great cost to oneself and one's political future — "this is not vanity," to say it with Ezra Pound. The lines spoken by Farinata in Hell ring way beyond Hell, and they are enough to guarantee his tragic worth. He is not just "the Heretic" or "any heretic," he is dramatically individualized and larger than his sin; he is superhuman by contrast with Cavalcante, the all-too-human sharer of his flaming tomb. That his generosity did not suffice to save him from damnation enhances, rather than diminishes, his stature, even in the Christian clash of human with otherworldly values. For all his theme of exemplary salvation, Dante is also, as Auerbach has it, a poet of the secular world — and without the stormy drama of this world's scene, the heaven-bound ascent and the (temporarily reached) heavenly perspective would collapse. Borgese has remarked that Dante's wrath survives the purgative phase of the *Inferno* and even of the *Purgatorio* [5] — luckily for the poem, I say, which lives on such dynamic contrasts to the extent that they mobilize for us the otherwise all-too-rigid architectural symmetry.

Far from discounting the essential contribution of scholars like Montano (or Singleton) to a unified reading of the *Comedy*, I propound a flexibly contrapuntal interpretation, which will allow us to grasp the tragic complexities of each climactic episode even while integrating it in the total process of Dante's fictional ordeal. Tragic dignity attaches to such figures as Francesca, Farinata, Pier delle Vigne, Brunetto Latini, Ulysses, because in each of them we witness the mystery of a lofty nature doomed by sin, and what could be more tragic to a Christian soul? We could also talk of the mystery of liberty and of the drama of temptation. (And yet, if we cling to the theological argument, what choice did Francesca have? Or how could Dante know that Ugolino was really damned? Couldn't a last-minute repentance have saved him, and was the poet authorized to assume fictional omniscience concerning the secret intercourse between Ugolino and his God? Isn't it, rather, that the poet claimed a poet's license in placing those hypothetical damned in his Hell, since he needed them, and, what is more, they needed him as an evoker and claimed their chance to speak through him?) At any rate, tragic or just pathetic (as Ciacco, Cavalcante, and Ugolino undoubtedly are), these sinners are eminently human, with all that flesh is heir to. Our sympathy for them is not wasted, our appreciation of their suffering humanity can even survive the harsh theology that assigned them to everlasting doom — though this does not mean that we have to break up the poem into unrelated fragments.

Each sinner rehearses his life, or his catastrophe, for Dante, to whom they are stations in a pilgrimage, moments and instruments of a purification, of a self-recognition and eventual salvation. Yet they are all individual souls, God's highest work. In each of them Dante the pilgrim can mirror something of himself, at least their common fallible humanity, and more specifically some inclination which might drag him too into the abyss — but for the grace of God (and my watchful will) there go I. Paolo and Francesca ring a crucially autobiographical note for the *stil nuovo* poet who had wandered after several *donne dello schermo*; they are figures of his possible destiny, hence his response. Farinata, the heroic antagonist, is also what Dante might become if he heeded without restraint his own political and intellectual pride. Pier delle Vigne, as a wronged servant of his state, is in a way a counterpart of Dante, who through him purges the possible temptation of suicide in the face of injustice, and who without infringing on his Christian dogma vindicates Pier's memory on earth — Pier was not guilty of treason,

> per le nove radici d'esto legno
> vi giuro che giammai non ruppi fede
> al mio signor, che fu d'onor sì degno!

> for the new roots of this trunk
> I swear to you I never broke my loyalty
> to my great lord, who was so worthy of honor!

That cry *de profundis* is not meant to debase its utterer or to elicit snobbish condescension on the part of the reader. Brunetto Latini is a father figure, a momentary counterpart of Virgil as teacher, local embodiment and not caricature of the pervasive teacher motif on which so much of the whole poem's action is predicated; he is a *cara e buona immagine paterna*, and Dante acknowledges his debt to him. Again, there is something of the best of Dante's youth connected with him, and if the unity of the *Comedy* depends on despising Ser Brunetto, I have little use for that unity, and I invoke the poet's better knowledge against his dogmatic intentions.

Let us not forget that if Brunetto is damned, so is Virgil; that Dante put to use Brunetto's *Treasury*, and that if figures like Brunetto represent something to be left behind, they also embody or utter something which will stay with Dante: the prophecy of his exile, the auspice of literary and moral triumph, tragically proffered by him who could not triumph, and who, like a lesser Virgil, did as

> . . . quei che va di notte,
> che reca lume dietro e sé non giova,
> ma dopo sé fa le persone dotte.

> . . . he who goes by night,
> who carries a lamp behind and does not help himself,
> but shows the way to those who follow him.

Even if we read an irony into Dante's touching avowal,

> . . . ad ora ad ora
> m'insegnavate come l'uom s'etterna,

> . . . by the hour
> you taught me how man makes himself eternal,

the irony is structural, not immediate, and moreover it is tragic; a reminder of how the living can use the dead, an example of the complex relation of an open present to a closed past. The "eternity" Ser Brunetto taught Dante to strive for was a humanistic immortality, thus not the true eternity, which only Beatrice can help him to secure. For himself, Brunetto Latini has been able to gain only the eternity of damnation. In Purgatory Dante will formulate a memorable self-criticism in the humility of the artist who is learning to relativize the value of earthly fame from a higher perspective than Hell could afford:

Oh vana gloria de l'umane posse!
   com poco verde in su la cima dura,
   se non è giunta de l'etati grosse!
Credette Cimabue ne la pittura
   tener lo campo, e ora ha Giotto il grido,
   sì che la fama di colui è scura.
Così ha tolto l'uno a l'altro Guido
   la gloria de la lingua; e forse è nato
   chi l'uno e l'altro caccerà del nido.
Non è il mondan romore altro ch'un fiato
   di vento, ch'or vien quinci e or vien quindi,
   e muta nome perché muta lato.
Che voce avrai tu più, se vecchia scindi
   da te la carne, che se fossi morto
   anzi che tu lasciassi il pappo e 'l dindi,
pria che passin mill'anni? ch'è più corto
   spazio a l'etterno, ch'un muover di ciglia
   al cielo che più tardi in cielo è torto.

How vain the glory accruing to human powers!
   how shortly it keeps its verdant dominance
   when not helped by the grossness of bleak ages!
Cimabue thought himself master of the field
   in painting, and now Giotto is acclaimed
   so that the former's fame is quite obscured.
Just so one Guido took from the other Guido
   the glory of the language; and one may live already
   who will drive both of them from their own nest.
The rumor of the world is only a gust
   of wind, which blows now this way and now that,
   and changes name with changing of direction.
What increment of fame will you obtain
   by departing from life in your old age
   rather than at the time of baby talk,
within a thousand years? which is a shorter
   lapse of time, by comparison to eternity,
   than a twinkle of the eye versus the slowest of heavens.

(*Purg.* XI, 91–108)

Yet it is the vanity of conceitedness and not the value of art that Dante is
here learning to reject; the intersection of history and eternity is his con-

stant problem, and if with him, like the Christian he is, eternity emerges as the final judgment of history, it is not because history is irrelevant. Humanistic fame of the kind Brunetto taught him to acquire will still be on Dante's mind when, high up in Paradiso, he says:

> ritornerò poeta, ed in su 'l fonte
> del mio battesmo prenderò cappello.

> I will return as poet, and on the font
> of my own baptism I will crown myself.

Thus the valuable part of Brunetto's experience and teaching stays with Dante to the very end, and how could it be otherwise when we consider that in terms of his faith, earth is an arena and not a shadow, and that the *Inferno* affords glimpses of the earthly values to be rescued from the wreckage of history, those very values which accrue to the theologically damned yet morally respected figure of beloved Virgil. When Beatrice takes over as Dante's educator (and as judge of history), she does what the Church did with the Roman Empire: she comes to integrate and save even while superseding, to raise and not to destroy. Just as Dante the narrating poet will never have to retract his tribute of affectionate esteem to Virgil, so he won't have to unsay what he so heartily says to the lesser mentor Brunetto. I find it hard to separate Dante the knowing poet from Dante the passionate pilgrim in Canto xv of the *Inferno*. His warm words to Latini have the hindsight of Heaven; they are not spoken tongue in cheek. The chasm across which they are uttered defines the tragic scope of the whole episode.

This suggests a far more mobile and subtle relation between pilgrim and narrator (or between persona and author) than the rigid dogmatic separation of the two can admit; Dante the narrator relives certain crucial moments of his ordeal in unison with the naïver Dante he was while experiencing them, and they in turn were a reliving of certain decisive phases of his own earlier life, which the action of the poem, and the writing of the poem as such, bring to consummation. It would be wrong to believe that the privilege of otherworldly vision has definitively freed Dante from the burdens of earth. At the very moment of inditing his poem he has returned to earth, and the pathos of earth will intermittently assail him even while going through the *Paradiso*, for the supreme vision was glimpsed and lost, and only death will bring final liberation. We could speak of several Dante personae (the bewildered pilgrim through Hell, by implication Dante's fiery youth; the serener visitor of Purgatory, by implication a wiser, sadder Dante of mature years; and the liberated traveler into Heaven, foretaster of permanent bliss), and of the changing relation of Dante the author to these personae, with each of whom he may momentarily identify even though he is wiser than they. A stable attitude does not prevail everywhere; the posthumous wisdom of the writer returned from the other world yields time and again to outbursts of passion, and these appear as present comment of the writer on the world he takes so much to heart, violent interjections of the imperious pen at its relentless task.

We have in the *Comedy*, then, both a self-transcendence and a frequent reimmersion of the author in his past experiences, which he can recapture in a kind of historical present, not only to judge, but also to respond, as Ishmael does with the crew of the vanished ship. Between Ishmael and his life on the "Pequod," a whirlpool; between Dante and his earlier life, a light that failed, though it gave guidance. Did this hard-won wisdom make him harder or mellower? It is a postexilic Dante we see at work, a man committed to his vision, not to an abstraction. I am not prepared to accept the closing lines of Canto xv of the *Inferno* as contemptuous of Brunetto and destructive of his dignity; "quegli che vince e non colui che perde" ("the one who wins and not the one who loses"), yes, an unseemly haste, forced by the circumstance of Hell, but conveyed by an image of victory, ironical though it may be. If we go by theology in the abstract, then Dante's placing of Brunetto in Hell is a highly arbitrary gesture, founded on arrogant hypothesis; how could Dante know that the aged scholar had not repented his sin before death, in the sanctum of his soul? But of course Dante needed Brunetto in his ordeal, and even more in the rehearsing of his life — autobiography being one of the essential dimensions of the poem. The occasion for Ser Brunetto's damnation is not discussed at all in the episode; Dante is not really interested in showing us how bad a sodomite can be, because if that had been his concern, he could have easily picked some likelier candidate.

Florence and Florence's destiny, Dante and Dante's future, Ser Brunetto and the value of learning and teaching — these are the pressing concerns of our poet, and it is no use pretending that he is more insufferably righteous than he actually manages to be. Ser Brunetto's sin is a private affair; God took care of that, and how sad it is that such a fine man should have fallen! But to Dante the poet, that man is more than an abstract example of punished vice; he appears in his best aspect, he is almost incongruous in Hell, and this makes the meeting a more poignant ordeal for our pilgrim (and for the struggling writer). The whole situation reminds us that, whatever George Steiner may say in *The Death of Tragedy*, it is simply not true that Christianity made tragedy impossible. When the destiny of an immortal soul is at stake, beyond the horizons of earth, tragic possibilities deepen. Dante's "other world" brings this world into sharper focus; the tension between the two is part of Dante's challenge as a poet, the mainspring of his creativity.

And nowhere does this tension vibrate more keenly than in the Ulysses episode of Canto xxvi, where the damning sin furnishes the occasion for introducing a heroic figure whose bearing is anything but contemptible (as the alleged sin would require, instead, if the chief purpose of Dante in conjuring the much-traveled Greek warrior were to exemplify an abstract vice).[6] As John Nist has recognized in a very personal (and partly myopic) essay,[7] Ulysses mirrors something of Dante's own roaming life, Dante's leaving his family behind, Dante's intellectual curiosity and the dangers it once entailed. Unlike Dante's, of course, Ulysses' thirst for boundless knowledge will result in physical and metaphysical shipwreck. The horizon of infinity is not available to human effort, "argomenti umani," unaided by Divine Grace. And yet how grandiose is that hopeless effort! Ulysses' venture into the unknown may have blinded Romantic critics like De Sanctis to the nonhumanistic underlying attitude of Dante in evoking the twin flame; but the poem's unity gains nothing by demeaning the "virtue" of the pagan hero, a virtue Dante himself approves of within the larger framework of Christian revelation:

> fatti non foste a viver come bruti,
> ma per seguir virtute e conoscenza.

> you were not made to live the life of brutes,
> but to follow the way of valor and knowledge.

One must be temporarily deaf to poetry to misread the tragically inspired lines:

> e, volta nostra poppa nel mattino,
> dei remi facemmo ali al folle volo

> and, turning our stern toward the orient,
> we made wings of our oars for the mad flight

as John Ciardi does (despite his other accomplishments as a translator) when he minimizes the value of "folle" ("mad") the way a Sunday school teacher would: "we made wings of our oars for our fool's flight." [8] The "madness" of Ulysses, no matter how self-judging that term can be, is no petty thing; Dante did not conceive a petty figure, indeed he showed in him the greatness of which the pagan world was capable, because only thus could the failure of Ulysses acquire its full significance in the context of a work which is engaged in the search for ultimate values. Ulysses' destruction by the God-whipped maelstrom in sight of Purgatory's mountain confirms this view; the noble hero almost makes it, in defiance of the inviolable decrees emanating from what is to him "Altrui," an unknown and alien power. Melville's Ahab will be one of his descendants.

If, in Ulysses' fatally misguided thirst for worldwide experience, through an epically straightforward style that shuns all uncertainties, Dante portrayed something of himself, he counterbalanced the Greek navigator with the antithetic figure of Guido da Montefeltro, who is basically "other" than Dante, for Guido interests the poet as a real case of moral ambiguity, damning casuistry and devious weakness. With all due caution about clichés, one might see in Guido the prototype of the modern Hamletic antihero, as contrasted to the ancient hero who, Ahab-like, is lost through his overweening assurance and not through bad conscience. Theologically, Ulysses and Guido are on the same level, and they are meant to illustrate fraud; poetically, they are at the antipodes of each other, just like Farinata and Cavalcante, and they afford Dante a chance to wield language masterfully. The counterpoint of Guido's tortuous sentences — a moral portrait in themselves — to Ulysses' headlong utterance cannot be lost on the reader:

> S'io credessi che mia risposta fosse
> a persona che mai tornasse al mondo,
> questa fiamma staria senza più scosse . . .

> If I thought that my answer were to a man
> who was ever going to return to the world,
> this flame you see would stop shaking forever . . .

The irony of Guido's self-deception with regard to his interlocutor is a dramatic touch of the first order, and his final perdition at the hands of the "logician devil" appropriately caps his story. Style evokes, style judges, style objectifies; there is no reason to discard De Sanctis' idea that European drama-to-be (especially Shakespeare's character study) was seminally contained in Dante's portrayals.

Style changes to suit each epic, or pathetic, or ironic portrait, and it can even mimetically descend to the bottom of abomination as in the episode of Mastro Adamo and Sinon; yet style retains its fundamental identity even while becoming other, just as Dante becomes somehow "other" (through compassion or fear, wonder or anger or disgust) only to become more fully himself. In every relevant figure he recognizes what is other and what is himself, and his poetry serves as both necromancy and exorcism. Thus his poetry is "experience," not of the unpeopled world as Ulysses would have it for himself, but of the other world, and of this world through the other. There is no need to reduce each heroic or pathetic figure to small size in order to save the coherence of the whole. This coherence is so strong that it thrives on the structural balance of thrust and counterthrust, as a Gothic cathedral does. Style decides, every time, style creates, and it creates by transcending the theological intention, by using it as a support, not by conforming to it as to a blue print. This way a world is born — or reborn — in and around Dante's individual pilgrimage; and it is a full-sized world, not a parade of moralistic phantoms. Calvary and resurrection, Dante's ordeal culminates in a momentary recognition of the divine plenitude which every singular will, be it through strength or weakness, fatally had to miss by persisting in its isolation. Damnation is self-confinement in the singular form of existence; salvation is openness to communal infinity. Poetry is what accomplishes the impossible transition from the former to the latter pole, from the compressed and finally choked energy of Hell's funnel to progressively released energy, beyond the zero point where the first reversal of perspective occurs.

CHAPTER V

PATTERNS OF MOVEMENT IN
THE *DIVINE COMEDY*

IT IS no sin to heed the promptings of chance. An arresting passage in *Purgatorio* II sent me back, through sheer contrast and analogy, to one in *Inferno* XVII; then as I read on, in this further retracing of Dante's journey, to *Paradiso* I, some of the well-known lines brought back to my mind those previous ones in such a way that they crystallized into a special cluster of sound, imagery, and meaning within the immeasurably larger context of the intricate poem.

A gestalt I am now trying to descry arose from the following specific couplets, and developed around them:

> e, discarcate le nostre persone
> si dileguò come da corda cocca.

> and, once he had unloaded the two of us,
> he vanished like an arrow from the nock.
>
> (*Inf.* XVII, 135–36)

> ond'ei si gittar tutti in su la piaggia:
> ed el sen gì, come venne, veloce.

> so they all threw themselves upon the beach:
> and off he went, as fleet as when he came.
>
> (*Purg.* II, 50–51)

> ma folgore, fuggendo il proprio sito,
> non corse come tu ch'ad esso riedi.

> but no bolt of lightning, as it flees from its source,
> would race as you did in returning to it.

(Par. 1, 92–93)

If these memorable fragments can be shored up to establish a connection that makes specific sense, it is because they all kinetically portray, or better, act out some kind of swift movement. The first quotation effectively concludes a transitional canto in which Geryon, an allegorical embodiment of Deceit, provides for Dante and Virgil the much-needed aerial transportation, over a forbidding ravine, from the last circle of violent sinners to Malebolge, the accurately subdivided circle of fraudulence. In the above two lines, Geryon is caught in the act of unloading his exceptional passengers and darting back right away to his outpost. The second quotation also describes the speedy departure, right after arrival, of a supernatural agent charged with conveyance of souls: the pilot-angel who shuttles between Purgatory beach and the mouth of the Tiber to bring to their temporary home the spirits of those deceased that, though not damned, have some purging to do. For his busy job he employs a transcendental boat powered by his sail-like wings. The third quotation, finally, occurs at a crucially transitional point in the action of the poem, when Dante is lifted into the sky, at lightning speed, from the top of Purgatory mountain, to begin his exploration of Paradise. Since this sudden upward thrust cannot be directly perceived by Dante himself, who is rapt in contemplation of Beatrice's sun-staring eyes, it is she who informs her astonished charge of the giddy motion under way.

If Dante did not have a special genius for climactic concentration, it would not do to focus like this on one- or two-line excerpts from episodes wide apart; it would be wanton surgery. I know of no other poet who can bring to a consummation the development of a whole canto, or the essence of a human destiny, as he does in the minimal units of narrative poetry: a tercet like Pia de' Tolomei's, or even a single line. Style in his verse appears as a structural force of compression that captures locally, in its appropriate version, the whole informing idea. The archetypal architecture of the entire *Comedy* is already making itself felt in our quotations, which happen to be from each of the three canticles, even if their respective encasing episodes do not bear a relation of narrative symmetry to each other. Obviously, the narrative counterpart of the pilot-angel would be, in Hell, Charon the angry boatsman of *Inferno* III; while the dynamic relation of Beatrice to Dante in *Paradiso* I would seem to echo, on its own heightened scale, the initial action of Virgil in extricating Dante from the dark wood: "Allor si mosse, e io li tenni retro" ("Then he moved, and I followed in his footsteps," *Inf.* II, 136). Geryon is clearly a link in the story, and but for Dante's visualizing power his whole episode would have remained a stopgap; it doesn't certainly stand out, as say, the Francesca episode or the Pier delle Vigne one does. Yet Geryon is an airborne Charon, and in a poem that dramatizes the idea of passage and transmutation he cannot ultimately be irrelevant; both he and the pilot-angel, no less than Charon, are rescued from the status of mechanical contraptions by the force of poetry, which confers upon them thematic value. Treated by a less pervasive imagination, these angels and demons could not have risen above the lifelessness of more or less clever stage props. If this is true, the quality of movement exemplified in our selections must have some local relevance to each respective kingdom of the Beyond in which the action takes place. The three quotations would not have struck the imagination of this reader, to vibrate in a dissonant chord, if somehow a truly *infernal* stress did not make itself felt in the verbal rhythm of the first one to offset a symmetrically *purgatorial* physiognomy in the second and a culminating *paradisal* trait in the third.

Swiftness in movement, graphically caught in all three of them, is the thematic relation that makes it possible to encompass them in a basic harmony. If we can slow down this swiftness for the purposes of focused analysis, comparative examination of the passages in their several contexts will be more pointed as a result. The method, provided it is tactfully used, should not be more pedantic than the slow-motion pictures by which competent sportsmen study in detail the technical performance of track runners.[1]

Geryon's described action is above all, poetically speaking, a matter of rhythmical embodiment. The two hendecasyllables in question move at antithetic pace: the heavy slowness of the first actually triggers the rapidity of the second, which is enhanced in its turn by the strong foil. This effect results, in the first line, from Dante's choice of what is the rarest of stress patterns in Italian hendecasyllables, namely, a combination of three accents on the fourth, seventh, and tenth syllables ("e, discarcáte le nóstre persóne"), which, compared with the two prevalent patterns of fourth, eighth, and tenth, and sixth and tenth, makes a decidedly retarded cadence. The following line shoots through a fourth-eighth-tenth accentual series: "si dileguó come da córda cócca." Of course, the stress pattern does not work by itself in abstraction from meaning and sound. The body of words, along with their contextual arrangement, concurs in the effect; otherwise how could anyone account for the strange fact that the *Purgatorio* line mentioned above exploits precisely the same retarded cadence (fourth, seventh, tenth) of the heavy *Inferno* line with a contrary result of incomparable fleetness? Let juxtaposition speak for itself:

> e, discarcáte le nóstre persóne.
> ed el sen gì, come vénne, velóce.

Leaving aside for the moment the Purgatorial line, to which I shall revert later, I should like to point out how the markedly harsher consonants of its Infernal counterpart are at the core of mimetic slowness. Sibilant, plosive, and vibratory sounds cumulate into thick syllables of the unmelodic kind Dante defined as *rime aspre* ("harsh rimes") and functionally employed throughout the *Inferno* to fit its cruelty. Moreover, here the bristling syllables have a way of clustering into long-drawn words like "discarcate" ("unloaded") whose meaning and phonetic physiognomy both add to the retardation effect. This corpulent wording, hardly to be found in the Purgatorial ambience, makes us feel all the heaviness of the Hell-bound monster and the toil to be undergone by Dante not just in dismounting from its bulky back after the scary aerial ride, but in climbing down deeper and deeper through Hell toward the bottom of the dark pit where matter and sin reach their maximum condensation: the point "whither weights are from all over drawn." Since Dante in his symbolic language identifies heaviness, darkness, and opacity with evil, as the negative of weightless light, it is easy to see that the atmosphere of density created by the use of *rime aspre*, to be climaxed in the last circle of Hell where Lucifer is stuck in ice, is structurally relevant to the imaginative metaphysics of the whole poem. We can here feel the pulse of the overall informing idea.

Indeed the sense of bulk and toil is effectively conveyed by the sonal organization of the whole Geryon incident. Here is a telling sample, from line 79 through line 93, where Virgil persuades Dante by word and example to mount the repulsive monster for a short bareback ride:

Trova' il duca mio ch'era salito
  già su la *gro*ppa del *fie*ro animale,
  e disse a *me*: "Or sie *for*te e ar*di*to.
Omai si scende per sì fatte scale:
  monta dinanzi, ch'i' voglio esser mezzo,
  sì che la *co*da non *po*ssa far *ma*le."
Qual è co*lui* che sì *pre*sso ha'l ri*pre*zzo
  de la quartana, c'ha già l'unghie smorte,
  e triema tutto pur guardando il rezzo,
tal divenn'io a le parole porte;
  ma vergogna mi fè le sue minacce,
  che innanzi a buon segnor fa servo forte.
I' m'asset*tai* in su *que*lle spal*lac*ce:
  sì volli *dir*, ma la *vo*ce non *ven*ne
  com'io credetti: "Fa che tu m'abbracce."

I found my leader who already rode
  the ferocious animal bareback,
  and he said to me: "Now be strong and bold.
By now such is the stairway we must climb down;
  mount here in front of me, for I want to be
  between you and the tail, lest it harm you."
Just like the man who is so close to the shivers
  of ague that he already has pale nails
  and trembles even looking at the shade,
just so I became at hearing those words;
  but his threats filled me with shame,
  which makes a servant strong in his lord's presence.
I sat as best I could on those hideous withers:
  this I meant to say, though my voice did not
  come out as I wished: "Do hold me in your arms."

Apart from the intrinsically heavy words, notably those with rhyming "-ezzo" endings that anticipate similar harsh sounds in the circle of the icebound sinners, it is the frequency of retarded hendecasyllables (as italicized in the lines above) that makes the rugged verbal medium express fatigue and anxiety. A few lines below, another retarded hendecasyllable describes very mimetically, in the guise of Virgil's command to Geryon, the nature of the slow-wheeling flight to come:

> . . . "Gerion, moviti omai:
> le rote *lar*ghe, e lo *scen*der sia *po*co:
>
> . . . "Geryon, now you start moving:
> let the gyres be wide, and the going down imperceptible:

The same rhythmical mimicry appropriately emerges in the immediate sequel, which portrays Geryon's slow preliminary movements and then, after his sudden self-propelling whiplash, Dante's fear and the braked flying of the monster that maneuvers to a perfect landing:

> Come la navicella esce di loco
> in dietro in *die*tro, sì *quin*di si *tol*se;
> e poi ch'al tutto si sentì a gioco,
> là 'v'era il *pet*to, la *co*da ri*vol*se,
> e quella tesa, come anguilla, mosse,
> e con le branche l'aere a sè raccolse.
> Maggior pa*u*ra non *cre*do che *fos*se
> quando Fetòn abbandonò li freni,
> per che 'l ciel, come pare ancor, si cosse;
> nè quando Icaro misero le reni
> sentì spennar per la scaldata cera,
> gridando il padre a lui: "Mala via tieni!";
> che fu la *mia*, quando *vi*di ch'i' era
> ne l'aere d'ogni parte, e vidi spenta
> ogni veduta fuor che de la fera.
> Ella sen va notando lenta lenta:
> rota e dis*cen*de, ma *non* me n'ac*cor*go
> se non ch'al *vi*so e di *sot*to mi *ven*ta.
> Io sentia già da la man destra il gorgo
> far sotto *noi* un or*ri*bile *scro*scio,
>
> As a small ship eases itself out
> by backing up, he got himself out of there;

and when he felt he had full elbowroom
he bent his tail against his own chest, and
    by stretching it eel-like he propelled himself
    and gathered the air to his body with the paws.
I think no greater fear can have arisen
    when Phaeton let the reins go out of control
    so that the whole sky seems to have burned out,
nor when poor Icarus felt his back being plucked
    bare of feathers by the melting of the wax,
    while his father cried out: "You're on the wrong route!";
none greater than my fear when I realized
    I was immersed in air, with all view barred
    save of the beast.
It swims on very slow:
    wheels and goes down, yet I cannot sense it
    but that the air fans my face and lower limbs.
I already heard the waters on my right side
    make a horrendous roar under us,

Dante's aeronautical imagination proves every bit as lively and exact as Leonardo's; he has overlooked no detail of the concrete experience to be evoked, from the visual to the tactile, kinetic, and aural impact. The alliteration in the line "se non ch'al *viso* e di sotto mi *venta*" combines with the rhythmical impedance to express the rush of thick air on Dante's face and body. The density of this murky medium prompts the poet to say, two lines above, that his animal aircraft "swims" very slowly ("sen va *notando* lenta lenta") rather than flies.

On the other hand this prevalent impedance effect, so relevant to the psychophysical quality of the scene, alternates with the rapidity of Geryon's takeoff and of the ruinous flights of Phaeton and Icarus, conjured by fear in the clinging aeronaut's mind. The contrast, throwing into strong relief the dominant atmosphere, is the more effective because it relies not just on description and imagery, but on appropriately placed quick lines like "e quella tesa, come anguilla, mosse" and "né quando Icaro misero le reni" to offset dynamically the retarded ones. Dante's fear of a fall from great heights is very plausible in the immediate context since this happens to be his first airborne trip; his fear also has something to do with the obsession of sin that is still burdening him, but in retrospect it acquires an ironic flavor, for Geryon is really anticlimactic to the sky-soaring Icarus or Phaeton. The mood of suspense, however, is brilliantly sustained by the repressed cry that comes through the sequential unit "Ícaro mísero" just before taking direct shape in Daedalus' desperate warning to his runaway son ("Mala via tieni!"), which Dante the uneasy passenger can almost think he hears while the winged dragon carries him down into an impenetrable darkness.

To make his fear even more archetypal in that helpless plight, Geryon evokes in the poet's alert mind first a maneuvering ship and then a convulsive eel, thus suggesting a submersion that is directly contrapuntal to the act of flying though appropriate to the downward direction of the flight itself, which is a slow plunge into the dark. The connotation of seawater is sustained, as we saw, by that tactical verb "swimming," which had already described Geryon's first appearance at the end of the previous canto (XVI, 130–36):

> . . . 'i' vidi per quell'aere grosso e scuro
> venir notando una figura in suso,
> maravigliosa ad ogni cor sicuro,
> sì come *tor*na co*lui* che va *giu*so
> talora a solver l'ancora ch'aggrappa
> o scoglio o altro che nel mare è chiuso,
> che 'n su si s*ten*de, e da *piè* si rat*trap*pa.

> . . . I saw through that thick, dark air
> a shape come swimming up,
> fit to astonish even the firmest heart,
> such as sometimes a diver will rise back
> to the surface after disentangling the anchor
> from a reef or other hindrance under water:
> he stretches from the waist up, and pulls in the feet.

Here the transition from "thick and dark air" ("aere grosso e scuro") to the menacing liquid element is effortless, and the simile of the diver surfacing from the hard job of disentangling his boat's anchor from some impediment on the sea bottom aptly clinches the point to prepare us for imminent developments in the next canto. The diver's physical strain is well rendered by the retarded cadence in the fourth and last lines quoted. Dante's personal anguish and his concern with the knot of sin to be perilously untied contribute to the weird strength of this elaborate depth image, even if it refers primarily to Geryon's mode of appearance, to his threatening deviousness, to his needed services, and to his peculiar system of locomotion.

Fear of the dragon and of the submersion of which it is going to be the vehicle, abhorrence of reptile sliminess, and the suddenness of treachery are all present in the dynamics of the line (xvii, 104) that gives us Geryon's propulsive outstretching of his previously coiled tail in the eel simile. The mercurially slippery word for "eel" ("anguilla") accounts for such an effect, which constitutes a thematic variation on the crouching-craning motion of the diver to whom Geryon is compared at first in the quoted conclusion of Canto xvi. If we consider how Dante, in describing the composite beast's wheeling flight in its terminal phase (Canto xvii, 126–32), introduces the antiphonally graphic simile of the wayward hawk, tired by too much time on the wing, we shall see that he has been playing on the two sets of alternating images in polyphonic style: on the one hand, the more literally appropriate series of air-wingedmen-falcon, and on the other, the contrapuntal series of sea-diver-ship-anchor-eel. For they interlock, offsetting each other, instead of truly identifying in a perceptual resolution, even if convincing tonal transitions are provided by that initial relation of thick air to deep water; as for the diver image, it is directly antiphonal to the falling airman's (Phaeton, Icarus). That diver is, of course, imagistically pivotal to the local situation, and to the overall one too; for, as the quotation from Canto xvi makes clear, he goes up and down ("suso" and "giuso"). That isn't only what Geryon himself does in his shuttling service; it also describes what Icarus and Phaeton have done, although they have gone up and come down only once, to be sure, and it points to Dante's alternately rising and falling mood, caught as he is between fear and hope through the ordeals of Hell. Moreover, it has to be remembered that he is now going down the funnel of Hades in order to reemerge eventually through its bottleneck hole and start rising to the stars. More important, it seems that the poet can afford to describe Geryon's movements in terms of contrasting similes — some human, some birdlike, some relating to fish — because the monster combines all these attributes in his body, having the face and torso of a man, the wings of a huge eagle, and the tail of a scaly dragon. Since this newfangled sphinx stands, allegorically, for Hypocrisy, ambiguity and deceit inhere even in its first appearance, when it seems to be swimming and is actually flying, and in the imaginative impact the whole episode evinces through a canon-like development.

Part of this is the scorpion simile Dante uses in Canto XVII, 25–27, to sketch the workings of Hypocrisy's poisonous tail:

> Nel vano tutta sua coda guizzava,
> > torcendo in su la venenosa forca,
> > ch'a guisa di scorpion la punta armava.

> In the void his tail lashed out for its whole length,
> > twisting upward the poisonous fork
> > which was armed on the tip just like a scorpion's.

Apart from the way in which composite imagery is here supposed to depict the composite nature of the beast, quickly compared to a beached boat and then to a bellicose beaver before a provisional climax is reached in the impressive entomological figure, the darting scorpion tail fits as a musical variation the dynamic theme we have been tracing on the spur of our first cue. A slowness appropriate to an apparently earthbound bulk whips itself into action by contracting and then violently distending its mass lengthwise; thus the sinister movement of the scorpion varies the swimming rhythm of the diver who "stretches upward, and gathers up his feet," and will be echoed by the eel convulsion at line 104 of Canto XVII, finally to be resolved, after additional intervening slowness imparted by the wheeling-falcon image, in the striking bow-and-arrow figure of the canto's last line. Enough has been said on the verbal-rhythmical dynamics of its immediate antecedent, which acts as a foil to its own swiftness; we can now observe how the two antithetic lines are intimately tied by plosive alliteration (dis-carcate . . . come da corda cocca) combined with liquid vibrants and with an ominous insistence on the dark vowel *o*, itself echoing throughout the flight sequence where the following triple rhymes stand out: poco-loco-gioco, tolse-rivolse-raccolse, mosse-fosse-cosse (reinforced by "Fetòn abban*donò*" in the body of an intermediate line), accorgo-gorgo-sporgo, scroscio-scoscio-raccoscio, pone-Gerione-persone. The concluding double rhyme rocca-cocca comes as a natural clincher; and we shouldn't overlook, in the body of the verse, such horizontal chromatic sequences as: "per cen*to* *ro*te, e da lu*n*ge si po*ne*;" "*co*sì ne pu*o*se al fon*do* Gerione;" and other echoing notes interspersed liberally in the hawk-simile part.

Dark coloring and reiterated sharp consonants give body to these truly infernal lines, the last two fitly capping the canto with a sonal resolution that seems to sum up and release its pervasive essence. The fast arrow-like pace of the very last line results from the accurate choice of short words in syntactically direct and unpunctuated alignment ("si dileguò come da corda cocca"), while the toiling slowness of the last but one, so effective in the juxtaposition, is a matter of longer verbal units clotted into an absolute ablative between two bracketing commas ("e, discarcate le nostre persone,") in retarded hendecasyllabic cadence, even though the syllabic sounds are the same as in the last line. What we get as a consequence is the hard stretching of the bow ("e, discarcate . . .") followed by its sudden release, in which words like "corda" actually render the whir of the snapping string, and the repeated plosives mimic the sharpness of the departing arrow. Iconically, this image climaxes the previously noted ones that thematize the double movement of contraction and distention: the surfacing diver, the scorpion, the eel (and the riding poet himself when he alternately cranes and huddles to cling more firmly to his mount; the verb "raccoscio" at line 123 recalls the analogous "rattrappa" as said of the diver in the last line of the previous canto). But the climax is obtained by discarding any animal comparison in favor of the bow and arrow, which abstracts in heightened form the tautness and violence of the effort involved in all those movements. Swiftness in Hell cannot be effortless or graceful; it is tied to mass, to untranscended density and weight, which only violent strain can rescue from earthbound sluggishness. Geryon is never so strongly presented as when he disappears ("si dileguò") like a whizzing arrow. This dynamic instant supersedes in its finality the laborious analytical description of the monster's heterogeneous parts as given at the beginning of Canto XVII. We see and feel the self-launched beast as a pure projection of mass. The canto has been spiraling through its descriptive phases to this tremendous fore-shortening in acceleration, which Brancusi would understand in terms of his figurative abstractions. Thus my initial selection of two lines for a comparative discussion within the total context of the *Comedy* would now seem far from whimsical, since these lines (and more particularly the second one) consummate the pertinent episode in a way that is revelatory of Hell's own essence.

The angel who ferries souls to Purgatory, as an earlier juxtaposition of distant lines may have shown, typifies an utterly different kind of speed. Unlike infernal Charon, he is a boatsman who needs "neither oar nor sail" (*Purg.* II, 32) for propulsion, since fanning his "eternal pinions" (line 35) beautifully suffices to that purpose. And the contrast with Geryon's writhing and snapping couldn't be more poignant. The celestial ferryman's motion is not a matter of reptilian tension and release, for it is continuous, drawing upon a constant source of liberated energy. As a result, we get in the focal line (*Purg.* II, 51) that concludes his brief appearance an effect of graceful gliding, dynamically conveyed by the short, light words, accentually and syntactically grouped in wavelike balance. The spirant alliteration on the last two words (*venne, veloce*) imparts a keen breeziness to the line; on pronouncing it, our lips find themselves going through the motions of blowing, and we kinetically feel the ocean wind in the angel's wings: "ed el sen gì, come venne, veloce." Free from the verbal and syllabic corpulency of its rhythmical counterparts in the *Inferno*, here the retarded hendecasyllable makes for effortless movement — an effect we should vainly look for in the sharp tautening of Geryon's bow-and-arrow line, instinct as it is with massbound energy.

Broader confirmation may accrue to these localized remarks from further analysis extending beyond our initial verse focus to encompass all of the pilot-angel's performance in Canto II, with its contrapuntal correspondences to some traits of the comparable Infernal episodes. For instance, just like the last two lines of Geryon's canto, lines 50–51 of *Purgatorio* II tell of an unloading followed by the immediate departure of the conveyance:

> ond'ei si gittar tutti in su la piaggia:
> ed el sen gì, come venne, veloce.

Yet, if line 50, in describing the rush of spirits disembarking on Purgatory beach, employs thicker sounds than the next one and thus acts as a tactful foil to the latter's fleetness, the contrast is not between straining weight and sharp shot, as in Geryon's final lines, but between animated crowding and speedy lightness. In both cases we have, between two antinomially contiguous lines, a relation of resilience, and the resilience is appropriately violent to the point of cruelty in Hell, but a manifestation of ease in the Purgatorial locale. Alliteration bridges in each case the two contrasting elements of the conclusive rhythmical gestalt, with vastly different overtones: the ponderous "discarcate" of *Inferno* xvii echoes in the antithetic "dileguò" ("vanished") of the next line as well as in the wiry sequence "come da corda cocca" ("like an arrow nock from the bowstring"), while in the Purgatorial counterpart the parallel innervation of sound links "si gittar" ("threw themselves") and "piaggia" ("beach") in line 50 with the short verb form "gì" ("went") in line 51. If Geryon has to catapult himself into the air by sharp exertion, and the motions of dismounting from his bulky back fatigue his wary passengers, no such strenuousness attaches to the corresponding actions of the fleet angel and of his eager purgatorial charges. "Gì" resolves in a suggestion of final quickness the comparatively denser cues of "gittar" and "piaggia," but these in their turn are far from heavy, implying as they do a readiness of unforced movement and perhaps even the soothing plash of waves on the reached shore.

Both of the last lines in question kinetically enact a fast disappearance which, like others in the great poem, takes us by surprise and establishes forever in our memory the figure caught at vanishing point. The quality of movement displayed in disappearing is really a dynamic portrait of each figure involved. The dynamic portrayal recapitulates and supersedes all the previous description, because images and sounds converge all along onto the "negative" climax. Thus we saw how the last line of Geryon's canto consonantally and vowel-wise rehearses in foreshortened acceleration the *rime aspre* of the whole episode; similarly, the very unharsh rimes of the pilot-angel's episode gravitate on its mid-canto conclusion to establish a lyrical tone attuned to the wistful dreaminess of the *Purgatorio*:

Ed ecco qual, sul presso del mattino,   13
  per li grossi vapor Marte rosseggia
  giù nel ponente sovra 'l suol marino,   15
cotal m'apparve, s'io ancor lo veggia,
  un lume per lo mar venir sì ratto,
  che 'l mover suo nessun volar pareggia.   18
Del qual com'io un poco ebbi ritratto
  l'occhio per domandar lo duca mio,
  rividil più lucente e maggior fatto.   21
Poi d'ogne lato ad esso m'appario
  un non sapea che bianco, e di sotto
  a poco a poco un altro a lui uscio.   24
Lo mio maestro ancor non fece motto,
  mentre che i primi bianchi apparser ali:
  allor che ben conobbe il galeotto,   27
gridò: "Fa, fa che le ginocchia cali:
  ecco l'angel di Dio: piega le mani:
  omai vedrai di sì fatti officiali.   30
Vedi che sdegna li argomenti umani,
  sì che remo non vuol né altro velo
  che l'ali sue tra liti sì lontani.   33
Vedi come l'ha dritte verso il cielo,
  trattando l'aere con l'etterne penne,
  che non si mutan come mortal pelo."   36
Poi, come più e più verso noi venne
  l'uccel divino, più chiaro appariva;
  per che l'occhio da presso nol sostenne,   39
ma chinail giuso; e quei sen venne a riva
  con un vasello snelletto e leggiero,
  tanto che l'acqua nulla ne 'nghiottiva.   42
Da poppa stava il celestial nocchiero,
  tal che parea beato per iscripto;
  e più di cento spirti entro sediero.   45
"*In exitu Israel de Egypto*"
  cantavan tutti insieme ad una voce
  con quanto di quel salmo è poscia scripto.   48
Poi fece il segno lor di santa croce;
  ond'ei si gittar tutti in su la piaggia:
  ed el sen gì, come venne, veloce.   51

And look, as in the imminence of dawn   13
   Mars glows ruddy through the thick haze
   down West over the ocean's line,   15
just so there appeared to me, quite recognizable
   should I see it again, a light streaking so fast
   across the sea as to outpace any flying thing.   18
And after turning my eyes from it for a moment
   to ask the appropriate questions of my leader,
   I saw it had grown alike in light and size.   21
Then from each side of it there came into view
   something white, I did not know what, and then
   another whiteness like it issued from the underside. 24
Still my teacher was keeping his silence,
   while the first whiteness turned out to be wings:
   as he then well knew who the oarsman was,   27
he shouted: "Do, do go down on your knees:
   there is God's angel: and do fold your hands:
   henceforth you will see more such officers.   30
You see he spurns any human device,
   so that he needs no oar, nor any sail
   but his own wings to reach so distant shores.   33
See how he has stretched them out toward the sky,
   to ply the air with those eternal feathers
   which never molt as mortal plumage would."   36
Then, as the divine bird came closer and
   closer, he appeared in fuller splendor;
   so that my eyes could not sustain the sight   39
so close, and I looked down; and he came ashore
   with such a slim vessel and light
   that the water sucked in no part of it.   42
The heavenly boatswain was standing astern,
   radiating such bliss as Scripture intimates;
   and more than a hundred spirits sat within.   45
"*In exitu Israel de Aegypto*"
   they all sang out in perfect unison
   with that psalm's sequel as is written down.   48
After that he made the sign of the holy cross;
   so they all threw themselves upon the beach:
   and off he went, as fleet as when he came.   51

Though onomatopoeia is no sound-constant as such, of course, but a variable depending on meaning and context, I'd risk the remark that the climactic spirant alliteration of line 51 (*venne, veloce*) is strengthened by previous recurrence in the strategic words I have marked. Among these, some seem to stand out, like the five forms of the verb "vedere" ("to see") in lines 16, 21, 30, 31, 34; the two *v*-alliterating forms of the reciprocal verb "apparire" ("to appear") in lines 16 and 38 (two more forms of the same verb, without the *v* sound, occur in lines 22 and 26); the three forms of "venire" ("to come") which, in lines 17, 37, and 40, anticipate the final "venne" of line 51; the twice used preposition "verso" ("toward"), pointing once to heaven (the angel's real home) and once to the onlookers on the beach (his present destination); and finally, such isolated but important words as "mover" ("to move," line 18), "volar" ("to fly," line 18), "vasello" ("vessel," line 41), "velo" ("sail," line 32), "voce" ("voice," line 47). Semantically, these words plucked from the syntactical context on hand might design a Klee-like abstraction of the essential goings-on! The alliterative clusters they magnetize, then, can hardly be irrelevant. Taking both meaning and sound into account, I'd say there are three such primary clusters, namely, one comprising lines 16–18 (the angelic boat's dim appearance), another centering on lines 31–34 (Virgil's explanation to Dante of who and what the apparition is and how the boat moves), and a third one innervating lines 37-42 (the angel's dazzling approach and landing). The three sonal-semantic units, in crescendo order, are musically recapitulated in inverted form by the transparent concentration of the last line.

One could even say that all the lines of force gravitate toward the last word as such: that uncannily apt "veloce" which gives us the grace, and not just the velocity, of the angelic yacht, because it resumes in its light sounds the phonetic physiognomy of "velo" ("sail") in line 32, and also of "volar" ("to fly") in line 18 and "ali" ("wings") in lines 26 and 33. This compels us to observe that the alliterative impulsions streaming through the passage are not limited to the airy *v* series, but include at important points the complementary liquid series of *l*, which appropriate consonantal echo, indeed, works within each of the clusters I have tried to isolate for analytical purposes. And since we are reading, as far as possible, contrapuntally, it may not be beside the point to recall how visual, aural, and kinetic form, in the lines describing the angelic ship's swiftness, closely recalls the memorable line of *Inferno* XXVI in which Ulysses recounts the eager rowing of his shipmates bent upon "making wings of the oars for the wild flight" "Dei remi facemmo ali al folle volo . . ."). Compare with that lines 32–33 of the present context:

> sì che remo non vuol né altro velo
> che l'ali sue tra liti sì lontani.

Or also, at some remove, lines 17–18 and 51. If we listen even more closely, we shall find that the Ulysses line expresses a crescendo of strenuous and successful effort, while no effort is involved in the gliding ease of the angel's speed. The digression is less digressive than it seems, for Ulysses, like the angel, was bound for Purgatory (unawares), when the whirlpool sucked him down with his ship; lines 130–32 in *Purgatorio* I, right before our episode, commemorate his shipwreck by implication, in stating that the approaches to Purgatory are out of bounds for any living navigator:

> Venimmo poi in sul lito diserto,
> che mai non vide navicar sue acque
> omo che di tornar sia poscia esperto.

> We then came to the deserted shore
> which never saw any man ply its waters
> who could afterward find his way back home.

Geryon is twice compared to a ship, and then to a hawk in his wheeling flight, with the metaphoric exchange between the element of air and the element of water setting the keynote at the outset, in the diver simile; the pilot-angel is a "divine bird" (line 38) propelling a boat, and no submersion fear is implied, for his "slim and light vessel" (line 41) just skims the water's surface without dipping below (line 42). He is then clearly antiphonal to both Charon, with his heavy boat, and Geryon himself; Dante's imagination works with symmetries. These, however, would remain mathematical skeletons unless he brought them to life, as he does here, with his matchless gift for perceptual grasp. Thus we see an intimation of sails in the whiteness of the approaching ship on the inviolable ocean, until the dazzle turns out to be wings, with a weird plausibility of miracle. The miracle is there above all in the etymological sense of an event to be ad-*mired*, and, in the literal terms of the story, it inverts what would otherwise be, in a more common situation, the metaphoric likening of a boat's sails to bird wings. The inversion, in perfect keeping with the supernatural agent at work here, will gain added relevance from one more direct comparison with the great *Inferno* line of Ulysses, where human endeavor, straining itself to its limit, metaphorically changes the normal means of navigation into desperate wings; whereas in the Purgatorial context an emissary of Paradise appears at first to be using the "argomenti umani" ("human devices") of oar and sail before this is declared to be an optical illusion masking the reality of celestial wings. The visual as well as dynamic affinity of sails and wings sustains that imaginative elaboration throughout, as it does in a closely comparable string of nautical-angelic images to be traced in modern Hart Crane's *The Bridge*, especially the sections "Ave Maria" and "Atlantis."

The apparitional evidence of the phenomenon Dante reports rests largely on his using the verb "to appear" ("apparire") no less than four times in predicative connection with "light" ("lume," line 17), "whiteness" ("un non sapea che bianco," line 23), "white wings" ("bianchi . . . ali," line 26) and "luminous" ("chiaro," line 38). In this verb, to be repeatedly found in key position throughout the *Comedy* and, long before that, in the *Vita Nuova*, Dante stresses the positive meaning of "coming suddenly into sight" above the negative and ironic one of "to seem." The suddenness of apparition characterizes, of course, the first use of this verb in our passage, while after that it takes on another shade of meaning: "to manifest oneself" in an intensity of revelation which proves too much for Dante's mortal eyes, as it will, again and again, in the *Paradiso*. Optical precision marks the graduality of this visual surprise, with our poet's eyes from the beach catching first a distance-dimmed light on the horizon, then taking in an indefinite white luminosity whose real shape and nature will manifest themselves only later, when Dante's mental categories will manage to recognize and classify it as an object, beyond the astonishment of the uncategorized chromatic sensation — and Virgil must help, for Dante has never seen such objects before.

The visual and semantic factors of such poetically recreated hypothetical perception are closely allied to sound-mimesis. Some of its consonantal aspects have already received analytical treatment here, but the interplay with vowel effect is paramount. The frequency of the long, open *a* can hardly be irrelevant to the impact of the passage at hand, when we reflect how it occurs twice in the verb "apparire," which somehow attracts whole constellations of *a*'s. A line like "mentre che i primi bianchi apparser ali" ("while the first whiteness appeared now to be wings") provides the most striking example. Others would be traceable in lines 22–24, with words like "lato," "appario," "bianco," "altro" thrown into dominant relief by stress pattern; or in line 33, with "ali" echoed by "lontani"; or in line 38, where the final word-cluster "più chiaro appariva" certainly stands out. And among the rhymes we find -atto, -ali, -ani, -aggia. The genius of his native language prompted Dante to play on the sustained fullness of this open vowel, as if, with as many syllables as possible and without disfiguring the inherited words, he were uttering the "Ah!" of wonder. It is no accident that the expansive vowel should make itself heard as pure exclamatory gesture in Virgil's exhortation to his disciple in lines 28–30:

> gridò: "*Fa, fa* che le ginocchia cali:
> ecco l'angel di Dio: piega le mani:
> omai vedrai di sì fatti officiali.

Alternating with narrow and light-colored vowels like *i* and *e*, the *a* thus sets the tone for the chromatic pattern of our Purgatorial episode, just as the dark-colored *o*, reinforced by occasional *u*'s, was seen to predominate in the murky air of Geryon's hell ambience, not only in the concluding tercets, but right from the start, in Canto XVI (line 130 onward):

> ch'i' vidi per quell'aere grosso e scuro
> venir notando una figura in suso,
> maravigliosa ad ogni cor sicuro,
> sì come torna colui che va giuso . . .

A tonal echo of this dark appearance strikes our ear in the comparable part of the *Purgatorio* episode, where the angel first shines at horizon level on the sea with the ruddy light of Mars as seen "through thick haze" ("per li grossi vapor"). "Grossi vapor" recalls "aere grosso e scuro" ("thick and dark air") and spreads its *o* note around in neighboring words like "rosseggia," "ponente," "sovra," "suol," "ancor," "lume," before the light tones take over. At the same time the contrast matches the resemblance, for Geryon looms into sight as a swimming shape of darkness, soon to plunge Dante into a thicker darkness in which he will be momentarily blind, while the angel appears right away as a dim star whose light will rise to unbearable pitch, threatening Dante's visual powers with the blindness of dazzling clarity, not darkness (lines 38–40). If so, then the last two lines of our passage rehearse that sequence in inverted order, but only through the chromatic impact of vowels: "gittar . . . la piaggia . . . ed el sen gì . . . venne, veloce." Quite unpedantically, the series returns from open *a* to dark *o* through a string of narrowing light sounds (*e* and *i* pronounced according to Italian phonetics); and since the ruddiness of Mars ("Marte rosseggia") was said to characterize the angel's early gloaming on the horizon, by *o*-centered words, when our voice comes to rest on the *o* of "veloce" the synaesthetic suggestion of a light fading into dim red is pretty strong. Dante knew nothing of what modern physicists call the Doppler effect, but he had good eyes and good ears, and he certainly turned them to account here for a dynamic evocation of wide spaces. His synaesthesia has little in common with Rimbaud's and is probably instinctive rather than planned, even though we know that his use of "harsh rimes" in appropriate contexts was deliberate, and an unfailing musical ear obviously guided him in his verse construction to set up the kind of admirable complex patterns I have been endeavoring to identify here.

As is to be expected, no machinery, whether of serpent tail and dragon wings or of angelic pinions fanning the earth's atmosphere, proves necessary to engineer Dante's upward flight from the summit of Purgatory into heaven. He now has eaglelike Beatrice in lieu of a winged dragon, and since purification has been attained and the thicker air of the lower layers is left behind, the celestial intermediary has no need of adapting her resources to an external vehicle as the angel did in ferrying his load of souls across Dante's mythicized Atlantic Ocean. As *Paradiso* i tells us, she just stares into the sun and relays its beam to her lover, who thereupon shoots aloft with her at lightning speed without realizing it. He merely wonders at the deluging sun, which seems to invade the whole sky with its blaze, but cannot directly sense his own uncanny movement — one reason being that his optical reference is Beatrice moving along at the same pace, and another, that following her lead he has averted his eyes from the mountaintop (on which they were initially poised) to the dawn-lit sky. And at this height, air is no longer to be felt. Beatrice herself has to explain to the stunned poet what really happened, thereby inaugurating her recurrent dissertations on appearance and reality:

> ma folgore, fuggendo il proprio sito,
> non corse come tu ch'ad esso riedi.

> but no bolt of lightning, as it flees from its source,
> would race as you did in returning to it.

It is to Dante's credit that he has thus avoided the embarrassment of describing the moment of the unbelievable takeoff. He has taken us once again by surprise, as he did, to a lesser extent perhaps, in the two previous episodes. For this is the hardest transition, both in terms of spatial movement and of poetical development. From earth to Heaven is a qualitative leap, whose intrinsic infinity can only be bridged by a velocity approaching what was believed to be the instant propagation of light. The earlier transition, from Hell to Purgatory, was skillfully described in terms of an inversion of gravity: here all weight is shed, and the pull of spiritual gravity is free to operate. Dizzy speed is effectively expressed by the sonal duplication "fòlgore-fuggendo" — in which the Italian word for "lightning" projects the verb "flee" from its own phonetic insides — and by the quick alternation of *f* and *g* which suggests a zigzag motion. The chromatic series appears in each of the two focused lines with a basic *o-e-i* pattern, but acts less strongly than the *f* alliteration, which in its turn is reinforced by the emphatic stress on the first syllable of "folgore," almost at the beginning of the line. Indeed this initial accent of the relevant hendecasyllable upsets the normal rhythmical balance by overshadowing the canonic ones, which fall on the sixth syllable ("fuggendo") and on the tenth ("sito"). This way the lightning dominates the two lines in question, because of the rhythmical suddenness that leaves everything behind on its trail. (It is this chiefly that differentiates the *Paradiso* line from a famous *Inferno* one which compares to lightning the green lizard darting through a path at the height of summer:

> Come 'l ramarro sotto la gran fersa
> dei dì canicular, cangiando siepe,
> folgore par se la via attraversa,

> As the green lizard under the great flail
> of dog days' heat, darting from hedge to hedge,
> flits lightning-like across the path,

In *Inferno* xxv, 79–81, the word "folgore" is less strategically placed in the sentence even if it dominates its own line.)

The lightning simile in our *Paradiso* line, besides, is offered only to be negated in the next, with the kind of heightening negation that is well known to mystics and theologians as *via negativa*. On the semantic level, this establishes the transcendent quality of movement in Paradise as against its matter-bound manifestation in Hell (where Geryon's final dash is likened to a discharged arrow), while in *Purgatorio* the pilot-angel's swift gliding on the marine reaches, being compared only to itself without further ado ("he went as swiftly as he had come"), seems to fit a median position in the scale, at least as far as direction goes. Discursive meaning and image, as here sketched, match the rhythmical behavior of each culminant line, which emphasizes their differences in much the same way. For we realize, by choosing to compare them closely enough, that the *Inferno* line capping the whole of Geryon's canto gravitates accentually toward its terminal part: "si dileguò come da corda cocca." (The stresses fall on the fourth, eighth and tenth syllables; the movement described is upward and oblique, and reverses a slow downward one.) Instead, the three stresses of the Purgatorial line, on the fourth, seventh, and tenth syllables, are equally distributed on the three syntactical members of the clause and thus suggest a decidedly horizontal movement: "ed el sen gì, come venne, veloce." But in the *Paradiso* line both the important accent and the pivotal word are at the beginning, the stress pattern involving the second, sixth, and tenth syllables; the stress displacement certainly matches the quasi-instant vertical propagation used for the simile. If we place the three lines in an ideal series, we shall find that the shifting of stress and emphasis from the end part to the beginning corresponds to the inversion of gravity that takes place in passing from the subterranean to the heavenly kingdom. Farfetched as this inference may sound, it finds additional support in the fact that while both the *Inferno* and the *Purgatorio* lines are self-contained clauses, each terminating its own sentence, the *Paradiso* line, syntactically unself-contained, projects and resolves into the next one.

At this point we may note with some guarantee of relevance that an inversion of movement is precisely the subject of our *Paradiso* couplet. What it says is that the lightning, fleeing earthward from its proper "site" (the sphere of fire, that is, the sky), did not speed so much as Dante did in returning ("riedi") to his own (Heaven, the original home of the soul.) The double statement is thematically anticipated by a tercet in this very canto (lines 49–51), which figuratively describes Dante's response to Beatrice's example in looking at the sun in terms of a rebounding sunbeam that flits up again from the reflecting surface "like a pilgrim wanting to return":

> E sì come secondo raggio suole
>   uscir del primo e risalire in suso,
>   pur come pellegrin che tornar vuole . . .

> And as a second ray of light comes out
>   of the first, to rise back toward the height,
>   quite like a pilgrim wanting to return . . .

Purified Dante is homeward bound for God. In line 75 he says to Divine Love: "tu 'l sai, che col tuo lume mi levasti" ("you know it, who by your Light lifted me up"). "By the strength of your light you lifted me;" but that "levasti" is a verbal concentrate worthy of Dante the craftsman and thinker we know, for it denotes not just the positive action of raising the pilgrim into the sky or the negative one of taking him away from the earth, but even more the spiritual causation of "making him light" (Latin "levis," hence "levare" and "levitate"). Having overcome the gravitational pull of thick matter, sin, and hatred, Dante now responds to the contrary attraction of Love "that moves the sun and the other stars"; and yet this spiritual movement originates in himself as well as in its goal, in the form of a purified "desire" which is the same as the cosmic force propelling the heavenly spheres in their eternal rotation (lines 76–84).

Even if he is now beginning to share in the joyful illumination of Paradise, stupor and bafflement still overwhelm him at the unforeseen experience, and Beatrice dutifully takes it upon herself to dispel the "grossness" of his temporary delusion (lines 88–93). This occasions her explanation of the expanding light and music from the sun in terms of Dante's just-started space trip, and if we keep in mind the total specific contexts of the earlier quotations from the previous canticles, we shall notice how the same modifier "grosso," which defined in *Inferno* xvi the constant murkiness of the thick air Geryon "swims" through, and in *Purgatorio* ii the temporary haze dimming a star on the horizon, here in *Paradiso* i refers to the residual clumsiness that veils the untrained mind in the presence of celestial phenomena, a kind of mental haze, of course.

> . . . Tu stesso ti fai grosso
> col falso imaginar, sì che non vedi
> ciò che vedresti se l'avessi scosso.

> . . . You embroil yourself in grossness
> through false imaginings, so you fail to see
> what you would have seen had you shuffled it off.

The "false imaginings" are literal acceptance of the sense data, which in the Purgatorial episode discussed here would have led Dante to self-mystification if Virgil had not clarified things for him, as Beatrice does now. An essential aspect of the movement reenacted by our chosen passage is the transition from confused sight to true vision. This is a shock at first, as is the passage from cosmic and mental grossness to Paradisal rarefaction, which involves purity and intensity of being. No wonder that a trait of cruelty should linger on at the beginning of the *Paradiso's* first canto, when the poet invokes Apollo, god of poetry (and of the sun he and Beatrice are said to have been gazing at), and in so doing praises the divine patron of his art for having skinned ambitious Marsyas, defeated in a musical contest:

> Entra nel petto mio, e spira tue
> sì come quando Marsia traesti
> de la vagina de le membra sue.

> Enter into my breast, and breathe therein

> as you did when you pulled Marsyas
> out of the sheath of his own limbs.
>
> (lines 19–21)

If we remember that "vagina" means sheath as well as the feminine genital organ, the action of "unsheathing Marsyas from his own limbs," as expressed in Dante's Italian, may imply a rebirth along with the fabled death, and the suggestion finds an additional basis in the verb "trasumanar" ("transfigure") which, at line 70, epitomizes the simile of Glaucus, the Greek fisherman transformed into a sea-god, as applied to the inner change Dante experienced at the moment of receiving from Beatrice the relayed light of the sun. And, since Dante confesses that the process of transfiguration is beyond words, we see another echo of the Marsyas myth in the contest the poet is undertaking by the act of going on to write. A celestial violence therefore reverberates on the lightning image by which Beatrice negatively describes his upward dash.

This leads us to infer that the Paradisal couplet chosen for focal comment, despite its unique physiognomy, rehearses in its transcending way the hellish violence of Geryon's movement. A bolt of lightning is an arrow of fire, and the bow-and-arrow simile indeed occurs shortly after (lines 118–26) in connection with Divine Providence, then in the next canto (lines 23–25) to describe Dante's own flight into lunar heaven. Hegel would say that the *Paradiso* "aufhebt" ("negates and fulfills") the *Inferno* and *Purgatorio*, and Dante himself would use in this respect the above-mentioned verb "levare." We have now seen, by an alternately focusing and expanding method of comparison, how the short passages initially selected for explorative discussion can be juxtaposed to exemplify a qualitative progression of movement. Both poetically and metaphysically, motion accelerates to vertigo point when it reaches Heaven, the reign of completely liberated energy. But by the same token, it progressively approaches the peace of the Unmoved Mover, quiet source of all movement. This paradox is implied in the emphasis on the verb "fissare" ("to gaze fixedly"), which denotes the way Dante and Beatrice are going to establish direct contact with the cosmic energy that will send them aloft. The lightning simile strives to contain and resolve the paradox by suggesting instant speed. Another form of the paradox is that the utmost intensity is to be found in extreme rarefaction, at the opposite pole of earth's density. Yet the rarefied spheres contain the earth, and the abstract poetry of the *Paradiso* presupposes the concreteness of "falso imaginar." Our chosen lines are arrows spanning this polarity, and they could be illustrated by an artist like Paul Klee, whose *Pedagogical Sketchbook* seems to trace the essential dynamics of abstracted reality in a way not uncongenial to Dante. My tentative approach, I hope, will have shown how it is possible to trace the flight of those arrows in a reading that will not make the poetry subservient to its raw matter, whether theological or historical, but rescue theology on poetry's own terms. Poetry survives in its own right and so can afford to carry theology or time-bound philosophy on its shoulders. The best way to the *Comedy* is still through poetry, without, of course, discounting the necessary information that is adjunctive. In a Pythagorean mind like Dante's, poetry could feed on abstractions, without losing its local, individualized presence.

CHAPTER VI

PURGATORIO, CANTO V
THE MODULATIONS OF SOLICITUDE

It is not true of many another canto, as it certainly is of *Purgatorio* v, that its thematic structure recapitulates the movement of the whole *Divine Comedy*. It does this by looking back to the earth of the living and eventually reechoing the infernal world, while at its climax foreshadowing Paradise; indeed a paradisal anticipation can be overheard in the canto even before the transfigured voice of Pia de' Tolomei comes to suggest heavenly peace as an antiphon to the remembered turmoil of murder, battle, and storm. Few cantos exhibit such variety of tones, and no other so thoroughly rehearses the fundamental gesture of the *Comedy* from the perspective of Purgatory — a privileged perspective for our poet, who can here enjoy the double advantage of closeness to earth, to human history with its passions, and openness to heaven. We might rephrase this by pointing out how this closeness to the physical world is also a distance. The empire of passion — a slavery in Hell — is now left behind and viewed at one remove, with the liberty warranted by final hope. Yet this hope is bound up with memory, and love with suffering — we are "no longer down there" but also "not yet up there"; we are in a middle kingdom, a kingdom of impermanence between two extremes — and as such indeed the ideal kingdom of artists, who significantly abound on the slopes of this island mountain. A further consideration will show that this transitory stage between two worlds (the one of despair and the one of ecstasy) is the more nearly human world, the one where man, although he has left his flesh behind, must labor to transcend its residual heritage.

In Canto v transitoriness is even more poignant because we are still in Ante-Purgatory — on the threshold of Heaven's threshold, so to speak, in a kind of no-man's-land where the souls feel their earthly ties along with the urgency of an admission to the hierarchy of purgative suffering. The relief at knowing themselves saved is counterpointed by recurrent nostalgia, as unforgettably focused by the beginning of Canto VIII. Nostalgia grips Dante and Casella upon meeting each other on Purgatory shore, so that stern Cato has to break up what is an emotional and aesthetic indulgence to urge the new arrivals on to their assignments.

A similar sternness prompts Virgil in turn to scold his easily distracted ward at the beginning of our canto, when the thronging souls' cries of wonder at Dante's corporeality (he is the only one there to cast a shadow) cause the unghostly one to slow down:

> . . . vidile guardar per maraviglia
> pur me, pur me, e 'l lume ch'era rotto.
> "Perché l'animo tuo tanto s'impiglia"
> disse 'l maestro, "che l'andare allenti?
> che ti fa ciò che quivi si pispiglia?
> Vien dietro a me, e lascia dir le genti . . ."

> . . . I saw them gaze in astonishment
> at me, at me, and at the light I broke.
> "Why do you let your mind be so embroiled"
> the master said, "that you slow down your step?
> and what are all those whisperings to you?
> Follow me, and let wanton people talk . . ."

Virgil's sententious admonition here, exhorting Dante to keep his purpose more firmly in mind, sounds excessive at first by comparison with the slight occasion for it (in the same way, one resents Cato's censorious intrusion upon the lovely gathering in Canto II). Our sympathy is with the spontane-

ous behavior of the childishly curious souls, and with Dante's equally spontaneous reaction:

> . . . e seguitava l'orme del mio duca,
> quando di retro a me, drizzando il dito,
> una gridò: "Ve' che non par che luca
> lo raggio da sinistra a quel di sotto,
> e come vivo par che si conduca!"
> Gli occhi rivolsi al suon di questo motto,
> e vidile guardar per maraviglia . . .

> . . . and I followed in the footsteps of my Guide,
> when from behind, pointing the finger,
> one cried out: "See, there seems to be no ray
> of light on the left side of the lower wayfarer,
> and he has all the appearances of life!"
> I turned my eyes at these words,
> and I saw them gaze in astonishment . . .

Actually, our pilgrim is emerging from the midst of the negligent souls,
and his solicitous guide has reason to warn him against any waste of time.
Dante has just taken his leave of lazy Belacqua (Canto IV), and the natural
action of turning around and slowing down his gait at the voice of curiosity
is too natural for comfort in view of the self-purifying task that awaits him
in this realm of purification. At the gate of Purgatory proper, the angel will
tell Dante that there is no turning back. As against the solicitude and ascetic
purposiveness required by the situation, Belacqua was a comical portrait of
the *allzumenschlich* man, of non-self-transcending naturalness. And a comic note — of the refined quality compatible with the purgatorial atmosphere
— rings on right here at the beginning of Canto V, down to Dante's blush at
his master's reproach: the self-mortification of the poet renders a kind of
poetic justice to Belacqua. We shall find more examples of this purgatorial
humor later on, when Virgil and Dante momentarily conspire to keep eager
Statius in the dark about the revered Latin's identity, or when (XXIV, 2–24)
Forese shows his friend Dante the Rabelaisian pontiff who is now purging
his immoderate taste for "l'anguille di Bolsena e la vernaccia" ("the eels of
Bolsena and the vernaccia wine"). And at the beginning of Canto VI, as a
kind of comic relief from the high pitch reached in Canto V through the

tragic voices of Jacopo, Buonconte, and Pia, we shall see Dante again involved in a situation of humorous import when the anxious souls crowd around him to wrest promises he knows he cannot keep, feeling as he does like a winning player beset by the less fortunate ones.

To be sure, the comic note is never an end in itself, but only modulates consummate transitions to lyrical transport, as at the end of Canto XXI, when Statius embraces Virgil unexpectedly recognized "trattando l'ombre come cosa salda" ("treating shades as if they were a solid thing"), or at the outset of Canto VI, where the animation of the garrulously insistent petitioners around Dante turns out to provide a sharp foil for the affectionate meeting of Virgil with his proudly solitary fellow poet from Mantua and for Dante's own passionate invective against strife-ridden Italy. Here in Canto V the comical start will gradually introduce the complex choreography that is to culminate in the sustained trio of two warriors and a woman whose epitaph rings forever in our mind's ear. In ranging through such a vast gamut of tones, Dante's gift for dramatic modulation shows to advantage as he reattains a pitch worthy of the *Inferno*'s strongest moments, yet with an ease, an airiness, which would have impossible there. This ease springs from the new acceptance of human nature as something to be improved, but also understood — hence the airy nature of humor here. It also arises from the detachment with which life on earth is viewed — hence the airy nature of tragedy here. The Ante-Purgatory spirits who died violently and repented at the last moment are still recent dead, still very much of earth, yet not so bound to their earthly roots that they cannot rise above them in the very act of describing their earthly end. A cathartic serenity softens the notes of pity and horror here, whereas horror and pity held full sway in Hell.

In such a context, ease is only the other side of solicitude, or else the initial comedy could not lead so naturally to the crescendo of earnestness that brings the canto, as a subordinate organic unit of the long poem, to its resolution. Consider the comedy of manners, the ritual of etiquette, that provides the initial movement: the curious souls attracting Dante's attention, Dante's response (a mixture of embarrassment, amusement, and vanity, as

expressed by that "pur me, pur me") eliciting Virgil's reprimand ("No time
to lose!"), Dante dutifully falling into line as a scolded schoolboy. Then
there occurs a renewed interruption — harder to ignore because it comes,
this time, from a flock of souls walking in front of and across our visitors'
path, not behind, and also because these souls seem less idle and gossipy than
the others. They are brought up short in their absorbing litany by the unexpected discovery of a living visitor in their realm:

> E 'ntanto per la costa di traverso
>   venivan genti innanzi a noi un poco,
>   cantando *"Miserere"* a verso a verso.
> Quando s'accorser ch'i' non dava loco
>   per lo mio corpo al trapassar de' raggi,
>   mutar lor canto in un "Oh!" lungo e roco.
>
> Meanwhile across the ledge
>   there came folks a little in front of us,
>   singing *"Miserere"* line by line.
> When they noticed that I blocked the sunbeams
>   with my opaque body, they changed
>   their singing into a long and hoarse "Oh!"

Again, it is a comical note that elicits dramatic movement and plausibility:
Dante's "realism" (to use Luigi Malagoli's term), Dante's observance,
Dante's spare language, which is all things and actions and thus makes the
essential innuendos possible. At this point, the proceedings cease to be casual and formalize themselves into a kind of courtly choreography, with the
new group of souls sending two messengers to find out who our two pil-
grims are, and the messengers returning to their senders with Virgil's diplo-
matic reply — a reply which shows some relentment from his earlier refusal
to get involved with these curious people, without however failing to make
the point that Dante's time is precious:

> . . . "Voi potete andarne
>   e ritrarre a color che vi mandaro
>   che 'l corpo di costui è vera carne.
> Se per veder la sua ombra restaro,
>   com'io avviso, assai è lor risposto:
>   faccianli onore, ed esser può lor caro."

. . . "You may go now
  and report to those who sent you here
  that this man's body indeed is real flesh.
If they stopped just to see his shadow,
  as I think they did, they now have their answer:
  let them honor him, for it may help them, too."

Virgil's diplomacy is a matter of solicitude for his pupil, whom he is trying to shield from importunate curiosity. There is condescension in his
message to the eager souls, and just as he reproached Dante for indulging in
idle diversion, he now emphasizes to the crowding inhabitants of the place
the importance of the distinguished foreign visitor. The exhortation to
honor Dante may, however, imply more than a plea for discretion: it leaves
the door open for an interview if the souls here met have more serious busi-
ness in mind than childlike curiosity. Thus, by a carefully worded after-
thought, Virgil the severe mentor becomes once again the tactful intercessor, his severity being definitively mollified by the meteor-like swiftness
with which the two messengers flit back to report his words to their group,
and by the group's quick response:

Vapori accesi non vid'io sì tosto
  di prima notte mai fender sereno,
  né, sol calando, nuvole d'agosto,
che color non tornasser suso in meno;
  e, giunti là, con li altri a noi dier volta
  come schiera che scorre sanza freno.

I never saw lighted vapors so swiftly
  streak through a terse sky in the first dark of night,
  or at sundown any clouds of August,
as they did in returning up there;
  and, once arrived, with the others they turned
  toward us, like a squadron with loosened rein.

Apart from the airy, almost paradisal quality of the similes employed to
depict the messengers' rapidity and their senders' promptness in forcing an
interview upon our exceptional visitor, it is hard to miss in their action a
touch of humor which seems consistent with their bodiless nature. This
purgatorial smile compounds loss and deliverance. (What does it mean to

have shed a body without yet attaining the ultimate fulfillment of Heaven? Small wonder that the bodiless ones fuss about Dante's corporeal integrity, and that the theme of flesh unexpectedly present and flesh too suddenly relinquished runs through the whole canto, counterpointing smile to sadness!) The humor is not lost on Virgil the impatient but benevolent old-timer of the Beyond vis-à-vis these newcomers; at the same time, our stern master of ceremonies would not countenance the sudden unrestraint of these recent dead, who still have to undergo the refining ordeals of Purgatory and still belong in a no-man's-land, and he would not plead their cause with Dante, as he does in lines 43–45, if he did not sense in their haste (an otherwise unseemly form of behavior for him) a candid expression of zest. Curiosity was a regrettable form of self-indulgence, but it actually sparked solicitude, and this affords a mutual reward in the initially casual encounter. It is here, at the hinge of dramatic action, when external movement rises to its climax, that comedy modulates into deep earnestness, with Virgil withdrawing from conversation to let Dante take over.

"Questa gente che preme a noi è molta": these people are not to be put off, and they must not be, for their urgency is an imperious prayer, "e vegnonti a pregar." The exchange between them and Dante can only be defined as passionate courtesy; the diplomacy of exploration yields to the effusion of prayer, the heightened form of solicitude, which includes the dead and the living and makes Dante an intercessor in his turn between the two worlds. This justifies pragmatically the dramatic device of building up Dante's person from the start by having him function as the center of converging interest from all sides. There is appropriate dramatic progression in the way Virgil passes on to Dante the role of interceding for the dead with the living, and this progression develops further as Dante hears out the soliciting chorus and in so doing yields in his turn the center of the stage. The dead — for whom it is a little like returning to life to have the privilege of speaking to a man of flesh and blood — first address him as a unanimous chorus, to state their condition and general request; they want to be recognized or at least known, so that their plight and their need for supporting prayer may be reported to whoever cares in the world they so abruptly left:

"O anima che vai per esser lieta
  con quelle membra con le quai nascesti"
  venian gridando, "un poco il passo queta.
Guarda s'alcun di noi unqua vedesti,
  sì che di lui di là novella porti:
  deh, perché vai? deh perché non t'arresti?
Noi fummo tutti già per forza morti,
  e peccatori infino a l'ultima ora . . ."

"O soul that goes toward final beatitude
  with the same limbs with which you were born,"
  they cried to me, "do slow your gait a little.
Look if you ever saw any of us before,
  for you could bring news of us back there:
  oh, why do you walk on? why don't you stop?
We were, all of us, violently killed,
  and sinners all, down to our last hour . . ."

Then, after Dante denies having ever met any of them before, and assures them of his willingness to help, in the name of that peace which through Virgil "di mondo in mondo cercar mi si face" ("from world to world I am made to pursue"), the chorus individualizes itself in a succession of three personal voices summarizing three unique destinies. This is the full release of the dead folk's urgency ("questa gente che preme a noi è molta . . ."), and here the poetry of the episode gains full momentum with the utmost sharpening of dramatic focus. The initial groping of curiosity and wonder has become dawning cognition and final recognition, even if not of the kind that previous personal acquaintance makes possible in the case of a Latini, a Casella, or a Forese. The latter kind, of course, would have demanded a continued dialogue between poet and interlocutor, with the intimate touches that are out of place in this different context, where the voice of each self-revealing figure supersedes that of its intent evoker.

If the breathless sequence of the three tragic stories, punctuated only by Dante's question to Buonconte about Buonconte's burial, rhythmically embodies the release of mounting pressure, the fullest expansion of that delayed release has to be seen in Buonconte's prolonged description of the devil-conjured storm and flood which disposed of his forlorn corpse. The

onrush of his words mimetically parallels the fury of the torrential waters, and throws into sharper relief the epigrammatic composure of Pia's elegy:

> "Deh, quando tu sarai tornato al mondo,
>   e riposato de la lunga via"
>   seguitò il terzo spirito al secondo,
> "ricorditi di me che son la Pia:
>   Siena mi fé; disfecemi Maremma;
>   salsi colui che 'nnanellata pria
> disposando m'avea con la sua gemma."

> "Please, once you have returned to the world
>   and taken your due rest from the long journey,"
>   the third spirit said, following up the second,
> "remember me, who am la Pia:
>   Siena made me; and Maremma unmade me;
>   he knows, who before that had put on me
> his ring and gem by way of bridal pledge."

Here the expansive momentum of release makes room for an ingathering of the voice, an orchestral etherealization resulting from diminished volume and higher register — fit climax for the dramatic progression we have been tracing in the elaborate unfolding of this rich canto. After Jacopo del Cassaro's grim account of his bloody death, and Buonconte's story of the power that Hell wields on earth, Pia de' Tolomei's feminine gentleness brings a glimmer of paradisal peace in the stormy context. Unlike her rugged male companions, she avoids grisly details and — in prefiguration of the *Paradiso*'s style — gives us the purified essence of her destiny on earth ("Siena mi fé; disfecemi Maremma"). This shows even in her choice of the most symbolically comprehensive verb for the action of death ("Maremma unmade me") as against the specific realism of "I fell" on the part of both Jacopo and Buonconte: "Corsi al palude, e le cannucce e 'l braco/ m'impigliar sì, ch'i' *caddi* . . ." ("I ran toward the swamp, and the reeds and mud entangled me, so that I fell . . ."); "e quivi/ *caddi* e rimase la mia carne sola" ("and there/ I fell and my flesh remained alone").

Thus gentle Pia, midway between Francesca and Piccarda, crowns this foreshortened epic of medieval Italy (the dimension Vico saw as dominant in our manifold poem) with her unwarlike song; and she does that the better because she reveals herself as the very essence of solicitude in this canto where solicitude provides the keynote against a background of the world's ravages and neglect. Jacopo and Buonconte urge Dante to obtain prayers for them from the survivors; she thinks first of his fatiguing journey, as a sister would, and of the rest he will have to take before busying himself with his embassies from the world of the dead. Her greater detachment from earth and selfishness shows also in the discretion of her request to Dante, whom she merely asks to remember her, while Jacopo gives specific directions as to what to do for him in his native town of Fano, and Buonconte laments that "Giovanna o altri non ha di me cura." Jacopo even sighs for the world he left when he considers that, if he had not taken the wrong path to escape his murderers, he would "still be there, where one breathes." It is an understandable trait in such a man of action that he should fleetingly regret the lost chance for further action on earth, while Pia, a passive victim, only thinks of herself in passive terms, even stylistically ("Siena made me; Maremma unmade me; . . . he knows who . . . had put his wedding ring on me"). It is likewise understandable that she, a woman, should refer to her murderous husband (without of course mentioning his name, as if to exorcise him in the very act of bringing him into the picture) and wistfully think of the wedding ceremony.

But all the canto has been a ceremony enacting the progression of solicitude, as those dead well know who remember their "deserted flesh" and their untended name among the living ("non ha di me cura . . ."). Dramatic characterization has undergone a gradual heightening to ritual choreography and choral song, as led by choragus Jacopo and concluded by the soprano voice of Pia. Between Belacqua's laziness in Canto IV and Dante's outburst of patriotic outrage in Canto VI (where the ruinously factional "Monaldi e Filippeschi, Montecchi e Cappelletti" are branded above all as "uom sanza cura," men without civic solicitude*), the awakening and inten-

---

* My interpretation of the expression "uom sanza cura" (*Purg.* VI, 107) must be weighed against the equally plausible reading which makes it singular instead of plural and vocative instead of appositive, thereby referring it to the previously addressed German Emperor Albert I rather than to the strife-ridden Italian families. See, for instance, Thomas Okey in his translation, *The Purgatorio of Dante Alighieri* (London, 1901), p. 67. But even so, my structural point about the word *cura* holds good.

sification of "cura" is aptly placed in Canto v. As an ambassador of the dead, Dante speaks to the living, and if he cares for the individual destiny of each purging soul, he cares even more for the communal destiny of Italy and Christianity, which embraces the living and the dead. But only a poet — especially a poet among poets here in Purgatory — can be trusted with such a mission, and the occasional reluctance he and Virgil show to the thronging souls that want to be heard is only ironic dramatization of this solicitous care. The souls crowding around Dante in Cantos v and vi are characters in search of an author. Like Pirandello's figures in the play by that name and in a short story related to it, these souls solicit their prospective author because they want to exist more fully. It is a double deliverance they expect of him: that he obtain prayers on their behalf to shorten their waiting period in Purgatory, and that he renew their memory on earth — by giving them a local habitation and a name in his poem. If he cannot satisfy all of them, this only dramatizes the magnitude of his task as a poet, as the intermediary *zwischen zwei Welten*, and his awareness of the impossibility of doing total justice to his mission. But the fact that some of these restless ghosts do find their author in Dante seals his success, while objectifying for us the progress of solicitude as the drama of poetry taking shape right here, in this Purgatorial Limbo, on the threshold of a threshold — where the poet's concern for his prospective creatures is most urgently needed, and where it coincides with his concern for the world they once shared.

PART TWO *The Legacy*

CHAPTER VII

DANTE'S PRESENCE
IN AMERICAN LITERATURE

ONE could almost say that Dante has been to modern American poetry what Shakespeare was to Goethe and the German Romantics: an awakener and a constant guide. However, in the nineteenth century, which saw the rise of Dante studies in America, the situation was a bit different if not actually reversed; Dante did mean something in the creative sense to prose writers of Hawthorne's and Melville's caliber, in a way perhaps also to Poe, but hardly to those we now consider the best poets of the time. Dante in fact did not perform a vital function for the nineteenth-century forerunners of Pound, Eliot, Stevens, Hart Crane, and Robert Lowell, though he was widely read in American literary circles, and not only in translation.[1] The Transcendentalists and the "Boston Brahmins" among others, as J. Chesley Mathews has recently reminded us,[2] were well acquainted with him, and one need only mention Longfellow's translation of the *Divine Comedy* or James Russell Lowell's very readable essay on Dante's life to realize how close the Florentine's heritage was, culturally speaking, to these sensitive men of letters. Longfellow in particular acclimatized Dante at Harvard and thus established there an uninterrupted tradition of Dante studies which, through Charles Eliot Norton and Charles Grandgent, was to reach T. S. Eliot on the one hand and Charles Singleton on the other. One can follow step by step this American pilgrimage of Dante in Angelina La Piana's book.[3]

But philology as such is not my concern here. Academic culture apart, the fact remains that the two major American poets of the century, Walt Whitman and Emily Dickinson, were unaffected in their creative practice by whatever knowledge of Dante they had. It is surprising to learn that Whitman admired Dante's spareness (along with his directness), for nothing in Whitman's verse could be called Dantean, and of course his avowed intent was to get away from the strict formal traditions of European literature (which he identified with the class-bound heritage of feudal dogmatism), the better to sing the regenerating all-inclusiveness of fledgling democracy in a very un-Dantesquely effusive chant. Dickinson's Dante, to judge from her rare references,[4] was D. G. Rossetti's Pre-Raphaelite stylization, and it is unlikely that she ever went further than the *Vita Nuova* in her reading of Dante. If she had, she would have found something congenial to her starkest existential poetry in the sinewy style and vision of the *Comedy*.

Poe's acquaintance with Dante's writings, we can infer from the documentation of Mathews, was both deeper and broader than Emily Dickinson's, to the point of leaving obvious traces not simply in a few quotations or references, but on the shaping of a poem like "The City in the Sea" and of the *Inferno*-like nightmares of *Arthur Gordon Pym*. Even if he did not know his Dante so well as did his contemporaries Emerson, Thoreau, and Longfellow, I feel inclined to question Mathews' conclusion that Poe's "interest in Dante seems to have been shallow." The infernal aspect of Dante's poetry cannot have failed to appeal to the Gothic author of so many tales of horror (mannerisms apart). One might even venture to descry an archetypally Dantesque trait in "A Descent into the Maelstrom."

The same suggestion can be advanced with greater likelihood for that other maelstrom in which Melville sinks Captain Ahab's "Pequod" at the end of *Moby Dick*:

And now, concentric circles seized the lone boat itself, and all its crew, and each floating oar, and every lance-pole, and spinning, animate and inanimate, all round and round in one vortex, carried the smallest chip of the Pe-quod out of sight . . . and . . . the bird of heaven, with archangelic shrieks, and his imperial beak thrust upwards, and his whole captive form folded in the flag of Ahab, went down with his ship, which, like Satan, would not sink to hell till she had dragged a living part of heaven along with her, and helmeted herself with it.

Now small fowls flew screaming over the yet yawning gulf; a sullen white surf beat against its steep sides; then all collapsed, and the great shroud of the sea rolled on as it rolled five thousand years ago.

Compare with this epic conclusion the final lines of Ulysses' own account of his equally hell-bound shipwreck in *Inferno* xxvi, 137–42:

> Ché de la nova terra un turbo nacque,
> E percosse del legno il primo canto.
> Tre volte il fé girar con tutte l'acque;
> A la quarta levar la poppa in suso
> E la prora ire giù, com' altrui piacque,
> Infin che 'l mar fu sopra noi richiuso.

> For a whirlwind arose from the new land,
> and it struck our vessel in the bow.
> Three times it whirled her around with all the waters;
> the fourth time it made her stern rise up
> and the stem go right down, as it pleased Another,
> until the sea was sealed again above us.

The evidence available confirms that Melville had read the *Inferno*, in Henry Cary's then current translation, by 1849, and unmistakable references crop up in most of what he wrote from then on, *Moby Dick* included. But rather than count references and talk of "influence" here, we should speak of an elective affinity which made Melville recognize a vital part of himself, across a yawning gap of history, in the Italian poet's "power of darkness." One learns only from those one loves, as Goethe said to Ecker-mann. Melville would have conceived his Faustian Ahab even if he had never heard of Dante's Ulysses, but having met that quite Faustian figure certainly made a difference to the author of *Moby Dick*, who, with his gift for mythical analogies, can only have found a spurring similarity in the metaphysical catastrophe of Ahab's medieval forerunner.

Dante's Ulysses and Melville's Ahab are Heaven-defying seekers of experience, of knowledge at any cost, and they are rewarded by the same nemesis. It was fortunate that Melville came to read the *Inferno* in the very years in which the myth of *Moby Dick* was taking shape in his imagination, for the Ulysses figure as reinvented by Dante in his "lucky ignorance" of the Homeric source, and possibly compounded with a blaspheming hero of hatred like Capaneus, powerfully contributed to summoning into sharp focus the haunting phantom of the whale-hunter from Nantucket. The latter's Shakespearian, Miltonic, and Byronic genealogy would not have stood in the way of this final conjuring, since the age (unlike ours) tended to see Dante through Romantic eyes. The bold conjunction of Dante with Shakespeare and indeed Byron occurs in the essays of Francesco de Sanctis, the critic who recovered Dante for the nineteenth-century liberal sensibility even as he was throwing new light on the whole of Italian literature.[5]

Shakespeare certainly nurtured Melville's imagination much more pervasively than any other author, Dante included, and the Hamlet- and Lear-like aspects of Ahab make the latter a more complex figure than Dante's Ulysses. Likewise, Melville's style, especially in *Moby Dick*, tends to Shakespeare's Elizabethan, nearly baroque sumptuousness — a far cry from Dante's concision. Yet in the passage I have quoted from *Moby Dick*, the exuberance of Shakespearian cast spends itself until it tapers off into the spare finality of the last paragraph, whose content and cadence parallel the solemnly placating rhythm of Ulysses' concluding line in Dante. Compare "and the great shroud of the sea rolled on as it rolled five thousand years ago" with "Infin che 'l mar fu sopra noi richiuso" ("until the sea was sealed again above us"). In both instances, the lines of force of an eloquent utterance converge in a weirdly serene resolution, just as the whirlpool in each scene finally levels off after engulfing a defiant crew to restore God's elemental peace over any human transgression. This may illustrate the complementary uses to which Melville could occasionally turn the Shakespearian and the Dantean pattern in his own imaginative projection of experience.

Dante became Melville's scenographic and psychological reflector, if not his stylistic one, when he strove to portray destructive passion in the hell of urban alienation in the reference-studded *Pierre; or, the Ambiguities*, the story of an otherwise explicitly Hamletic artist. Dante also stood him in good stead later on for the depiction of a new kind of inferno (nascent industrial exploitation) in the short story, "The Tartarus of Maids." The *Inferno*-like nature of the initial scenery here is not determined just by an outspoken "Dantean gateway" in the steep gorge that leads to the impervious mountain recess harboring the devilish paper-mill, but also by details like "Plutonian, shaggy-wooded mountains" (an intentional reminiscence of the Dark Wood), by names like the "Devil's Dungeon," and by the "turbid brick-colored stream, boiling through a flume among enormous boulders," which, on account of its strange color, is called "Blood River" — a clear allusion to Phlegethon.

But the bulk of the story transcends the obviousness of such stage props by showing us an unexpectedly quiet, subtle kind of hell where everybody is polite while the relentlessness of the humming machinery slowly consumes the doomed girls tending it. "Inverted similitude," to quote the author, emphasizes this social horror by ironically comparing the machines to an animal, or to a harp, and the white pulp they process, to human sperm, while in the final phases of production one of the working girls who take care of ruling the blank sheets of finished paper is herself "ruled and wrinkled" prematurely as if she were just a sheet of paper. A ghostly whiteness dominates — how much more frightening than the darkness of the initial landscape! The lifeless takes on demoniacally lifelike traits; the human is assimilated to the lifeless.

In Marxist terms this would be called alienation, the reduction of man to merchandise (and Melville feels obliged to emphasize his point by observing that "Machinery — that vaunted slave of humanity — here stood menially served by human beings . . ."). The sinister inversion of roles is effectively expressed by functional metaphors, in a language of much greater sobriety than *Pierre*'s; of course, the moral situation itself is more lucidly focused than that novel's melodrama, for here the hellish thing is the absence of passion, as against the excess of passion there. Thus in this very modern story we see a post-Romantic Melville using Dante as a springboard for an original experiment, rather than as a source to echo and amplify as he had done in the less mature *Pierre*. Melville's ironical use of specific Dantean references in a dislocating context of his own strikingly foreshadows Eliot's system.

Next to Melville, his friend Hawthorne is the other conspicuous case of a nineteenth-century American writer who in some of his work responded creatively to Dante's example because he felt a kinship with the medieval allegorist. Allegory as a constructional device to make a story reflect moral universals was something the two Americans shared with the thirteenth-century Florentine they both liked so well, though he did not have to be their exclusive source for it, since they had it closer to home in the heritage of Edmund Spenser, John Bunyan, and the Puritan colonials. Further grounds of affinity were the sense of evil, the problem of damnation, the biblical background with a germane prophetic outlook, and, in Hawthorne's case, an unrelenting sobriety of style. Like Melville, Hawthorne too received a few cues from Dante: for instance, in *The Scarlet Letter*, in the *Italian Note-Book*, and in *The Marble Faun*, where, as Mathews appropriately notes, the theme of the two sinning lovers inextricably entwined, along with the moral symbolism of darkness and light, tangentially evokes for us the image of Paolo and Francesca. They had loomed much more closely behind that other pair of fated lovers, Melville's Pierre and Isabel, eight years before.

A more interesting instance of Hawthorne's use of a Dantesque theme, whether deliberate or instinctive, is provided by the short story, "Young Goodman Brown." The candid townsman of colonial New England, going out into the surrounding dark forest at night to discover there, in a witches' sabbath presided over by the Devil, the revelation of universal evil, obviously finds himself much in the same predicament as Dante's pilgrim persona at the outset of *Inferno*. For, like the fictional Dante in the poem, young Goodman Brown is etymologically *bewildered*, lost in a moral wilderness that has its literal counterpart in the scenery of a Dark Wood haunted by threatening apparitions. The likeness extends to the uncertainty, coupled with hallucinatory vividness, of his experience (was it a nightmare? was it actual fact?), if we but recall Dante's similar touches in presenting his transcendental adventure from the start as a vision more real than ordinary reality, yet unaccountably entered:

> *Io non so ben ridir com'io v'entrai,*
> *Tant'era pieno di sonno* a quel punto
> Che la verace via abbandonai . . .

> *I cannot quite explain how I entered there,*
> *so slumberous was I* about the moment
> that I left the true way . . . (*Inf.* I, 10–12)

> . . . *la vista che m'apparve* d'un leone.
> Questi *parea* che contra me venesse
> Con la test'alta e con rabbiosa fame,
> Sì che *parea* che l'aere ne temesse . . .

> . . . *the sight, which appeared to me*, of a lion.
> He *seemed* to be coming against me
> with head reared up and with a raging hunger,
> so that the very air *seemed* to be afraid . . .
>
> (*Ibid.*, 46–48)

I have italicized the more pointedly visionary traits of Dante's language. In both cases, we have a sudden, inexplicable transition from normalcy to apocalypse, from the waking state to a dreamlike one which is actually an awakening to deeper, troubling awareness, so much so that the abnormal vision thus attained will crucially refocus the persona's perspective on the norm of reality: in young Goodman Brown's case, unlike Dante's, this will result in a permanent distortion that leaves no hope.

Thus Hawthorne perceptibly departs from his "source" in making damnation an untranscendable state of mind, rather than just a purging phase, for the spectator persona, with the added touch of a truly hellish (and exquisitely modern) subjectiveness in the ambiguity that hovers forever on Brown's incommunicable experience. His loss of faith is appropriately allegorized by the pun on his wife, Faith, who appears to him truly lost and damned in the nocturnal revelation. Here again is a radical reshuffling of the Dantesque situation by what Melville called "inverted similitude," since no help is forthcoming from Catholic Dante's heavenly ladies or guiding poet, as befits a Calvinist hell of the mind which can admit of no intercessors in the individual conscience's stark confrontation of gratuitous doom versus gratuitous election. Yet, in spite of his Catholicism, medieval Dante appealed to the Puritan in Hawthorne as well as in his worldlier friend Melville, and in general the continuing presence of a more or less overt puritanical tradition may help to explain the greater fortune Dante has had so far with Anglo-Saxon creative writers than with his fellow Italians. Of the modern Italian writers, only Eugenio Montale can be said to have Dante in his blood.[6] Pirandello was also drawn to him, but to a much more limited extent. Renaissance humanism and its aftermaths caused the puritanical aspects of Dante to be rather disregarded in the mainstream of Italian literature.

To return to "Young Goodman Brown," I must point out that the Dark Wood theme there is hardly "derived" in any univocal sense from the *Divine Comedy*, since it constitutes a variant of that pervasive forest-town polarity which appears, with different overtones, throughout the structural fabric of *The Scarlet Letter* no less than in some short stories from the earlier *Twice-Told Tales* and *Mosses from an Old Manse*. If in "Young Goodman Brown" the night wood stands for overt and the town for covert hellishness, in the spirit of a New England folklore which Robert Frost was later to use in less drastic ways, in *The Scarlet Letter* the forest stands for the perilous freedom of unblessed nature, and the town for the cruel limitations of civilization; both are inadequate choices for the questing protagonists, and Hester finally settles significantly on the border of wilderness to express her removal from both conditions in the sort of independent commitment she can make to civilization itself.

Thoreau at Walden, despite his freedom from the obsession of sinfulness, was himself a kind of Hester mediating between the closed world of civilization (the city) and the open world of nature (the woods); indeed these insistent images in American literature express the ancestral experience of the Puritan settlers in the virgin continent, to be repeated by generations of pioneers in the face of comparable hardships. But this, finally, is an archetypal experience of man the founder of civilizations. And one basic reason why Dante could reach the imagination of his nineteenth-century American admirers and help it to find a literary focus, was that he too, in his theological terms, had formulated the same perennial alternative between town and wilderness, civilization and nature, corruption and regeneration. The two complementary images of city and forest develop and intertwine throughout the long itinerary of his poem, from Dark Wood to Wood of the Suicides to Eden Forest on Mount Purgatory to the heavenly Garden of Paradise, from corrupted Florence to City of Dis to the celestial Rome and Jerusalem. Our Bible-trained Americans could hardly fail to recognize the pattern and draw from it an additional incentive to ambitious creation.

Thus if Dante contributed, along with the Bible and with Shakespeare,[7] to shaping the imaginative experience of some of the finest American writers during what has been called the American Renaissance of the nineteenth century, this proves their happy selectivity, which is part and parcel of originality in art. "Reverence for the archetype," to say it in Melville's words,[8] helped to bring forth creativeness instead of stifling it, especially since that reverence went hand in hand with moral courage, when to rediscover literary archetypes was itself a pioneering act. The radical temper of American literature in its first flowering phase could be sustained by an involvement with Dante, who, depending on the approach, may be felt either as tradition-bound or as revolutionary.

Little wonder then that Dante should become the literary Bible of the founding fathers of twentieth-century American poetry, T. S. Eliot and Ezra Pound, at a time when the residual restlessness of that pioneer spirit which had long spent itself in its coast-to-coast transcontinental surge was already driving several of the keenest artists of Anglo-Saxon America into the reverse surge of expatriation. They were pioneers of a sort, trying to mold a new, stronger tradition for English poetry by venturing into whatever geographically or chronologically remote areas of accomplishment seemed to promise a suitable reward; hence their need to break with an immediate milieu of sterile deliquescence. Iconoclasm was sparked by the search for deeper roots and broader horizons.

It is no mere coincidence that the title of Pound's first book of verse, which he published in Venice in 1908 soon after interrupting his just begun teaching career at home,[9] was *A Lume Spento*, straight from *Purgatorio* III,

132. Manfred, the speaker of that line in the *Comedy*, is talking of the injustice and neglect wreaked upon him in the world he left behind on earth, to contrast it with the "green hope" Divine Providence has disclosed for him in the world that has received him; Pound, thoroughly dissatisfied with the academic and literary situation in the homeland, was looking forward to a cultural rebirth in the Old World. It is likewise no coincidence that "Prufrock," T. S. Eliot's first poem to be published (in 1915, thanks to Pound's prevailing upon Harriet Monroe, the editor of *Poetry* [10]), bore as its epigraph six lines quoted in the original language from *Inferno* XXVII. The lines borrowed from Dante establish a link between the objectified persona of Prufrock, in whom Eliot modulated the fears and frustrations of the age, and the tortuous Guido da Montefeltro.[11] Prufrock's lines are also spoken from a (disguised) hell. The inscription in Eliot's volume, *Prufrock and Other Observations* (1917), dedicated the whole book to one physical victim of war's hell by using (again in the original Italian) Statius' affectionate lines to his fellow poet and master Virgil in *Purgatorio* XXI, 133–36.[12] After the war, *The Waste Land* would appear with the famous dedication to Pound, whom the author calls "il miglior fabbro," "the better shaper" (of his mother tongue), in the very words a fine Italian poet applies to Arnaut Daniel in *Purgatorio* XXVI, 117; Eliot was thinking also of Pound's partiality for Provençal poetry.

Dante, in short, presides over the literary exordium of each of these revolutionary exiles in search of a valid tradition, and he was to remain with them to the very end. This fact should be duly stressed against the hasty opinion that sees in French *symbolisme* the exclusive model, or catalyst, of Eliot's and Pound's writing. Laforgue (and then Baudelaire), on whom Eliot modeled his early style,[13] led him naturally back to the Metaphysicals and to Dante in actual poetical practice, as his essays confirm. There was no need to "lead him back" to Dante as far as theory was concerned. As to Pound, his interest in Rimbaud, Corbière, and Laforgue was far less decisive than his dogged emulation of Browning, whose rugged, uneven dramatic monologues could be refined to the point of approaching Dante's own taut style. After all, the *Comedy* consists largely of concentrated dramatic monologues as well.

It may be of some interest in this regard that in "Sestina: Altaforte," one of his early poems (from the 1909 collection entitled *Personae*), Pound dramatized Dante's Bertran de Born (*Inf.* xxviii) in Browningesque fashion, thereby joining thematically two of his exotic literary loves (Dante and the Provençals) through the good offices of his direct English ancestor. Of course the Provençal troubadours, whom Pound has abundantly discussed, translated, and paraphrased, were themselves germane to Dante, and it was probably Dante that introduced him to Arnaut Daniel.[14] With Guido Cavalcanti and other *Stilnovisti*, the Provençals seem to form, for Pound, a Dantesque constellation — which sounds historically plausible enough, and even more so stylistically. Ever since his essays on *The Spirit of Romance* (1910),[15] which contain his first championing of Dante, Pound has reiterated his belief that Provençal troubadours, Italian *Stilnovisti* (of whom Dante was initially one), and Chaucer hold the secret of regeneration for the stale modern Muse, thanks to their perennial lesson in verbal concision, visual clarity, and metric resourcefulness. Along this line he went as far as making Dante the supreme master of verse style over what he considered the verbose lusciousness of Renaissance Shakespeare. That perhaps helps to explain a certain Pre-Raphaelite tendency in Pound's early verse; indeed several of his *Personae* poems are not exempt from the related *art nouveau* aestheticism which marked the work of so many European contemporaries, despite his austere prescriptions in matters of style. His lyrics often are graceful stylistic exercises rather than personal statements. Thus for instance a melodic, decorative piece like "Blandula, Tenulla, Vagula," which on the other hand foreshadows the paradisal sections of his late *Cantos*. And even the severity of his aesthetics, which restrains the decorative bent, owes something to Walter Pater's request that artistic expression be refined of all dross to "burn always with this hard, gemlike flame." The best result will be "Hugh Selwyn Mauberley," of 1920.*

The early Pound is an eclectic, striving to appropriate diverse alien ex-

---

* For a documented and sensitive study of Pound's beginnings as a poet, with much relevance to my present points, see Thomas Jackson's *The Early Poetry of Ezra Pound* (Cambridge, Mass., 1968), which became available too late to be taken into account in my discussion.

periences in poetry, whether as versifier, critic, or translator. But he is a
demanding eclectic. Dante remains his touchstone, even when, in a radical endeavor to purify poetry of all frills and superstructures, he would
pare it down to the sheer atom of vision: the image, understood as the
"emotional complex of perception in an instant of time." That is the Imag-
ist phase of the last pre-World-War-I years, with his editing of the 1914
anthology *Des Imagistes*, his polemical gestures in *Ripostes*, his dictates to
fellow poets, "A Few Don't's by an Imagiste." Verse written according to
this extremely reductive poetics, like "In a Station of the Métro" and T. E.
Hulme's slim "Collected Poetical Works" which Pound was to incorporate
in his own enlarged volume *Personae* as exemplars of his radical principles,
shows all the shortcomings of such a stance. Yet it represents, along with
the supporting theory, a threshold of experiment which Pound had to reach
so he could consummate his own aestheticism and rebuild poetical discourse
anew.

The war years are intellectually turbulent for Pound. He and Wyndham
Lewis formulate Vorticism, with the *Cantos* soon coming to exemplify
that new avant-garde theory in the effort to overcome the atomistic and
unhistorical poetics of Imagism by a dynamic junction of images. The poetics and attendant practice are reinforced by the aesthetic discovery,
through Ernest Fenollosa's work, of the Chinese ideogram, which Pound
assimilates to the Saxon kenning as a technique for perceptually presenting the manifold in a unified form. He translates Li Po and other Chinese
lyricists in *Cathay* (1915), he tackles the No plays,[16] he makes Confucius'
Oriental Enlightenment a cornerstone of his social theories. Dante comes
into this "vortex" because of the *Cantos*,[17] which are to be Pound's *Divine
Comedy*. Thus, from image to vortex, from the supposed minimal unit of
imagination to its maximum expansion, we see the restless experimentalist
abandon the concentrated lyric of *poésie pure* for the most ambitiously inclusive epic effort of our times. He is no savage iconoclast like the Futur-
ists; he wants precision, sharp edges, no fuzziness in diction, and he invokes
Gautier's poetics for this, but of course the chief example of clear-cut style
is still Dante.

Dante stays close to the indefatigable author of the *Cantos*, through the nearly five decades their composition has taken so far, also because of an irrepressible doctrinal ambition (and didactic attitude) in economics, politics, sociology, with important references to certain medieval theologians who can support Pound's theories of social credit. The hub on which all these diversified interests turn is language, whose renewal and preservation is the poet's care and whose corruption portends the decay of society as a whole. Here too is a parallel to one of Dante's prime concerns, if we but remember the *Convivio*'s first chapter on the literary worth of the Italian vernacular and the final vindication of the same (till then humble) language in the *De Vulgari Eloquentia*. Like Dante, Pound has insisted on using the contemporary speech, without thereby renouncing the right to modulate it into literary elegance where demanded by the theme, and in fact his corpus of verse, especially in the *Cantos*, exhibits all nuances of linguistic usage, from the demotic (American slang) to the lofty, a trait the modern poet's work shares with the *Divine Comedy*. Dante's poem was revolutionary in its time: it broke with the convention of Latin as the mandatory medium for doctrinal or epic subjects, as well as with the classical prohibition to mix the low and the high style.

A related feature of the *Cantos* (and of Eliot's *Waste Land*, which Pound was instrumental in bringing to its final clipped redaction) is likewise Dantesque: the polyglot range of functional quotations from a number of relevant languages, which the author brings directly into his English context for the purpose of achieving dramatic immediacy of cosmopolitan scope. Greek, Latin, Chinese, Provençal, German, French are all called upon to yield their melodic or visual tribute to the madly ambitious poetical enterprise. Although Dante did not avail himself of this linguistic franchise to the same incredible extent, he did make Arnaut Daniel utter memorable Provençal lines in the *Purgatorio*, and he did let the saints in the *Paradiso* occasionally speak or sing Church Latin, while even demon Plutus and giant Nimrod in the *Inferno* vent their rage in appropriately incomprehensible gibberish. Polyglot verse was fairly common practice in the Middle Ages, anyway, throughout Christian Europe.

Along with that, we have to consider the cultural syncretism of the *Cantos*, which move back and forth between several areas of history: ancient Greece, Confucian China, Jeffersonian America, modern Europe, Renaissance Italy, medieval Provence. While duly taking into account the necessarily ampler spectrum of cultures made available to Pound by the exhaustive resources of information in the present-day world, I would also compare this aspect of the *Cantos* to the *Divine Comedy*'s amalgamation of classical, biblical, medieval European, and even Arabic lore, and more generally of myth and legend with contemporary historical fact — a medieval characteristic which partly meets Pound's modern requirements for epic inclusiveness. He himself said to his interviewer Donald Hall that

the first thing was this: you had six centuries that hadn't been packaged. It was a question of dealing with material that wasn't in the *Divina Commedia* . . . The problem was to build up a circle of reference — taking the modern mind to be the medieval mind with wash after wash of classical culture poured over it since the Renaissance.[18]

And though he added that he had tried "to make the *Cantos* historic . . . but not fiction," we should not take that word "historic" to mean mere documentary fact to the exclusion of significant myth, since myth, mediated by the literary sources Pound incorporates by translation or allusion, is woven into the arduous fabric of the poem to illustrate some form of experiential truth. Dante's distinction between the allegory of poets (fiction) and the allegory of theologians (truthful story) comes here to mind.

In a brilliant essay on "The Formal Structure of Pound's *Cantos*," Thomas Clark has contended that Pound's epic differs from Dante's, among other reasons, in having a circular rather than vertical direction:

Pound's struggle isn't upward, like Dante's, but circular. The poem begins as a spiral in wide arcs, marking a point every now and again with the statement of a theme. As the poem grows its movement is circular and inward toward a center, not upward: the arcs become smaller, the thematic material is crowded into closer and closer relation. Since Pound's conception of his material involves neither chronological nor spatial progression, vertical movement in the Dantesque manner is unnecessary . . . The coherence and splendor that he is trying to achieve won't be a place or condition achieved by *movement*: it will be static, a state of mind in the reader who is able to hold the whole poem as a unit, to put together all its parts. This is the *lux*, λαμπρά that Pound is after, and it is the major form of the poem: it has only an accidental correspondence to Dante's form.[19]

Yet the poet himself has acknowledged a basic, if free, correspondence of threefold pattern to the *Divine Comedy*:

I was not following the three divisions of the *Divine Comedy* exactly. One can't follow the Dantesque cosmos in an age of experiment. But I have made the division between people dominated by emotion, people struggling upwards, and those who have some part of the divine vision. The thrones in Dante's *Paradiso* are for the spirits of the people who have been responsible for good government. The thrones in the *Cantos* are an attempt to move out from egoism and to establish some definition of an order possible or at any rate conceivable on earth . . . There is no doubt that the writing is too obscure as it stands, but I hope that the order of ascension in the Paradiso will be toward a greater limpidity.

For the knowledge of contemporary reality is a knowledge of Hell and purgatory, with only possible glimpses of paradise:

It is difficult to write a paradiso when all the superficial indications are that you ought to write an apocalypse. It is obviously much easier to find inhabitants for an inferno or even a purgatorio . . . I am writing to resist the view that Europe and civilization are going to Hell.[20]

Even if it may be true, as Clark says, that Pound's use of Dante in the *Cantos* is colored by Homer's *Odyssey* (an important contributory source), I would limit that statement to the first part of the *Cantos*, in view of the undeniable fact that, with *Rock-Drill* and *Thrones*, direct references to the *Convivio* and *Paradiso* multiply to the point of innervating the verse's composite tissue. Neither Homer, nor Ovid (another basic source, corroborating the thematic metamorphosis on which the poem thrives), paramount though they may be, can be said to do what Dante, and Pound in his wake, tried to do: "descriver fondo a tutto l'universo." Be it added that Homer (indirectly, through Virgil's mediation) and Ovid (directly) were authoritative sources for Dante as well.

The *Cantos*' protean persona, insofar as it manages to remain a recognizable entity apart from the author's unmediated voice, certainly begins as an Odysseus launched through the itineraries of historical experience. But by the time of the *Pisan Cantos*, written in the humiliating confinement of a detention cage in 1945, the poet's own self shatters that mythical mask and all other masks, to speak out in his own name as Dante does when break-

ing the flow of epic narration to utter a personal concern — something
Homer never does:

> Pull down thy vanity
> Thou art a beaten dog beneath the hail,
> A swollen magpie in a fitful sun,
> Half black half white
> Nor knowst' thou wing from tail
> Pull down thy vanity
>   How mean thy hates
> Fostered in falsity . . .
>
> But to have done instead of not doing
>   this is not vanity . . .
>
> To have gathered from the air a live tradition
> or from a fine old eye the unconquered flame
> This is not vanity.[21]

or again:

> As a lone ant from a broken ant-hill
> from the wreckage of Europe, ego scriptor.[22]

Indeed I agree with Donald Davie that, contrary to his own theory of the
impersonal mask a poet should assume to gain aesthetic objectivity through
distance — a theory quite close to Eliot's thesis of the objective correlative
and Yeats' system of self and anti-self, Pound tends in his later work to be
a very personal poet. One direction of the *Cantos'* pilgrimage is from persona to person. It would not be the first time that a writer contradicts in
actual practice his own theoretical precepts. This explains the vehemence
of invective, which in *Canto* XLV, the "Usura" canto, reaches a Dantesque
tone in spite of the rather different rhythmic texture.

Pound's lifelong ideological fight against finance capitalism, with which
he identifies *Usura*, or the forces of exploitation undermining social order
and creativity, led him into sympathizing with fascism, just as it might
have led him to communism. One must keep in mind his fiery temper, in-
capable of compromise and liable to Quixotic delusions. The dragon *Usura*
is his Moby Dick, a mythomaniacal obsession; for in his concern for civilization he becomes both a Don Quixote and a Melvillean Ahab. This ex-

plains both his great generosity to fellow artists and his notorious blindness to certain appalling consequences of political mythomania. Incidental fanaticism apart, this attitude of Pound's to "usury" is itself a very medieval trait, and one that Dante would have understood. But Pound shows open medievalist tendencies also when he defends the qualitative thinking of medieval theologians on ideas like "light" and "*virtù*" against the dissecting abstractions of modern science. Hence his doctrinal interest in Cavalcanti, whose canzone "Donna mi prega" he has translated and inserted in the *Cantos*.

Pound's affinity for Dante is the more interesting in that it has not made for a literary imitation of the ancient master, but simply fostered an emulation of his accomplishment along radically new lines. Just as Dante substantially diverged from the Virgil he greets as his master and author, with the result that the *Divine Comedy* is no repetition of the *Aeneid*, but an original development made possible by that freely handled model in the changed cultural circumstances, the *Cantos* depart from their medieval model in many particulars of texture while competing with it in thematic scope. The suppression of narrative connectives in what Hugh Kenner [23] has defined a "plotless epic" unified by thematic recurrence in "fields of force" rather than by continuity of action would have confused Dante just as Dante's mixture of styles would have dismayed Augustan Virgil. Another feature Dante could never have accepted is the frequent insertion of historical documents untransformed into verse. The earlier poet did not align the raw material of poetry with the finished product, since song, unbroken song, was his standard. Much like atonal music, the discontinuities in rhythm and subject which stem from Pound's deliberate "ideogrammic" technique also reflect the convulsive quality of modern experience. The danger is that the "vortex" of ideas thus set in motion may accelerate centrifugally instead of cohering. Some of the material is intrusive, ideologically but not poetically assimilated.

In view of Pound's exquisite work as a translator of Horace, Propertius, Catullus, Arnaut Daniel, and Guido Cavalcanti, one wonders why he never undertook to translate the *Divine Comedy*. The answer might be that he did not think it feasible to improve substantially on Laurence Binyon's translation, which he warmly recommended and partly followed in the making. It is also imaginable that such a vast enterprise would have drained the energies he needed for his own demanding epos. Even so, Pound is one prominent poet and litterateur who has rescued Dante from the monopoly of professional Dantists to make an independent use of him and thereby render him newly available to contemporary readers.

Harvard-trained T. S. Eliot did not have to learn his Dante from Ezra Pound, but unquestionably Dante provided one of their closest mutual bonds, judging from the equally strong imprint he left on both men's thought and work. At the outset, as we have seen, the *Divine Comedy* appears in epigraphic excerpts meant to set the thematic keynote for Eliot's own conversational verse in Laforguean style. Given the stylistic difference, the Dantesque epigraph to "Prufrock" acts also as a foil to make us feel the distance of modern low-toned speech, wavering between song and prose, from the sustained *cantus firmus* of the classic source. Then lines or short passages from the *Inferno* and *Purgatorio*, all in translation except for the last one, strategically infiltrate the texture of *The Waste Land* to arouse crosscurrents of allusive resonance with the other literary sources thus laid under contribution—Baudelaire, Nerval, Wagner, Shakespeare and other Elizabethans, St. Augustine, the *Pervigilium Veneris*, and so on.

Thus the lines from *Inferno* III and IV at the end of Section I ("The Burial of the Dead") effectively interact with an acknowledged echo from Baudelaire to establish an infernal aura in the realistically observed London scene; and they do that the better because the poet has successfully disguised these sources by blending their tenor with the given context. At other points, he prefers stylistic and linguistic dissonance to assimilation, as when he lets Baudelaire brusquely address the reader in the original French from "Au Lecteur" at the very end of Section I, or when he allows Dante to speak his own Italian from the Purgatorial episode of Arnaut Daniel at the end of the last section. Here the direct quotation functions in a polyphony of compressed literary voices (English, Italian, French, Latin, Sanskrit), as if to seal the whole troubling vision with a cosmopolitan chorus of purgatorial hope in the midst of sterility, ruin, and despair.

Of course, the referential sounding board established by Eliot's direct or indirect quotations in his particular context implies a difference in identity, a distorted analogy of situations to emphasize that history does and does not repeat itself, that the old recurs in the new but is changed by it. Thus the unidentified girl speaking at lines 291–99 uses partly Pia de' Tolomei's voice to tell her squalid story of seduction without love. The sarcastic effect is to stress the modern woman's lack of tragic dignity vis-à-vis pure Pia. That is in Section III, "The Fire Sermon." The following section, "Death by Water," outlines in Phlebas the Phoenician a nonheroic Ulysses, the prototype of all normal navigators and of man qua navigator. That the section was inspired by Dante's Ulysses episode we know from T. S. Eliot himself,[24] though what he actually said to his literary interviewer for the *Paris Review* is that the whole original section having to do with a shipwreck of the Ulysses type was excised at the suggestion of Pound. If so, "Death by Water" must be considered the reworked salvage of the expunged piece. And when Count Ugolino's words are echoed by the Sanskrit thunder voice at lines 410–13, they supply a cue for meditation on the locked-in human mind, the true hellish condition: each man is a prison unto himself, and Bradley's philosophy of solipsism naturally comes into view.[25]

In the above-mentioned interview, Eliot had come to define *The Waste Land* as a "structureless" poem and to indicate in the *Four Quartets* a more mature accomplishment. Certainly the earlier poem gives evidence of a painful struggle to unify the chaotic "fragments" of reality through the available categories of a reinterpreted tradition. "These fragments I have shored against my ruins": the moral, intellectual ruins of a disinherited humanity that can "remember nothing," "connect nothing with nothing." "Tradition and the Individual Talent," the famous essay composed in 1919, three years before publication of *The Waste Land*, illustrates that poem's problems and procedure very well. The "individual talent" must function in an objective context larger than himself, and that means the whole Western tradition from Homer to Virgil, Dante, Shakespeare, and Baudelaire, not as academically imposed, but personally repossessed. The *Waste Land*'s dramatization of modern disintegrating humanity as a jarring chorus of windowless psychic monads that fail to relate to each other calls forth within its own context the need to counteract that eccentric pull by the concentric force of those other voices who knew how to master experience: the classics. That the parade of disembodied modern voices thus played off against their noble and ancient counterparts hovers on the verge of incoherence, and that the contrapuntally conjured sources, designed to lay bare the modern predicament of unrelatedness, tend to weigh down the poem (especially at the end), is the risk of such a radical attempt as *The Waste Land* was in its time.

Yet the poem has the virtues of its faults; it functions dramatically through the very suddenness of its successively emerging voices. And this is perhaps its most significant formal affinity to Dante's own achievement, if we but think of the strong effect the Italian poet knew how to elicit from the dramatic immediacy of his characters' revelatory talk. This is true especially in the *Inferno*, where often the sinners are not visually described at all but just self-evoked by the inflections of their speech: for instance Francesca, Pier delle Vigne, Ulysses, and Guido da Montefeltro. In the *Purgatorio* the same applies to the great trio of Jacopo del Cassaro, Buonconte da Montefeltro, and Pia de' Tolomei in Canto v. The apparitions often catch Dante the pilgrim by surprise, as in *Inferno* x, where Farinata is already fully present in the dramatic sense, before being seen, through the revealing words he unexpectedly addresses to the wayfarer. The occasional difficulty of Eliot's analogous strategy in a different context comes from the modern poet's renunciation of narrative transitions and unified action—a trait *The Waste Land* shares with the *Cantos* and *The Bridge*. The modern poets' option for an elliptical technique in narration and imagery in works of large scope is liberating in some respects, but also limiting. Whatever disappears from the page must be supplied by the collaboration of the reader; pushed to the limit, the technique can make for a cultural algebra beyond poetry, as indeed happens in parts of Pound's last *Cantos*.

The dramatic analogy I mentioned goes hand in hand with the stylistic modulations Eliot recurrently tries out to mediate between his "low" modern voices, whether aristocratically futile or crude in a plebeian way (compare *The Burial of the Dead* and *A Game of Chess*), and his lofty sources that act as foils to them. These modulations are part of the poem's strength, and they provide another important affinity with Dante's *Comedy*, which — in a more gradual way — also includes the low ("comic") and the elevated or sublime ("tragic") styles in its ample gamut. Once again we see that the "individual talent" (the modern poet) observes the "tradition" (Dante and the other classics) in such a way as not to copy, but to transform it. What I said of Pound's relationship to Dante is true of Eliot's: he relates to Dante much in the way Dante himself related to Virgil; and Virgil is for Eliot, as he is not for Pound, the prototype of the classic.

Tradition is a personal as well as collective responsibility, an ever renewed resumption of the old in the new, not a supine acceptance of what is there. New poems "change" the old; in fact, Eliot and Pound have taught many of us to read Dante in a new way. And it adds to our appreciation of Eliot's work, in the light of his lifelong closeness to Dante, that his plea for an originally interpreted tradition came from a revolutionary, even iconoclastic poet, the poet of "Preludes" and *The Waste Land*, who eventually earned his self-proclaimed "classicism" as a reconstruction along new lines of what he had destroyed.

Thematically as well as stylistically, Eliot's itinerary went from the "infernal" phase of "Prufrock," *The Waste Land*, and *The Hollow Men* through the purgatorial one of the "Ariel Poems" and *Ash Wednesday* to the almost paradisal one of *Four Quartets*, paradise here being a glimpsed fulfillment the persona invokes, rather than a grasped actuality. The *disiecta membra* of dispersive experience, which had gone into the mimetic kaleidoscope of *The Waste Land* as soon as Laforguean satire proved unequal to the task of fully apprehending the derangements of the contemporary postwar world, came to be progressively reintegrated in the ever more fluently singing style of "Animula," *Ash Wednesday*, and the *Quartets*. Eliot's conversion to the Anglican form of Christianity paralleled this process of stylistic reintegration, while Dante, a constant presence, kept summoning him to new achievement.

From the time of his essays collected in *The Sacred Wood* (1920) to the booklet on Dante of 1929 and the still later pronouncements on "What Is a Classic?" (1944), on Dante again in 1950, and on "Virgil and the Christian World" (1951),[26] we hear him pay to the Tuscan exile a tribute he otherwise reserves only for Shakespeare, since in his opinion "Dante and Shakespeare divide the world between them" and "there is no third." He differs from Pound in this regard as far as Shakespeare is concerned; yet he says of Dante in 1929 that he is the most profitably imitable poet and the finest model of style for writers in any language, and in his 1950 lecture he puts Dante above Shakespeare in one respect, that, having a genius equal to Shakespeare's, he did not allow himself with his language the liberties Shakespeare occasionally took with his. This is a tribute of high significance in view of Eliot's statement, in the same context, that the great poet is "the servant, rather than the master" of his language.

Statements on poetics (or poetical programs) and actual poetical practice do not necessarily correspond, but in Eliot's case the close link between his criticism and his poetry is obvious. His repeated tribute to Dante was no lip service, and there was pride as well as humility in his statement of 1929 that he would have been content with knowing that a dozen of his own lines matched Dante's perfection in verse. Already in *The Waste Land* we have seen him occasionally approximate a Dantean style by incorporating translated lines from the *Divine Comedy*; in *Ash Wednesday*, direct quotes from the *Purgatorio* and *Paradiso* appear with a brilliantly transformed cue from Cavalcanti's "Ballata dell'esilio," and the climbing "stairs" evoke the Purgatorial *cornici*. The voice of Arnaut Daniel is once again fleetingly heard in Section IV, while the "white sails . . . flying seaward/ Unbroken wings" of Section VI recall the same simile in *Purgatorio* II, 26, where the white sails of the boat carrying new souls to the mountain island of purification turn out to be angels' wings, "mentre che i primi bianchi apparser ali." Finally, Piccarda is heard toward the end: "Our peace in His will."

"Animula" in the "Ariel Poems" takes its initial cue from *Purgatorio* XVI, 85–88 ff. The vicissitudes of the "simple soul" ("l'anima semplicetta che sa nulla") through the temptations of life become here the odyssey of progressive frustration in a devitalized world which makes for spiritual inanition. The style is much more continuous than *The Waste Land* could afford, and at points touches a Dantesque firmness:

> The heavy burden of the growing soul . . .
>
> The pain of living and the drug of dreams
> Curl up the small soul in the window seat . . .
>
> Issues from the hands of time the simple soul
> Irresolute and selfish, misshapen, lame,
> Unable to fare forward or retreat,
> Fearing the warm reality, the offered good . . .

At the end, prayer once again. The poem might be renamed "Variations on a theme by Dante."

Where Eliot most closely approaches Dante's style, to the point of consistent emulation for the length of seventy-two lines, is in Section II of the fourth quartet (*Little Gidding*).[27] Here it is not just a matter of using sparse cues to suit the changing context, or of playing one variation on a set phrase, or even of constructing an analogous scenery. The whole passage is conceived and executed like a Dantean episode. The (unmasked) poetic persona meets a "dead master" in the dawn dusk of a smoky London street after an air raid; there is a recognition, the venerable shade being a "familiar compound ghost," "both one and many"—Virgil, Dante, Poe and Mallarmé, for instance, and then the dead poet warns the living one about the moral hardships he will have to face in the declining phase of his life and career; thereupon he vanishes.

The wartime urban scene is effortlessly presented in Purgatorial tones of the less airy kind, with the smoke from the bombed ruins vaguely recalling the smoke that envelops the cornice of the wrathful spirits in *Purgatorio* XVI, where Dante meets the wise Marco Lombardo. The meter freely recalls Dante's *terza rima*, for it consists of unrhymed tercets aptly suggesting the cadence of the *Divine Comedy*—a technique also adopted, for different purposes, by Wallace Stevens in *Notes Toward a Supreme Fiction*. The lines tend to be more self-contained than formerly, with a caesura recurring in the middle to create a balanced rhythm of Dantesque gravity:

> Between three districts // whence the smoke arose
> I met one walking, // loitering and hurried
> As if blown towards me // like the metal leaves
> Before the urban dawn wind // unresisting.

> And as I fixed // upon the down-turned face
> The pointed scrutiny // with which we challenge
> The first-met stranger // in the waning dusk . . .

At the same time, a mobility of pauses and syllables prevents the versification from falling into the set mold of imitative servility. It is Eliot, a unique modern voice, that we hear throughout, and not a literary pastiche (which *The Waste Land* occasionally skirts).

The phrasing has a wiry neatness Dante would have found very congenial, and at times it even vies with him in sententious earthiness:

> . . . Last season's fruit is eaten
> And the fullfed beast shall kick the empty pail.

> . . . Then fools' approval stings, and honour stains.

Here and there, a line or phrase brings specific details of the *Divine Comedy* to mind, without the pointed emphasis the *Waste Land* quotations have. Compare ". . . 'What! are *you* here?'" with *Inferno* xv: "'Siete voi qui, Ser Brunetto?'" ("'Are you here, Ser Brunetto?'") and ". . . I left my body on a distant shore" with *Purgatorio* v, "'Quivi/ Caddi, e rimase la mia carne sola'" ("'There/ I fell and my flesh remained, alone'"). The whole terminal part of the "dead master"'s address to Eliot's persona is patterned on the prophetic speeches several damned, or purging, or blessed spirits make to Dante concerning his future life on earth; except that here the prophecy deals with the harm which will come to the persona from himself and his own failings, not from the malice of others:

> Let me disclose the gifts reserved for age
> To set a crown upon your lifetime's effort.
> First, the cold friction of expiring sense
> Without enchantment, offering no promise
> But bitter tastelessness of shadow fruit
> As body and soul begin to fall asunder . . .

The readiest association here would seem to be with Cacciaguida's words to Dante in *Paradiso* xvii, 58–60:

> Tu proverai sì come sa di sale
>   Lo pane altrui, e com'è duro calle
>   Lo scendere e 'l salir per l'altrui scale.

You will find out how salty is the flavor
of another's bread, and how hard the course
of going down and up another's stairway.

But it is the sustained diction itself, rather than any specific reference, that establishes the ideal proximity. At the end of the episode, as if to seal the free alliance he has entered with his master Dante, Eliot brings in word of a "refining fire" which comes straight from the Arnaut Daniel episode in *Purgatorio* xxvi, 148 — a favorite of Eliot's. His purgatory is terrene life itself. I cannot leave this remarkable passage of *Little Gidding* without recalling also that the admonition of humility from a dead artist to a living one likewise finds its counterpart in *Purgatorio* xi, where the miniaturist Oderisi instructs Dante on the vanity of earthly fame. Celestial fulfillment will be adumbrated in the final part of this last quartet, where "the fire and the rose are one."

Eliot started from Dante and spent a lifetime in getting nearer him, to the point where he could afford to "write like Dante" while speaking most like himself. The performance of the section of *Little Gidding* just discussed is an admirable example of craftsmanship, but not a mere literary exercise, as was some of Pound's early verse. In fact none of Eliot's poems, not even the most composite ones, could be termed mere exercises; unless we meant by that the *askesis* of style and soul. The *Quartets* give us Eliot's mature voice, and its timbre is various but never abrupt or shrill as Pound's sometimes is in the last *Cantos*. One may consider the ease with which the *Quartets* can include the Dantean canon in their otherwise different score. Dante can be many things to many men, and he has helped to bring out what was most Eliotic in Eliot, what was most Poundian in Pound; for our two literary friends were, by temper and ideas, markedly different. One need only think of Eliot's religious inwardness versus Pound's interest in secular politics; of Pound's bent for doctrine and invective and Eliot's preference for prayer. It is also to be noticed how widely their careers diverged after the early twenties. Eliot went beyond the composite angularity of *The Waste Land* toward the smoother symphonic style of the *Quartets* and the controlled richness of his verse plays, while Pound kept harping on the contractile forms of the *Cantos*, apart from preaching his Confucian and Gesellist socio-economic theories. The former evolved toward greater and greater communicativeness in poetry, the latter has pushed his demands on the reader to the verge of arrogance.

Yet in their different ways they have both measured their experiments against the highest standards, Dante in particular, and nowhere does this show more conclusively than in Pound's attempt to write, with the *Cantos*, the "Summa poetica" of our time, the all-inclusive epic of civilization — an enterprise for which he was not so poorly equipped, despite the idiosyncrasy of some of his views. Eliot's modesty has secured a more consistent poetical success, down to the moving confrontation with Dante we have just seen. But the ambition to write the total poem, whether Dante-inspired or not, has spread from Pound, and to a lesser extent from the example of *The Waste Land*, to other American poets like William Carlos Williams, in whose *Paterson* Dantean references are not wanting, and Hart Crane, who came late to Dante, as his letters and his tribute poem called "Purgatorio" indicate,[28] only to find that his mythic projection of the modern city world as a hell and purgatory in the American epic *The Bridge* had an obvious Dantesque pattern, probably mediated to him by *The Waste Land*.

As to Wallace Stevens, whose use of a Dantesque structural paradigm to counterpoint the theme of *Notes Toward a Supreme Fiction* I have discussed elsewhere,[29] he would have not received this impulse from either Eliot or Pound. Both writers, on the other hand, have been important sources to Allen Tate, who worships the Middle Ages as a lost Eden of civilization even more than do Pound and Eliot.[30] He deliberately used the Dantean *terza rima* in one of his poems ("The Swimmers"), and he was at least partly responsible for communicating to Robert Lowell a pragmatic interest in Dante. Lowell's well-known bent for a highstrung, rugged language makes his focal use of lines and passages from the *Comedy* a matter of natural affinity. This tactic, which he chiefly learned from Eliot, can be illustrated by poems like "Exile's Return" and "The Soldier" in *Lord Weary's Castle* (1946) and "For George Santayana" in *Life Studies* (1946). "Exile's Return" throws the shadow of the *Inferno* over war-ravaged Europe by quoting part of a line Dante reports as inscribed over Hell's gate. "The Soldier" is a condensed paraphrase of the story of Buonconte da Montefeltro in *Pur-*

gatorio v, for modern reference. "For George Santayana" includes a passage translated from *Inferno* xv to suggest a direct analogy between the situation of Santayana, a revered master whose rejection of the ancestral faith was never reconsidered, and Brunetto Latini, who is outside the pale of salvation for different reasons. Lowell's brief conversion to the Catholic Church, his prophetic stance, and affinity for metaphysical poetry are all concomitants of a zestful participation in Dante's legacy, which seems to operate most fruitfully in what is the (partly) alien ground of the English language. To this day, indeed, Dante's legacy has helped to keep poetry alive in this language, and the tribute of Robert Duncan,[31] among the younger American writers of visionary and experimental verse, has come to reassert the continued viability of such a gift from a dead "foreign" poet to the living ones. Civilization thrives on just such intangible bequests.*

* As this book goes to press, it seems appropriate to mention that Robert Lowell has followed up his earlier Dantean cues by translating the whole of *Inferno*'s Canto xv (which features the encounter with Brunetto Latini), in the volume *Near the Ocean* (New York, 1967). Another relevant reference is John Bullaro, "The Dante of T. S. Eliot," in *A Dante Profile*, ed. Franca Schettino (Los Angeles, Calif., 1967). Finally, mention should be made of LeRoi Jones' autobiographical novel, *The System of Dante's Hell* (New York, 1965).

CHAPTER VIII

VICO AND DANTE

THERE would be reason to bring Dante Alighieri and Giambattista Vico together across the intervening gulf of six centuries, even if Vico's pronouncements on Dante were not there to elicit such a linkage.[1] The linkage, in fact, has implicitly or explicitly occurred a few times during the last 150 years. Not accidentally, in the two founders of modern Italian criticism, the liberal patriots Ugo Foscolo and Francesco de Sanctis,[2] zest for Dante's poetry went hand in hand with a pervasive affinity for Vico, and the same was true of Samuel Taylor Coleridge in England. Later in the nineteenth century Karl Werner, an Austrian scholar of more conservative views in politics and religion, had this to say:

Vico was a thoroughly national thinker, and he reflects in his creative activity the spirit and mentality of his own people just as characteristically as the Frenchman comes through in Descartes, the Englishman in Locke, the German in Kant. As against Descartes' spiritual rationalism, or Locke's empirically realist intellectualism, it is in the artistically formative mind that Vico recognizes the source of all true insight and the immediate shaper of man himself in the totality of his being . . . The world encompassed by Vico's thought is that of historical man, in which, as in Dante's great poem, all spheres of cosmic reality find their center; Dante is to him the prince of poets, Homer, returned in the Christian era and as such also the interpreter of his own vision; the Virgil whom Dante chose for his guide corresponds, as a representative of the purposively shaping human reason, exactly to the idea that Vico himself has of that faculty's essence . . .[3]

In 1963 the Swiss scholar Theophil Spoerri, in what promises to be an enduring contribution to the study of Dante's poetry and thought,[4] said that Dante's Dark Wood image is of a piece with Vico's idea of a primordial wood, from which the beastlike giants constituting the degenerated remnants of Gentile mankind long after the Flood started their arduous evolution toward civilization under the hidden guidance of an immanent Providence. It is from the Dark Wood of error, we may remember, that Dante's bewildered pilgrim persona finds his circuitous way to salvation and enlightenment, with some supernatural assistance. Unquestionably, I would add, both myths are historical reenactments of the Fortunate Fall, one in the guise of personal allegory, the other in the shape of that collective archetype or "imaginative universal" (*"universale fantastico"*) which Vico posits as the organ of expression and knowledge for the "heroic," or pre-rational, ages of mankind. For he was himself very much a poet, capable of reattaining in his own passionate meditation those bygone phases of turbulent imagining that, in his view, had fostered the greatest poetry; and no matter how trenchantly he may affirm in *The New Science* (II, 219) that philosophy and poetry are in effect mutually irreducible, an epic power of vision seethed at the center of his thinking. This power, to be sure, he shared with Dante, as Mario Fubini recognized in his systematic investigation of Vico's relationship to Dante.[5]

Fubini in turn took his cue from Croce's study of Vico's philosophy,[6] especially Croce's remark that for all its sketchiness Vico's interpretation of Dante's poetry was a revolutionary step into modern criticism because in Croce's opinion, no one before Vico had ever looked at the *Divine Comedy* in that poignant way. Since Fubini's point of departure is more specifically literary, his essay on Dante's relevance to Vico, no less than his entire approach to Vico's style as a writer, amounts to a landmark in Vico studies. Accordingly, before developing further aspects of the problem I shall try to summarize Fubini's main points.

Briefly, they are as follows: Through his frequent references to Dante (in one of the *Orations*, in the *De Universi Juris Principio ac Fine Uno*, in

The New Science, in the *Autobiography*, in the letter to Gherardo degli Angioli, and in the book review called "Discoverta del vero Dante" or "Discovery of the True Dante"), Vico evinces a predominantly historico-philosophical interest in the medieval poet, whom he sees as a new Homer, as the singer of Italy's "barbarous age," to illustrate his theory of recourses and of barbaric or "heroic" ages as the prime seedbed of great poetry. The literary aspect of the *Divine Comedy* remains subordinated, in Vico's vision, to this bird's-eye view of history, which involves certain distortions of fact, such as the unqualified description of Dante's Italy as barbarous, ferocious, and so on. It also entails a reduction of Dante's poetry to another piece of evidence for Vico's aesthetics of the primitive sublime, which is supposed to have found in Homer an unequaled embodiment; in general Vico makes it very clear that his Dante must be read in the light of his non-Augustan Homer: the less civil and urbane, the greater.

Yet it is this very reduction, this radical rejection of Dante's doctrinal superstructures in favor of the naïve, unfettered element in his imagination, that marks Vico as the ancestor of Romantic aesthetics and, by the same token, of nineteenth-century Dante criticism, in sharp contrast to the over-refined Arcadian taste of his own age, which set polish above power and thus could not stomach Dante's rugged greatness. And when, in the letter to Gherardo degli Angioli, he says that Dante's wrath in the *Divine Comedy* is like Achilles' wrath in the *Iliad*, Vico is throwing vivid light on what certainly forms a seminal nucleus of Dante's poetry, even though he fails to solve the problem raised by his identification of poetry with myth and with the barbarous, unintellectual ages of mankind.

Does civilization necessarily kill poetry? Vico, unlike Hegel, would not have answered this question in the affirmative, says Fubini, and the proof comes from Vico's otherwise misplaced faith in the poetical powers of his young friend Gherardo degli Angioli, whose craving for Dante's strong fare and its counterparts in the midst of an effete Arcadian-intellectualist epoch he assumed to bespeak the austere taste that promises fresh creativity. In Gherardo, Fubini rightly observes, Vico was projecting his own self-portrait, and when we read in the *Autobiography* how solitary, melancholy, and choleric Vico was, we recognize in the eighteenth-century Neapolitan thinker a very Dantesque type: proud, at loggerheads with his age, absorbed by an encompassing vision which his own time failed to share or understand, and possessed by an epic sense of the past. Dante certainly nurtured Vico, through an elective affinity, and even similarities of style are to be noticed, as for example, in Vico's predilection for the graphic idiom to seal a sweeping utterance. Vico's conception of a providential pattern in human history would also have linked him to Dante. The primacy of poetical imagination cannot be denied in Vico, and thus his penchant for Dante emerges into proper focus as the meeting of a poet-philosopher with a philosopher-poet.

The fact that in the "Discovery of the True Dante" Vico was evolving toward a less generically historical and more literary appraisal of his congenial author is not lost on Fubini, whose assessment of Vico's limitations versus his pioneering originality in the whole matter of Dante studies can hardly be contested. Hopefully, however, there is room for further consideration. For instance, a reading of the "Discovery of the True Dante" in sequential perspective makes one wonder why Vico should have failed to develop its full implications as an internal critique of some overly systematic claims made in *The New Science*. While reasserting his Homeric analogy and Dante's consequent dependence on the barbarous ages of medieval Italy, Vico now speaks of an "expiring" rather than a rampant "barbarism" in Dante's time, thus shading his earlier statement. From the historical viewpoint he passes on to a linguistic one to correct the thesis, likewise set forth in the letter to Gherardo, of a Dante gleaning idioms from all the Italian dialects — a thesis possibly derived, directly or indirectly, from Dante's own *De Vulgari Eloquentia*. Dante is now firmly moored to the Tuscan speech, which in Vico's estimate must have shared a number of current locutions with other Italian dialects anyway. Finally, the aesthetic value appears as a matter of uniqueness and originality: sublime poetry like Dante's "cannot be learned by skill or craft," it has priority over all rules. Dante's sublimity, elsewhere described as verging on the primitive and the grotesque, is now connected with a "loftiness of mind" which, instead of accruing from the temper of the age, sets the poet apart in his contempt for whatever "greedy . . . soft, effeminate men commonly admire."[7] This loftiness shows in the exclusive concern for glory and immortality (of the humanistic type) and in "a mind informed by great and public virtues — and above all by magnanimity and justice," such as the Spartan education, despite its lack of emphasis on literature, seems to Vico to have once fostered in people "whose daily expressions . . . would adorn the work of the most illustrious tragic and heroic poets."

Clearly, Vico has moved beyond the conception of a barbarous Dante, whose only title to poetical greatness would have been the awesome portrayal of his age's cruelest passions, to bring him a step closer to full civilization. Indeed the "Discovery of the True Dante" was written in the years (1728? 1729? 1730?) immediately preceding the academic address *De mente heroica* (*Of the Heroic Mind*, 1732), in which, partly owing to its pedagogic aim, the idea of heroism has shed its barbaric implications to denote a consuming passion for knowledge as the mainspring of civil virtue. There is thus a heroism of the philosopher, the civilizer of late ages, and a heroism of the representative poet, the civilizer of early ages; they share such basic traits, if we take for our texts the "Discovery of the True Dante" and *Of the Heroic Mind*, that one wonders whether the shaping spirit of imagination and the piercing spirit of speculation are not about to become one in Vico's mind.

They of course do in the poem he wrote in 1730 for Clement XII's accession to the papal throne,[8] where our thinker takes advantage of the official occasion to sing his own flight from the dejection of an aggravating earthly scene to the "inaccessible light" beyond the sky. This transcendental zone "girds and envelops the world," to figure forth for the astral pilgrim's eye the vicissitudes of timebound empires in timeless fashion: it is obviously the "ideal eternal history" Vico descries as a recurrent pattern governing human history in *The New Science*. In this poem, though, the exercise of timeless contemplation counts above all as a personal deliverance for the time-ridden, grief-burdened persona who, while "down there in the low world," could not make rhyme or reason of human wrongs because his outraged intellect vainly sought truth in human things seen in disjointed isolation ("tutte scevere e sole"); now instead a total perspective has superseded the partial one to reveal the essential goodness of an overall design which ceaselessly redeems the corruptions of history.

Here Vico is telling us of the cathartic value of *The New Science* for its author; but in so doing he is unmistakably echoing certain climactic moments of Dante's *Paradiso,* many of whose lines come to mind as we read of Vico's persona soaring "from sphere to heavenly sphere, from planet to planet and from star to star," while the constellations of Argo, Perseus, and Hercules dwindle below him and vanish (Stanza 1). In Stanza 2, lines 18–20 ("Oh quanto corto, oh quanto/ col suo lungo aguzzar l'occhio ne' vetri/ è quel che ne le stelle Urania osserva!" – "Oh how shortsighted indeed is Urania's observation of the stars, despite her intent peering through the [telescope's] glasses!") take their stylistic cue from *Paradiso* XXXIII, 121–23:

> Oh quanto è corto il dire e come fioco
> al mio concetto! e questo, a quel ch'i'vidi,
> è tanto, che non basta a dicer "poco."

> Oh how my words fall short of my concept,
> and how they dim it! and it in turn, compared
> to what I saw, is not even enough to say "little."

Again, lines 50–51 in Stanza 3 have an unmistakable Dantesque ring:

> Oh mio pur troppo infermo occhio mortale!
> che là nel basso mondo . . .

> Oh my so sadly feeble mortal eye!
> which down there in the low world . . .

One cannot help recalling Dante's turning back to look on the "aiola che ci fa tanto feroci" ("the patch of land which makes us so ferocious"), from the starry heights of Paradise. For Vico has earned the right to conjure Dante's style, not just episodically, but as a matter of "heroic frenzy," as another poet-thinker would have said; and here the heroism of the philosophical mind does incorporate the heroism of a poetical mind likewise committed to the experience of a total cosmic perspective. At this threshold, they become one.

To return to the "Discovery of the True Dante," we must also see that, no matter how Vico may occasionally soar toward that supreme identification, he is by no means surrendering his central idea of spontaneity, *Zeit-geist*, and *Volksgeist* as essential to poetry:

What was most peculiar to Dante's sublimity resulted from his having been born with the gift of genius in the era of Italy's expiring barbarism. For human talents are like those of the earth, which, if brought under cultivation after fallow centuries, produces at the outset fruits marvelous for their perfection, size, and abundance; but which, once tired from overmuch cultivation, yields only few, wizened, and small. And this is why, at the end of the barbarian period, there arose a Dante in sublime poetry, a Petrarch in delicate poetry, a Boccaccio in light and graceful prose: all three incomparable examples which we must by all means follow, but which we can by no means overtake. Whereas in our own highly cultivated era, such fair works of art as are being created may well raise in others the hope not merely of overtaking, but of surpassing them.[9]

At the same time, Vico no longer discounts the doctrinal-allegorical layers of Dante's work, but makes them contingent upon the alert reader's response, and his conception of a merely "Homeric," that is, primitive, Dante is now significantly qualified to take into account Dante's uniqueness and individual reality, as against Homer's composite, collective, anonymous reality in *The New Science*. If so, the recourse of barbarism in medieval history can no longer be seen as a literal repetition of the earlier cycle, but as a new phase with poignant analogies; the image of Sisyphus, implicit in the pattern of "ideal eternal history," must yield to that of a progressive spiral, and the poet becomes more a Carlylean hero than a deterministic function of his time. Besides, the allowance made for Petrarch's "delicate" poetry is revolutionary within Vico's system, if we consider that "delicacy" generally recurs in his vocabulary as a term of disparagement. Vico is averting or at least undermining a possible mechanization of his own grandiose system.

The qualities he sees in Dante, with due respect to historical juncture, are those he thought he saw at the potential stage in Gherardo degli Angioli and actually harbored in himself. Even more important, they are the very qualities that would appear in the new poets of an Italy Vico was never to see: aristocratic, choleric, liberty-minded Alfieri; rebellious, public-spirited Foscolo; melancholy, austere Leopardi; earnest, historically minded Manzoni.[10] The letter to Gherardo thus amounts to a prophecy of things to come, of the rebirth of Italian literature from the renewed experience of those "virtues" of which Vico saw little trace around him. Arcadian frills would not do. And the problem of the compatibility of strong poetry with humane civilization was the same that Schiller would one day see, and solve in his own way, in the *Briefe über aesthetische Erziehung* (*Letters on Aesthetic Education*) and in *Über naive und sentimentalische Dichtung* (*On Naive and Sentimental Poetry*). If civilization is just a passive consumption of the past, it is "soft," effeminate, barren; if it is a shaping spirit, then mankind does not have to relapse into barbarism in order to renew itself (though perhaps Vico would have seen a recourse of barbarism in the violent outbursts of the French and Russian revolutions).

The very fact that even a glance at one aspect of Vico's work calls into question so much of the culture of his time and of times to come is symptomatic of his exceptional stature, which enabled him to meet Dante as an equal. There are striking parallels between Dante's intellectual development and that of Vico. In a letter to Father Giacco (October 12, 1720)[11] he confesses to his resentment of those fellow citizens who only remember the "weaknesses and errors" of his youth, as if subsequent progress did not decisively matter; and this brings to mind the solitary years from 1686 to 1695 which he spent in the rural isolation of Vatolla sul Cilento as a tutor to the Rocca children, the years from which Vico's early acquaintance with meditation and anguish date, the years so laconically covered in the *Autobiography*, though from them sprang the canzone "Affetti d'un disperato" ("Emotions of a Despondent Soul"). This canzone, which is Vico's best verse composition, expresses, according to Fausto Nicolini,[12] a despondency out of tune with Catholic orthodoxy, and Fisch and Bergin[13] note that the years of intellectual torment at Vatolla must also have witnessed Vico's contacts with the freethinkers of Naples, some of whom were to get in trouble with the Inquisition. The heresy in question was connected with the Gassendian atomism[14] that found so much favor in Neapolitan circles at the time; indeed Lucretius, the poet of Democritean atomism, was one of Vico's favorite authors and main sources, so that, as Fisch and

Bergin remark, *De Rerum Natura*'s Book v affords a repertory of thematic cues for *The New Science*.

That being so, the "errors" of Vico's pensive youth are comparable to Dante's straying from the "right path" during the years between the *Vita Nuova* and the *Convivio* (possibly under the influence of Cavalcanti's Averroism), while the overcoming of doubts and "errors" in the universal vision of *The New Science* — which reaffirms the relentlessly purposive action of a historical Providence over any "Stoic" (that is, Spinozian) conception of Fate on the one hand and any "Epicurean" (that is, Hobbesian-Machiavellian-Gassendian) conception of mere Chance in human affairs on the other — parallels Dante's spiritual trajectory from the gropings of his youth and early virility to the encompassing synthesis of the *Divine Comedy*. Through the obvious differences we can descry a common pattern of intellectual development, and of singular integrity, in the inner careers of these two solitary writers who quarreled so much with their respective times because they were in search of a universal truth.

This truth they gained by personal suffering, one remaining a factual exile to the last, the other a spiritual exile in his own city. The note of estrangement rings out more than once in Vico's *Autobiography*: "With this learning and erudition Vico returned to Naples a stranger in his own land . . ."; "For these reasons Vico lived in his native city not only a stranger but quite unknown . . ."[15] Both were men of fiery temper and each felt the singularity of his life as a spur to conquer a vision so much larger than himself, a vision by which his entire progress would be tested and his singularity vindicated yet transcended. Hence Vico's application of the providential concept to his *Autobiography*, which becomes a pilgrimage towards intellectual truth. The ordeals and intercessions through which Dante the pilgrim progresses towards his kind of truth reflect a comparable design.

Of course, Vico's dialectic is not Dante's; Vico's idea of Providence is only a metaphor in comparison to Dante's Augustinian view of history, since the post-Renaissance humanist conceived of Providence as an immanent force, indeed as man's collective mind operating beyond the conscious motives of man's actions toward a rational order of society in *this* world; whereas Dante's conception involved a divine force intervening in human affairs from above and, on occasion, through miracles. Dante would have found it impossible to accept Vico's revolutionary statement that man makes his own world in history, indeed makes himself in the process and can therefore know the relevant laws from the "modifications" of his own mind. Dante was immersed in the mythology Vico tested by his critical solvents; Vico's proto-Marxist reduction of all myths to the merely human and social element was the reverse of Dante's transcendent faith. Yet Vico the dismantler of myth was a mythmaker of sorts, for he could not help fashioning his own myths in the process of describing the epos of aboriginal history. No wonder, then, that he should be attracted to Dante the mythographer, with whom he shared a dramatic sense of the mind's workings, an epic sense of human action, and a keen power of sensuous perception to embody his ideas.

Vico's philosophy, unlike Kant's, never hovers for long in the spheres of logical abstraction, but takes the characteristic form of vivid axiomatic insights, with corollaries of rushing eloquence which stand to their generating axioms as the movements of a Beethoven symphony stand to the sharp initial statement of their theme. Vico, like Dante, thinks in concrete terms, and the physical world is never far from his focus; we are never allowed to forget that Sir Francis Bacon, the philosopher of experience, is among his cardinal authors. Vico does not just talk about the origins, development, and crisis of civilization: he makes us see its crucial scenes and imaginatively participate in the choral action, even while taking his bearings in the vastest perspective he can afford.

"Men at first feel without perceiving, then they perceive with a troubled and agitated spirit, finally they reflect with a clear mind" — thus Axiom LIII, paragraph 218, of *The New Science*. The ternary rhythm of existential growth is the rhythm of knowledge, and it governs the cycles of human history — the *storia ideale eterna*. One could point out its affinity to the Aristotelian rhythm of tragedy from passion to epiphany, as reinterpreted by Francis Fergusson and applied by him to the structure of Dante's poem.[16] Whether in Vico's or in Aristotle's theory, what is envisaged amounts to a sequence of phases of consciousness which in turn may find their counterpart in the triad of Hell (unrestrained passion), Purgatory (the suffering that enlightens), and Paradise (pure vision of Being). A common dynamic pattern underlies the philosophical dialectic of the mature Vico and the poetical-theological dialectic of the mature Dante.

Vico, the secularist, is far from irreverent; he has the piety of humanity, whose unfolding through recurrent conflict is the drama of all dramas, the crowning essence of all poetry. He calls his critique of history a "reasoned civil theology," and though he still sets the history of the Chosen People apart from Gentile history, it is but a step from his conception to Hegel's final dictum that "all history is sacred history." He is moved, and moves us, by the imagined spectacle of fallen mankind, a lawless herd of "big beasts all stupor and ferocity," wandering aimlessly through the huge postdiluvial forest to be eventually stricken with numinous fear by the thunderbolts that a moisture-saturated sky finally flings at them as if it were an angry Zeus. With the dawning of religion from fear in the naïve mind of the bestial giants, the long journey toward civilization begins, and the inarticulate "cyclopes" are on the way to becoming human, social, rational. We move from the infernal to the purgatorial phase, from the Dark Wood of error and violence, from the City of Dis and Malebolge, toward a glimpsed order.

> And oh! how hard it is to describe
> This savage forest, harsh and impervious.
> So bitter is it, that death is scarcely more.
> But to deal with the good I found therein
> I shall speak of the other things I saw in that very place.

The providential pattern, ontologically externalized by Dante in accordance with his faith and epistemologically reduced by Vico to an indwelling force of the collective mind, operates from the start, turning to account the worst predicament to make a virtue out of necessity. To say it with Hölderlin, "Wo aber Gefahr ist, waechst/ Das Rettende auch" ("But where danger is, there grows/ Salvation also").[17]

If it is possible to use Dante as an illustration of Vico, and Vico in turn as a commentary on Dante's authenticity, it is because each writer, in terms of his cultural framework, grasps the archetypes of human experience. The poem of salvation can be read as an allegory of civilization; conversely, *The New Science* is itself something like an epic poem, divested of the supernatural aspects which had to go into the making of the *Divine Comedy*. Accordingly, the more recent of these two structures of vision incorporates a number of elements from the older one and transmutes them into its own fabric. The Forest and the City, opposed yet interchangeable, appear as fundamental images throughout the *Divine Comedy* as well as in *The New Science* and in the letter to Gherardo. Farinata, Capaneus, Ulysses, Ugolino, with the enormity of their passions, correspond to the "atheist giants" in *The New Science*, whom Jupiter's thunderbolts – a self-projected fiction of the susceptible primitive mind – will eventually humble into submission to the rudiments of law.

The similarity of images is counterpointed by the antithesis in philosophical conception, since Vico's social redemption in history supersedes here Dante's theological condemnation of his unredeemable rebels in the Beyond, and we could expect no less from the philosopher who revalued myth in the very act of applying to it his anthropological reduction, because he could both see through it and feel it as something alive. Again, mythical giants appear in the *Inferno*, and one of them, Nimrod, has to do with the Tower of Babel and the bewildering multiplication of languages – a theme of the utmost interest to Vico, as witness Section II ("Poetic Logic"), especially paragraph 445.

In Vico's own mythology, it is one of the traits of primitive giants that they are mute, as are the demons in Dante's *De Vulgari Eloquentia*, which makes speech the absolute privilege of man. Whether Vico ever read the *De Vulgari Eloquentia* is a matter of surmise, but the Giants' canto in the *Inferno*, which is directly related to that treatise, was not lost on him and fed his imaginative hypothesis on the origins of mankind. Both writers – the philosophical poet and the poetical philosopher – were focally interested in the theme of language, for, as we have seen, Dante gave us in the *De Vulgari Eloquentia* the first historical treatise on linguistics and infused the poetical action of the *Divine Comedy* with a unique linguistic awareness,[18] while Vico, in the section of *The New Science* called "Poetic Logic," practically founded modern language theory, anticipating Ernst Cassirer's *Philosophy of Symbolic Forms*. Concern with language actually informs most of Dante's treatises from the *Vita Nuova* to the *Convivio* and

De Vulgari Eloquentia, to come to a head in the writing of his major poem; with Vico, the same concern already asserts itself in *De Antiquissima Italorum Sapientia* of 1710, which uses a factitious linguistic archaeology to convey the author's metaphysics and theory of knowledge at this stage.

In this connection we can hardly forget that Dante and Vico likewise debated for a time with themselves whether to use the Italian vernacular or the time-honored Latin of scholars, finally deciding in favor of Italian in their respective crowning works. Here too Vico seems to rehearse his great predecessor's career. His *Autobiography* records his resolve to leave "Tuscan" and Greek and concentrate on Latin at a certain point of his life,[19] and we should remember that, just as Dante's Latin works *De Vulgari Eloquentia*, the *Epistles*, and *De Monarchia* preceded the vernacular *Divine Comedy*, so *The New Science* came after a long series of books Vico wrote in Latin: the six academic *Orations*, the *De Antiquissima*, and the *De universi juris principio ac fine uno* of 1720, which may be considered a first version of *The New Science* itself. Vico's Italian, besides, is not unlike Dante's in its grafting of Latinisms onto a strongly idiomatic stock, as well as in its predilection for energetic expressions focusing on verbs which at times verge on the peculiar. Style and vision, in both writers, evolve from a relative initial abstractness to the rich concreteness of the final works, the *Divine Comedy* and *The New Science*, into which they respectively gathered the full fruits of their ripening.

It involves no injustice to the necessary distinctions between the medieval poem of salvation and the early-modern philosophical epic of civilization to see them as mutually illuminating. Their relationship is dialectical. Dante's imagination builds on the very hypostases Vico's genetic theory unmasks, but because Vico is no thin-blooded rationalist, he interprets without devitalizing and leaves us with the life of pulsing experience, not just with abstract schemata. *The New Science* absorbs in its imaginative and rational economy that *Inferno* which, during the Enlightenment, was repelling bloodlessly fastidious tastes à la Voltaire. Cannibalism, immoderate lust, the "infamous promiscuity of things and of women,"[20] untold violence, down to fecal sordidness (for which see Malebolge in the *Inferno*, along with paragraph 369, Book II, "On Poetic Wisdom," of *The New Science*): these are the archaic experience of the human race, since the human builds on the brutal, and social chaos is the matrix of social order. Dante must go through Hell to get to see the stars again. Historical Providence is forever at work, transforming, not punishing or suppressing, the amoral forces of instinct; and myth, poetry, religion — these necessary fictions of childlike giants — are the agents of that providential sublimation. Thus we see that *The New Science* closely parallels Dante's poem by celebrating in its choral way the perennial purging process of mankind which, in the *Divine Comedy*, focuses on the pilgrim persona. Dante's Beyond has become Vico's Here and Now; Heaven and Hell, as Blake was to say in unconsciously Vichian style, reappear as psychological realities dialectically related: the pole of energy, namely, live instinctual matter, and the pole of reason or form, to shape that inner substance of wild instinct.

In the process, what Vico calls "the grossness of heroic minds"[21] sharpens itself by expressing its mythic fictions in the very first kind of cognitive experience there can ever be. If we discount the inevitable differences, such purification finds its counterpart in Dante's ascent from world to world. When he rises into the heady ether of Paradise in his earthly shape, he lacks terms to decipher the new experience, so that Beatrice tells him:

> . . . Tu stesso ti fai grosso
> col falso imaginar . . .

> . . . You embroil yourself in grossness
> through false imaginings . . .

> *Par.* I, 88–89

Beatrice has here taken over Virgil's function of providential guide to direct the pilgrim's growth; Vico's indwelling Providence performs the same function for the collective pilgrim, mankind, which must forever rise from its own volcanic abysses to the purgatory of humanization, and on to full self-knowledge. It is no accident that language here, as elsewhere, should clinch the point by sharp analogy, maybe even an intentional echo on Vico's part. For it is precisely the "false imaginings" that start the deliverance of primitive mankind from brutish "grossness." Vico left several lyrics which intermittently reveal his poetical gift, but he was never so much the poet as when he wrote the charged prose of *The New Science*. What an irony that there (Axiom LIII, paragraph 218) he should have declared poetry and philosophy mutually incompatible; for it was this very polarity that tensed the sinews of his writing and enabled him to relive Dante's vision on his own transmuting terms.[22]

CHAPTER IX

EUGENIO MONTALE'S
DANTESQUE STYLE

THE author of *Ossi di seppia* (*Cuttlefish Bones*, 1925), *Le Occasioni* (1939), and *La Bufera e altro* (*The Storm and Other Things*, 1956) is a spare, constant writer. Sheer firmness of style has enabled Eugenio Montale to face his share of historical and existential worries without flinching. Ever since *Le Occasioni*, which *La Bufera e altro* can be said to continue, his message varies or reiterates the well-known motifs: the storm does not prevail over him, the game between him and time goes ceaselessly on, and the "bottle from the sea" hasn't come to shore yet. Montale isn't the man to bring his poetry "up to date." No need for that, since the two essential terms of his discourse are the world and the self, in the dimension of time. Between these two poles there flares up now and then a metaphysical lightning, to punctuate a colloquy lasting a whole lifetime; it will be the revelation of nothingness, or the antithetical one of a transcendent mystery, while human history (in the sense of public events) has little to do with it, being at most a secondary component, an occasional background. Montale lives time with great intensity, but his is fundamentally a time alien to historiography; it is the individual's memory and the crumbling-up of the world.

If facts and figures of contemporary history appear in his poetry, it is only as a function of personal drama: such is the case of "Primavera hitleriana" ("Hitlerian Spring"), "Piccolo testamento" ("A Small Will"), and "Il sogno del prigioniero" ("The Prisoner's Dream"). Here, in the second half of *La Bufera e altro*, the poet, confronted by the public world, withdraws from it in horror or mistrust; whether Hitler or "red or black clerics" are involved, his conclusion is always the same: to defend the inner stronghold of the self from public encroachments, for the public world is always cruel, or false:

> Ognuno riconosce i suoi: l'orgoglio
> non era fuga, l'umiltà non era
> vile, il tenue bagliore strofinato
> laggiù non era quello di un fiammifero.

> Everyone recognizes his kindred: pride
> was no flight, humility
> was not cowardly, the thin gleam scratched up
> down there was not of a burning match.

Montale's historical pessimism is absolute: in "Piccolo testamento" he evokes a hellish Apocalypse shadowing our history with the wings of Dante's Lucifer, and the defense of values is entrusted to the individual, private and precarious, with a matchless effect of sorrowful contrast:

> Solo quest'iride posso
> lasciarti a testimonianza
> d'una fede che fu combattuta,
> d'una speranza che bruciò più lenta
> di un duro ceppo nel focolare.
> Conservane la cipria nello specchietto
> quando spenta la lampada
> la sardana si farà infernale
> e un ombroso Lucifero scenderà su una prora
> del Tamigi, del Hudson, della Senna
> scuotendo l'ali di bitume semi-
> mozze dalla fatica, a dirti: è l'ora.

> Only this iris can I bequeath to you
> to witness a faith that was fought,
> a hope that burned slower
> than a hard log on the hearth.

> Keep its powder in your handbag mirror
> when, in the general blackout,
> the dance will get infernal
> and a shadowy Lucifer will descend on a prow
> the Thames, Hudson, or Seine
> shaking his tar wings half maimed by
> fatigue, to tell you the time is up.

The myth of this black Apocalypse becomes Kafkian in "Sogno del prigioniero," where the victory of public evil is complete, the "purge has been going on forever," and the protagonist does not know whether "at the banquet" he is going to devour others, stuffed gooselike, or be devoured in his turn. His judgment on our age is clear: in Montale's view, our civilization is going to founder in an anonymous collectivism where there will be no place for the real carrier of values — the individual. These are the ideas Montale personally confirms in his fireside talk.

But however we may evaluate these particular texts, the protest against the world of organized politics is no accidental motif in him, for it issues directly from his *Weltanschauung*. At the roots of Montale's stoicism there lies the sense of time as a steady consumption, of existence as entropy, as an irreversible process of decay. In such Lucretian and Leopardian perspective, the soul has no way out, and it can find itself only in the utter intensity with which it experiences the events of climactic instants and of memory. Refusing the dispersal entailed by an official calendar, it will secede further and further into that authentic history which is the labyrinth of inwardness, ceaselessly questioned in suffering and dream. Montale's hermeticism has nothing whatever to do with a literary fashion; it is an existential attitude, a defense of the self, a veiling and unveiling of his spiritual integrity. That is why his voice remains actual today when the hermetic fashion is over.

In Montale faithfulness to the self and faithfulness to language are one and the same; if his message is generally one of despair, his honesty is rocklike, and one cannot say too often that after the corruption of the D'Annunzian influence, which had threatened to bone the Italian literary language, he has signally contributed to endowing it with a new spinal cord.

The remarkable thing about it is that Montale has been able to assimilate something of the best D'Annunzio, especially in the cycle "Mediterraneo" of *Ossi di seppia*. And as Luciano Anceschi observes in his preface to the anthology of modern Italian poetry, *Lirica del Novecento*, the "Crepuscolari" along with Giovanni Pascoli are two recognizable strains in Montale's discourse, which owed something to them in its molding phase, but — and this is what matters — he overstepped any provincial boundary to obey his European and cosmic feeling; and he could accomplish that because, beyond the worn, uncertain, or convulsive vocabulary of the moment, he found an access to Dante's rugged language. If Mario Praz[1] has been able to draw a persuasive parallel between the poet of "Il male di vivere" ("The Harm of Living") and the author of "Prufrock" and *The Waste Land*, such undeniable parallelism must also be recognized as something more than a mere fact of "waste land," for it is rooted in their *Wahlverwandschaft* for Dante — an affinity openly proclaimed by the Anglo-American poet and implied by the Italian one[2] in his word-choices, sound-orientations, and love for clear-cut vision, or even in some functional quotation, as happens for instance in "Mottetto" ("Motet") No. 8 (from *Le Occasioni*).[3]

Normally Montale's language has a vertebrate compactness going back to Dante's; fighting shy of the all-too-obvious music into which the Italian lyrical tradition had come to melt, it lowers its tone to become an intimate conversation averse to epic peals, high-strung melody, or set cadences. Montale came thus to disjoint verse and freely treat the eleven-syllable line, shrinking discourse into a sequence of intense hard passages, as in the "Mottetti," or modulating ample meditative sentences with a rhythmical ease of which the best examples can be culled from *Ossi di seppia*, especially "I limoni" ("The Lemons"), "Crisalide" ("Chrysalis"), "Mediterraneo," ("The Mediterranean"), and "I morti" ("The Dead"), but also from *La Bufera e altro* — witness the eloquence of "L'orto" ("The Garden") or "L'anguilla" ("The Eel"). He transposed sound onto an inner level, varying rhyme with dissonance, shifting it into the body of the line, where it will exercise a more secret charm, and he often sought in alliteration a sound-unity for the context — a unity to be reconstructed from within, by

valuing syllables and consonants to the extent of making them the vertebrae
of a poetical organism. In "Scirocco" ("Sirocco"), for instance (from *Ossi
di seppia*):

> l'agave che s'abbarbica al crepaccio
> dello scoglio
> e sfugge al mare da le braccia d'alghe
> che spalanca ampie gole e abbranca rocce

the vertebrae are contained in these words: *abbarbica* ("strikes root,"
"clings"), *braccia* ("the arms"), *spalanca* ("throws open"), and *abbranca*
("clutches," a verb). But the secret thread of this music is also intertwined
with the recurrence of the vowel *a* (to be pronounced, of course, like the
English broad *a*), so full of breath, whether by itself or linked with an *l*
consonant:

> oh alide ali dell'aria
> ora son io
> l'agave che s'abbarbica al crepaccio
> dello scoglio
>
> . . . .
>
> Oh, dry wings of the air
> now am I
> the agave that clings to a crevice
> of the sea cliff
> and escapes the seaweed-armed sea
> opening wide gorges and clutching rocks

We thus have an internal play on *alide* ("dry"), *ali* ("wings"), *aria* ("air"),
agave ("agave"), *alghe* ("seaweed"), *spalanca* ("throws open"); the skeleton of verse is clad with sound-flesh. Likewise, see the play of *l* sounds
(*mollemente*, "softly," *flabello*, "fan," *redola*, "grassy path," *libellule*, "drag-
onflies," *fardello*, "burden") in "Mottetto" No. 17; or in the ending of "Buf-
falo" (from *Le Occasioni*) the echoes of dry, plosive sounds (*specchi*, "mirrors," *schianti secchi*, "dry crashes," *schiene*, "backs"); or again, in the
ending of "Corno inglese" ("English Horn," from *Ossi di seppia*), the
counterpoint of sibilant and plosive consonants:

> nell'ora che lenta s'annera
> suonasse te pure stasera

scordato strumento,
cuore.

in the slowly darkening hour
would it were playing you too tonight
instrument out of tune,
heart.

Or again, in "Meriggiare pallido e assorto" ("Pale, Intent Noontide," from *Ossi di seppia*), aridity changed to syllable (*sterpi*, "briar," *schiocchi*, "clacks," *serpi*, "snakes," *crepe*, "cracks," *scaglie*, "flakes," *sericchi*, "creakings," *cicale*, "cicadas," *calvi*, "bald," *picchi*, "peaks," *cocci*, "shards," *aguzzi*, "sharp"); and in the first stanza of the next poem in the same collection, the telling insistence on *f* sounds:

> Non rifugiarti nell'ombra
> di quel folto di verzura
> come il falchetto che strapiomba
> fulmineo nella caldura.

> Do not seek shelter in the shade
> of that thick greenery
> like the headlong hawk that plunges
> lightning-like through the heat.

We are not in the domain of an obvious, all-too-external onomatopoeia, as so often happens in Pascoli, but in the field of a sound-magic which stakes all on the "atomic" element of the word to make speech "scabro ed essenziale" ("rugged and essential"), as the poet himself has it — that rugged essentialness, to be sure, which strengthens Dante's verse, as Ugolino's and Pier delle Vigne's cantos will abundantly show. Many are the clues to Dante's blood-inheritance in Montale, for instance, the sad solemnity of "I morti" in *Ossi di seppia*, and even more "Tramontana" ("North Wind"), from the same collection:

> Ed ora sono spariti i circoli d'ansia
> che discorrevano il lago del cuore
> e quel friggere vasto della materia
> che discolora e muore.
> Oggi una volontà di ferro spazza l'aria,
> divelle gli arbusti, strapazza i palmizi
>
> · · · · · · · · · · · · · · · · ·

Ogni forma si squassa nel subbuglio
degli elementi; è un urlo solo, un muglio
di scerpate esistenze: tutto schianta
l'ora che passa . . .

And now have vanished the rings of anxiety
that rippled the lake of my heart
and the vast seething of matter
that fades out to die.
Today an iron will sweeps the air,
uproots bushes, harries the palm trees,

. . . .

Every shape is shaken in the turmoil
of elements; it is one shriek, one bellow
of uprooted existences: everything is torn
by the passing hour . . .

Canto I of the *Inferno* is here intentionally brought up by that "lake of the heart" which is a metaphor Montale seems to cherish, and then the ghost of Pier delle Vigne speaks up in two verbs (*scerpare*, "to uproot," and *schiantare*, "to tear up") to invest all of existence with a tragic meaning. For the poem deals with the horror of uprooting, and its concluding note sings love for the roots a wild wind threatens to break; therefore the Dante reference, whether conscious or casual, focuses our modern situation in a total vision.

Attention should not be denied, in this poem, to the initial alliterations (*spazza*, "sweeps," *strapazza*, "harries," *palmizi*, "palm-tree clumps"), which illustrate the above remarks on the sound-harshness (Dante's *rime aspre*, harsh rimes!) used to give new bones to verse; but what is still more important, Pier delle Vigne shows up again in a poem from *Finisterre* (included in *La Bufera e altro*): "Personae separatae." We are in a hellish wood of "skeleton locusts," where hell is made by the estrangement of two human beings who formerly communicated and loved each other. But all at once their private sorrow widens to enclose the universal tragedy of mankind at war (*Finisterre* came into being during World War II), and the momentous passage is accomplished by a clipped hint, almost casually:

> . . . Troppo
> straziato è il bosco umano, troppo sorda
> quella voce perenne . . .

> . . . The human wood
> is too much torn, too hollow
> that perennial voice . . .

The skeleton trees become Pier delle Vigne's wood, that is, the whole human race — suicidal like Pier, and just as hardly punished and broken up. A remembrance of Paradise emphasizes horror:

> . . . La tua forma
> passò di qui, si riposò sul riano
> tra le nasse atterrate, poi si sciolse
> come un sospiro, intorno — e ivi non era
> l'orror che fiotta, in te la luce ancora
> trovava luce, oggi non più che al giorno
> primo già annotta.

> . . . Your shape
> was seen here to rest in the small gorge
> among the stranded nets, then it dissolved
> like a sigh all around — and there was not
> the welling horror, in you light still found light,
> today no longer, when at the blush of dawn
> night already looms.

This poem is among the most sustained in the whole book, and all of *Finisterre*, as a matter of fact, belongs to the best Montale. The poet of "Casa dei doganieri" ("House of the Customs Men"), "Dora Markus," "Eastbourne," "Notizie dall'Amiata" ("News from Mount Amiata"), and "Nuove stanze" ("New Stanzas") has lived up to his own accomplishment, just because he has never tried to be different from what he is. He has added valid items to his former poetical inventory, without straying from the variously deep, delicate, or fitful vein which as yet shows no signs of exhaustion. The "occasions" of poetry are numberless, as many as the moments of life; epiphany is always possible to the metaphysical realist who has no need to reinvent himself at each season. Never mind if, in *La Bufera e altro*, certain diary pages from "Intermezzo," "Flashes e dediche"

("Flashes and Dedications"), and "Madrigali privati" ("Private Madrigals") remain too private to deserve comparison with the strong pieces. In Montale the man, side by side with the stern mind that has seen through anguish, there lurks an elf addicted to light or even frivolous things: there is the humorist who never takes himself seriously and who loves animals; and the whimsical boy who may like operettas, street songs and Gozzano's baubles, and the ephemeral occurrence. And there is, finally, a coyness compelling him to veil his own intense feelings, afterward to liberate them in some cryptic line which is meant both as confession and concealment. These components of his personality are all to be found, in quaint or subtly creative synthesis, in the body of his poetry.

This is poetry where obscurity is never a trick, and where occasional signs of involution never betray complacent mannerism, but are part of the poet's inner drama: "Do not ask us for the word hewing from all sides/ our formless soul . . . Do not ask us for the formula that will open up worlds to you,/ but only for some crooked syllable, dry like a withered branch," he has said in *Cuttlefish Bones*. An existence as poverty, which, when confronted by nothingness, indefiniteness, shapelessness, can only rely on the props of *hic* and *nunc*, on the objects whose individuality is felt as utter suffering; but this sense of the individual as ineffable though minimal reality, carried away by time, this Heideggerian *Dasein als Nichtigkeit*, must try conclusions with the ghost of otherness threatening it from the outside as well as from within. Memory is the shelter of existence, private history in the chaos of public history, that *sensus sui* which alone can save us; yet memory itself ends up undermining the individual's identity, changing him into something else than himself:

> Trema un ricordo nel ricolmo secchio,
> nel puro cerchio un'immagine ride.
> Accosto il volto a evanescenti labbri:
> si deforma il passato, si fa vecchio,
> appartiene ad un altro . . .

> A memory quivers in the full pail,
> in the pure ring an image laughs.
> I accost my face to evanescent lips:

the past is distorted, it ages,
it belongs to another . . .

This was *Ossi di seppia*; and "Due nel crepuscolo" ("Two in the Twilight"), from *La Bufera e altro*, deepens the same experience in a turn of
classic accomplishment:

> . . . Ed io riverso
> nel potere che grava attorno, cedo
> al sortilegio di non riconoscere
> di me più nulla fuor di me: s'io levo
> appena il braccio, mi si fa diverso
> l'atto, si spezza su un cristallo, ignota
> e impallidita sua memoria, e il gesto
> già più non m'appartiene;
> se parlo, ascolto quella voce attonito.

> . . . And I, lying back
> in the impending power, yield
> to the spell of not recognizing
> aught of myself out of myself: if only
> I raise my arm, the act is changed,
> it shatters on a crystal, its memory
> paling unknown, and my very gesture
> belongs to me no more;
> if I talk, I listen to that voice astonished.

Estranging himself from himself in time, the individual cannot help estranging himself from his beloved, who suddenly becomes a cryptic Unknown,
a disquieting Other, or an empty remainder:

> . . . Ti guardo
> in un molle riverbero. Non so
> se ti conosco; so che mai diviso
> fui da te come accade in questo tardo
> ritorno. Pochi istanti hanno bruciato
> tutto di noi: fuorché due volti, due
> maschere che s'incidono, sforzate,
> di un sorriso.

> . . . I look at you
> in a soft glimmer. I don't know
> if I know you; I know I never was

> so divided from you as happens in this belated
> return. Few instants have burned up
> the whole of us: except two faces, two
> masks on which, with effort,
> a smile is engraved.

The sense of inner event, be it even destruction, is here expressed with a force that grasps the metamorphoses of consciousness. We are on the line of "Arsenio" and of the other poems quoted above; for "Due nel crepuscolo" dates back to 1926. Struggle against the formless, identity that alienates itself, metamorphosis of memory, threat or splendor of otherness: these are the main themes of Montale's *Bufera* phase, and they account for his apocalyptic thrusts. His vision is interspersed with negative epiphanies:

> Il soffio cresce, il buio è rotto a squarci,
> e l'ombra che tu mandi sulla fragile
> palizzata s'arriccia. Troppo tardi
> se vuoi esser te stessa!

> The wind gets stronger, darkness is ripped by gusts,
> and the shadow you cast on the shaky fence
> curls up. Too late now
> if you want to be yourself!

Since our fellow being's estrangement from ourselves into a complete otherness makes the distance between him and us yawn infinite, the message never arrives, the letter remains "unwritten," and life becomes an inability to disappear:

> Sparir non so né riaffacciarmi; tarda
> la fucina vermiglia
> della notte, la sera si fa lunga,
> la preghiera è supplizio e non ancora
> tra le rocce che sorgono t'è giunta
> la bottiglia dal mare. L'onda, vuota,
> si rompe sulla punta, a Finisterre.

> I cannot vanish or lean out again; belated
> is the ruddy workshop of night,
> evening draws intolerably on,
> prayer is torture and not yet
> among the rising cliffs has come to you

the bottle from the sea. The empty wave
breaks on the headland at Finisterre.

Taken though it is from De Vigny's *Bouteille à la mer*, the image of that
bottle entrusted to the surf declares the nature of Montale's utterance; it is
in a way the poet's self-consciousness, but not just on the aesthetic level,
since it has a broadly existential import: it expresses the desperate desire
and inability to communicate. Aesthetically less achieved, but motivated
by the same dramatic experience of otherness, is the surrealist poem "Nel
sonno" ("In Sleep"), where we feel as strangely persuasive, like a De Chir-
ico without trickery, the focal image of that "adversary" that "snaps his
helmet shut/ on his face." It is another mask of otherness, the impenetrable
face reality opposes to an individual estranged from everything; it is the
price of self-isolation (enhanced though it may be by the cruel circumstances of a hellish war).

But the mask of an inimical otherness covers other moments of experience
as well; in "Serenata indiana" ("Indian Serenade"), for instance, it is the
horror of a hidden identity of the beloved woman with the octopus, the
greedy and shapeless monster of the abyss:

> Fosse tua vita quella che mi tiene
> sulle soglie — e potrei prestarti un volto,
> vaneggiarti figura. Ma non è,
>
> non è così. Il polipo che insinua
> tentacoli d'inchiostro fra gli scogli
> può servirsi di te. Tu gli appartieni
>
> e non lo sai. Sei lui, ti credi te.

> If it was yours, this life that holds me
> on the thresholds — then I could lend you a visage,
> fancy you as a figure. But it is not so,
>
> it is not so. The octopus that pushes
> inky tentacles into the reef
> can use you. Unawares you belong
>
> to him. You are he, you think you are yourself.

The horror of this black witchcraft is convincing; the self is undermined, and the poet struggles in the endeavor to define the formless. We are in a Melvillean and Dickinsonian atmosphere, though Montale is not to be "derived" from those masters.[4] The theme of threatening otherness arising as a ghost before or within ourselves is basic in the two American poets, who on the other hand, in respect to style, temper, and background, would seem to resist mutual assimilation. Their thematic link, and the independent affinity of the Italian contemporary poet, are clarified by Eliot's words when, in *The Three Voices of Poetry*, he says poetry is a fight of Jacob against the angel — that is, a struggle against formlessness.

Ghosts of sea animals (medusae) appear in the magic mirror of "Gli orecchini" ("The Earrings"),[5] where their presence is conjured, in the ambiguous twilight atmosphere, by the corals of the earrings which defenseless feminine hands are buckling on. A double threat is presented by formlessness (the sea of twilight) and war (". . . the crazy funeral booms/ and knows that two lives don't matter"); we cannot help remembering that the dark foreboding of war inhered in several poems of *Le Occasioni*. Otherness as the black witchcraft of memory inspired "Il ventaglio" ("The Fan"), also concerned with war. It is one of those cryptical poems which moved readers like Edward Williamson to say that Montale occasionally gets too private for comfort;[6] but the central image, of memory visualized as a fan that opens and closes to cast a frightening spell on us, is unmistakably graphic. The concluding question ("Muore chi ti riconosce?" — "Does whoever recognizes you have to die?") brings us back to the fundamental theme of sphinxlike otherness. In the fond "Ballata scritta in una clinica" ("Ballad Written in a Hospital"), the experience of otherness is given by the threat of death:

> Attendo un cenno, se è prossima
> l'ora del ratto finale;
> son pronto e la penitenza
> s'inizia fin d'ora nel cupo
> singulto di valli e dirupi
> dell'*altra* Emergenza.
>
> I await a sign, if the hour
> of final abduction is near;
> I am ready and penance

> begins right now in the hollow
> sobbing of valleys and cliffs
> of the *other* Emergence.

Here the small things of his sick wife (her tortoise-rimmed eyeglasses, her wooden bulldog, her alarm clock with phosphorescent dial-hands), making the protagonist a recognizable portrait, emphasize the contrast with looming death, which Montale probably embodies in the mythical figure of Jupiter changed into a bull to abduct Europa. But the "bull-like god" ("l'iddio taurino") isn't only death, he is also a heathen totem of vital urge. The intriguing ambiguity is complicated by a possible reference to the zodiac, since the poet's statement that "the bull-like god/ was not ours" is followed by an invocation to "Ariete" (the Ram, Aries), who chases "the horned monster" (the Bull, Taurus) away. In between, a seasonal motif appears with the acknowledgment of the godhead (possibly Aries himself, but more generally the gentler, creative manifestation of the life force as against its destructive embodiments like the Bull) that "paints with fire/ the lilies of the ditch." In this connection it may help to notice that in "Gallo cedrone" ("Black Cock"), another poem from the same volume, Jupiter is explicitly identified with a black cock killed and buried in the womb of earth like a seed. Throughout the poem, as in "Dora Markus," the interplay of minute personal objects and huge cosmic forces energizes the imagery in a way one must recognize as uniquely Montalean.

The final stanzas of "Ballad" show our poet at his best:

> Hai messo sul comodino
> il bulldog di legno, la sveglia
> col fosforo sulle lancette
> che spande un tenue lucore
> sul tuo dormiveglia,
>
> il nulla che basta a chi vuole
> forzare la porta stretta;
> e fuori, rossa, s'inasta,
> si spiega sul bianco una croce.
>
> Con te anch'io m'affaccio alla voce
> che irrompe nell'alba, all'enorme

presenza dei morti; e poi l'ululo

del cane di legno è il mio, muto.

You have put on your night table
the wooden bulldog, the alarm clock
with phosphorescent hands
that cast a faint glimmer
on your half-waking,

the nothing that suffices to any who want
to break through the narrow gate;
and outside there goes up on the flagstaff
a fluttering cross, red on white.

With you I too lean out to meet the voice
that breaks out in sunrise, the enormous
presence of the dead; and then the howl

of the wooden bulldog is mine, mute.

These lines need little comment, unless it be to point out their overall movement from the small real and emblematic objects (the wooden bulldog is still to be found at the Montales') to the enormity of death, and then the return from that glimpse of immensity to the helpless bauble — the wooden bulldog — which is charged with the poet's whole sorrow to the extent of becoming himself, his own fidelity.

Toy dog and alarm clock are not casually photographed; they are emblems of faithfulness and of patient time about to end. That is clarified by the unexpected finale, which owes most of its poetical efficiency to the complex play of sounds and pauses. It is all a counterpoint of *u*'s, *l*'s and *m*'s; there is a poignant caesura between "mio" ("mine") and "muto" ("mute"), like a sob and a prolongation of the line beyond itself, in a heavy suspense. The vowel-echo arising from the stress on "ululo" ("howl") and "muto" evokes a hallucination only to negate it right away, but the negation retains an echo of the notion denied. The word "muto," though it means "silent," ends up howling too; silence becomes an internalized shriek.

Though it does not make easy reading, "Ezekiel Saw the Wheel," inspired by a spiritual and through it by the Bible, is good Montale, and it deals with his leitmotivs: the spell of memory, the effort to dig up the image of a beloved from the "mound of sand" that time's hourglass had heaped up in his heart, the assault of otherness as a ghost of the past in the present. Here the vision of the "threatening Wheel" is not only Ezekiel's wheel, but also "Eastbourne" 's desperate symbol ("Evil wins . . . the wheel won't stop") in *Le Occasioni* — of a piece with Leopardi's closed circle "of all heavenly and terrestrial things" which "ceaselessly turn around always to revert to their starting point," as drawn in "Night Song of a Wandering Shepherd in Asia." The initial "foreign hand" is menacingly transmogrified; it becomes a "claw" in the end, and the peach tree's petals are "turned to blood." It is interesting to notice that the image of the wheel as Karma, ineluctable fatality, appears also at the end of "L'orto," one of the best poems in *La Bufera*:

> . . . Se la forza
> che guida il disco *di già* inciso fosse
> un'altra, certo il tuo destino al mio
> congiunto mostrerebbe un solco solo.

> . . . If the force
> that guides the record *already incised*
> were another, certainly your lot and mine
> would be joined in one groove.

When the late critic Pancrazi stated his acceptance of Montale's "physical" poetry as given in *Ossi di seppia* and his refusal of the "metaphysical" *Occasioni*, he failed to see how our poet's existential symbolism spontaneously issued from his cosmic, physical sensibility and was at bottom the same thing.

"La primavera hitleriana," pushes to another limit the experience of otherness, as mystical nihilism in which to find a shelter from the horror of a perverted present:

> . . . Oh la piagata
> primavera è pur festa se raggela
> in morte questa morte! Guarda ancora
> in alto, Clizia, è la tua sorte, tu
> che il non mutato amor mutata serbi,
> fino a che il cieco sole che in te porti

> si abbàcini nell'Altro e si distrugga
> in Lui, per tutti . . .
>
> . . . Oh, the wounded spring
> is still a feast if it freezes
> this death to death! Look on high,
> Clizia, it is your destiny, you
> who, yourself changed, keep unchanged love in you,
> until the blind sun you carry in yourself
> may be dazzled in the Other and destroy
> itself in Him, for all . . .

In "Ezekiel Saw the Wheel" otherness was death, memory, woman, sphinx, and destiny; here it is the experience of Being itself, and the affinity with Heidegger's development is conspicuous, though Montale owes nothing to the German thinker. The author of *Sein und Zeit* (*Being and Time*) started with a philosophy of existence as finitude grounded upon nothingness; but in his last works, especially from the Hölderlin essay on, he has evidenced different motifs, turning upon the experience of Being as participation in a horizon of possibility through language. From nihilism to mysticism is not an inconceivable step; and Montale, even though he does not rely on an organized system of orthodoxy like Eliot, proves occasionally open to luminous apocalypses. The visage of Christ dawns in his verse: in "Iride" ("Iris") as Holy Shroud, in "Sulla colonna più alta" ("On the Highest Pillar"), in "L'ombra della magnolia" ("The Magnolia Shadow") as "the Bridegroom's stigmata." God is now mentioned, at least as a glimpse of personal revelation:

> La scatola a sorpresa ha fatto scatto
> sul punto in cui il mio Dio gittò la maschera
> e fulminò il ribelle.
>
> The jack-in-the-box has clicked open
> at the point when my God threw down His mask
> to blast the rebel.

That was from "Verso Siena" ("Toward Siena"), but see further (in *La Bufera e altro*) "Vento sulla mezzaluna" ("Wind on the Crescent"), "Nella serra" ("In the Greenhouse"), "Incantesimo" ("Spell"), "Verso Finistère" ("Toward Finistère"), and the surprising "Anniversario" ("Anniversary"),

where the poet kneels to adore a young life that blossoms to give him joy
and salvation, yet finally despairs of any possibility of sharing his own revelation with his fellow men, and for an instant sees himself as a

> . . . Dio diviso
> dagli uomini, dal sangue raggrumato
> sui rami alti, sui frutti.
>
> . . . God secluded
> from men, from the blood curdled
> on the high branches, on the fruits.

Needless to say, this identification with the suffering god is characterized
by the grief of being separated from mankind, not by any complacent
pride.

Therefore, if otherness can manifest itself as demoniac outbreak, alienation, threatening madness, it also has a divine and angelic visage. Like a
dolce stil nuovo poet — Guinizelli or the early Dante — our poet repeatedly perceives the winged figure of an angelic woman. Thus "L'orto"
starts with a "messaggera" ("harbinger") which closely recalls the etymology of "angel":

> Io non so, messaggera
> che scendi, prediletta
> del mio Dio (del tuo forse) se nel chiuso
>
> . . . .
>
> I don't know, harbinger
> who descends, beloved
> of my God (of yours perhaps) if in the enclosure
>
> . . . .

and in its last stanza speaks of "incarnate demons" and "foreheads of fallen
angels." The garden is the spellbound precinct of memory; the unknown
visitor, probably the Clizia of other poems, is both a Mnemosyne and a
soothsayer who had foretold the disaster of war:

> L'ora della tortura e dei lamenti
> che s'abbatté sul mondo,
> l'ora che tu leggevi chiara come in un libro
> figgendo il duro sguardo di cristallo
> bene in fondo, là dove acri tendine

di fuliggine alzandosi su lampi
di officine celavano alla vista
l'opera di Vulcano,
il dì dell'Ira che più volte il gallo
annunciò agli spergiuri . . .

The hour of torture and lament
that fell on the world,
the hour you clearly read as in a book
prying with your hard crystal look
down where acrid curtains
of soot rising on lightnings
of workshops hid from sight
the work of Vulcan,
the Day of Wrath that the cock often
announced to perjurers . . .

The conclusion heightens personal affection to apotheosis, in a climate of cosmic sorrow:

O labbri muti, aridi dal lungo
viaggio per il sentiero fatto d'aria
che vi sostenne, o membra che distinguo
a stento dalle mie, o diti che smorzano
la sete dei morenti e i vivi infocano,
o intento che hai creato fuor della tua misura
le sfere del quadrante e che ti espandi
in tempo d'uomo, in spazio d'uomo, in furie
di démoni incarnati . . .

O silent lips, dry from the long
journey through the path of air
that sustained you, o limbs I hardly
can tell from mine, o fingers that allay
the thirst of dying people and inflame the living,
o intention that created out of your measure
the dial-hands and now expand yourself
into human time, human space, furies
of demons incarnate . . .

Here the Manichaean denier of history confronts much more explicitly than in most of his other work the problem of history's creative source, which seems to take shape for him in a Neoplatonic figure, prophet, celebrant, and goddess in one, a feminine force to be envisaged as his mind's bride, for she is a visitant from untold distances and yet seems to spring from his innermost self. His separation from her is his doom, and coincides with the world's present separation from the creative and redeeming force.

Another angelic epiphany flashes in "L'ombra della magnolia" ("The Magnolia Shadow") as "cesena," a migratory bird unconquered by the "shudder of frost"; and the flight of the mysterious creature invites the poet to leap into transcendence:

> . . . Gli altri arretrano
> e piegano. La lima che sottile
> incide tacerà, la vuota scorza
> di chi cantava sarà presto polvere
> di vetro sotto i piedi, l'ombra è livida, —
> è l'autunno, è l'inverno, è l'oltrecielo
> che ti conduce e in cui mi getto, céfalo
> saltato in secco al novilunio.
> > Addio.

> . . . The others fall back
> and surrender. The file that thinly engraves
> will hush, the empty husk
> of the singer will be soon glassy dust
> under our feet, the shadow is livid, —
> it is autumn, it's winter, the Further sky
> that leads you, and into it I throw myself, a mullet
> leaping onto dry land at the new moon.
> > Good-bye.

Thus the persona tries to conquer otherness by facing migration into death. And we get the kind of ending that only a poet in deep sympathy with animal life can give us.

This "mullet" leaps with no less force than the eel ("L'anguilla"), which counts among Montale's finest things. The eel is understood in its mystery of living creature, ocean-traveler; and its irresistible penetration into the hardest upland recesses represents an inverted transcendence, a victory of life over death:

> l'anima verde che cerca
> vita là dove solo

> morde l'arsura e la desolazione,
> la scintilla che dice
> tutto comincia quando tutto pare
> incarbonirsi, bronco seppellito;

> the green soul that seeks
> life where only parched desolation bites,
> the spark that says
> everything begins when everything seems
> to burn to charcoal, a buried stick;

It would be pedantic to submit Montale to a systematic Freudian interpretation, but can we exclude the possibility that under the triumphant vitality of these lines there may seethe a phallic image, motivated by the explicit ritual of regenerating fecundation?

> L'anguilla, torcia, frusta,
> freccia d'Amore in terra
> che solo i nostri botri o i disseccati
> ruscelli pirenaici riconducono
> a paradisi di fecondazione . . .

> The eel, a torch, a whip,
> a dart of Love on earth
> which only our ravines or the dried-up
> Pyrenean brooks lead back
> to paradises of fecundation . . .

In view of Montale's pervasive myths of aridity, stoniness, and irreversible decay, even the episodic welling up of such a countervailing symbol may gain focal significance.

The eel symbol, puzzlingly enough, has both phallic and feminine connotations, since at the end of the breathless one-sentence poem it becomes a "sister" (or incarnate emblem) of the very erotically earthy woman who in that poem emerges as the addressee of the whole utterance, and who has certainly to do with the protean "Fox" (Volpe) of an entire section of La Bufera. Thus the terrene embodiment of the feminine principle takes its place in Montale's poetry as an antiphon to its angelic manifestation, Clizia, who in turn does not function only as sublimated Eros if we remember certain warm moments of the "Mottetti," or even the ending of "L'orto," as quoted above. Yet on the whole, sublimation, transcendence, is Clizia's pull.

Thus she hovers in the doomed cosmos of "La frangia dei capelli" ("The Bangs") as a winged "migrating Artemis . . . unhurt/ among the wars of stillborn people"; her "restless forehead" merges with the whole sunrise to engulf the sky in its own light. Attention should be paid to the drastic judgment passed on our destructive age, bellicose and "stillborn" — Eliot would have spoken of "hollow men" here. Even if not directly named, Clizia haunts the poet's world and can be evoked by the most casual cues of workaday reality, as in "Giorno e notte" ("Day and Night"), which posits a vague identity between woman and skylark:

> Anche una piuma che vola può disegnare
> la tua figura, o il raggio che gioca a rimpiattino
> tra i mobili, il rimando dello specchio
> di un bambino, dai tetti . . .

> Even a flying feather can draw your figure,
> or the ray playing at hide-and-seek
> in the furniture, the light rebounding
> from a child's mirror on the roofs . . .

Then the sunrise-announcing bird, that is, the angelic harbinger of light and vanquisher of darkness (as the title itself points out), is shot down to death:

> . . . — e ancora le stesse grida e i lunghi
> pianti sulla veranda
> se rimbomba improvviso il colpo che t'arrossa
> la gola e schianta l'ali, o perigliosa
> annunciatrice dell'alba . . .

> . . . — and the same screams again and the long
> crying on the veranda
> if there suddenly bursts the shot that reddens
> your throat and breaks your wings, O daring
> herald of dawn . . .

and then daybreak is no longer a triumph of light, but a doomsday blared by barracks bugles on the silent waiting of cloisters and hospitals:

> e si destano i chiostri e gli ospedali
> a un lacerìo di trombe . . .

> and cloisters and hospitals are awakened
> by a rending blare of bugles . . .

Once again, the emblematic background of the poem contains a strong judgment on the evil of this age and shows Montale to be historically aware in his quarrel with history.

The image of angelic woman dominates "Il tuo volo" ("Your Flight") in a hermetic fire of disdain, but here perhaps the elliptical mode has reached an extreme, so that the intelligibility of the poem suffers somewhat, as if in certain climactic moments of vision the writer no longer cared to be understood by his readers, or by most of them. Among Dante's predecessors, the Provençal troubadours, this was a deliberate strategy employed to protect delicate messages from intrusive eyes, and it was called "sealed composition" (*trobar clus*). We find several examples of *trobar clus* not only in Arnaut Daniel (whom Dante read and admired), but in Dante's fellow poets of the *dolce stil nuovo* school, especially Cavalcanti, and in Dante's own lyrical work, from the *Vita Nuova* to the *Rime*, not to speak of the *Convivio*, which as a self-commentary throws much intriguing light on the subtle procedure. Despite all the obvious differences and the many intervening centuries, the analogy of method between the modern poet (operating at the time in the context of Florentine hermeticism) and his remote Florentine ancestors holds pretty well. Mallarmé's concomitant impact can only have strengthened the appeal of Provençal-Cavalcantian-Dantesque *trobar clus* for a writer who, like those medieval masters, resorts to the style of concealment for a variety of reasons, personal as well as political.

Just as the angelized lady of the thirteenth-century Florentines took on such ethical, philosophical, and religious attributes that she often became in their verse a mere doctrinal hypostasis (with the possible intimation of heretical overtones), Montale's Clizia wavers between the erotic, the prophetic, and the theological levels, until we realize that she personifies for him the very principle of gnosis, in defiance of public orthodoxies. She is that ineffable truth, rooted in a personal experience, which gives the lie to the official version of reality, and in this sense she constitutes an even more radical conception than Dante's Beatrice (who, at least in the *Divine Comedy*, came to confirm and not only to challenge). Montale in his modesty has invoked less ambitious angelic ladies than Beatrice as sources or parallels to his Clizia, as his "Imaginary Interview" will show.[7] The fact remains that, whether we liken Clizia to Beatrice herself or to the *donna gentile* which the *Convivio* maintains to have been an allegory of Philosophy (but it cannot have been a harmlessly academic one!), we have to return to Dante's doctrinal love poetry to understand what Montale has essayed in his choice of an unfashionable hypostasis for the focal point of his poetry from the nineteen thirties on.

Trobar clus and gnosis-apotheosis, then, would seem to form a closed circle in which the hypostatic vision precipitates the hermetic style, and it in turn refines its instruments the better to crystallize the vision. The alternation of lyrical verse and prose commentary in Dante's pre-*Comedy* career is a restless cycle of dreaming the truth and probing the dream, which had fatally to result in the coeval searching-and-seeing the truth that was his crowning epos; with Montale, dreaming and probing, seeing and testing are one in the act of poetry. This will enable us, for instance, to get closer to the secret of the forbidding poem "Iride," which is avowedly transcribed from a dream. Surrounded by an Oriental symbology which has to do with her Jewish origin, Clizia appears to the (heretically Nestorian) persona as the Christ-bearer going "through the night of the world" to pursue His redemptive work; and the final part of the poem shows her metamorphosis from real person, temporally and spatially determined, to timeless image: "but if you return it is not you, your history/ has changed . . ./ you have no yesterday, no today, no tomorrow."

She is again a Christ-bearer, in the shape of a swallow perched on a pillar in Palestine, in a shorter piece, "Sulla colonna più alta." Here she makes Christmas, transforming "the black diadems of briars into mistletoe," and, as the privileged creature she is, she humbles the earthbound birds, ravens and blackcaps, to the point where an epiphany in black occurs. The style reminds us of the "Motets":

> Ma in quel crepuscolo eri tu sul vertice:
> scura, l'ali ingrommate, stronche dai
> geli dell'Antilibano . . .

> But in that twilight you were on the top:
> dark, wings encrusted, exhausted by
> Anti-Lebanon frost . .

On a different keynote, we have in "Proda di Versilia" ("Versilian Shore") one of the most sustained pieces in the whole *Bufera* volume; here spellbinding memory brings back the dead, and the spell is wrought by a white sail, visually changed into a Dantesque angel from the *Purgatorio*:

> I miei morti che prego perché preghino
> per me, per i miei vivi com'io invece
> per essi non resurrezione ma
> il compiersi di quella vita ch'ebbero
> inesplicata e inesplicabile, oggi
> più di rado discendono dagli orizzonti aperti
> quando una mischia d'acque e cielo schiude
> finestre ai raggi della sera, — sempre
> più raro, astore celestiale, un cutter
> bianco-alato li posa sulla rena.

> My dead, whom I pray that they may pray
> for me, for my dear living ones as I in my turn
> for them invoke not resurrection but
> only completion of the life they had
> unexplained and inexplicable, today
> more seldom descend from the open horizons
> when an affray of waters and sky discloses
> windows to evening beams, — ever more seldom,
> celestial hawk, a white-winged cutter
> lays them down on the sand.

(Canto VIII of the *Purgatorio*, at line 104, tells of two angels who, like "astor celestiali" or celestial hawks, rout the tempting snake; while Canto II sings of the pilot-angel who ferries the souls to shore.)

The three stanzas following this introductory one (which is directly linked to "I morti" from *Ossi di seppia*) minutely evoke a particular landscape together with the poet's childhood. There are three fundamental effects, or rather three tones which by their succession create the magic of this poem: the lofty Purgatorial one of the beginning; the realistic one of the middle (where Montale paints in Brueghelian vein, and Brueghel happens to be a favorite painter with him); and finally the fable of the last stanza, with its allusion to Alice in Wonderland and the gloomy ending:

> . . . tempo che fu misurabile
> fino a che non s'aperse questo mare
> infinito, di creta e di mondiglia.

> . . . a time that was measurable
> until there yawned this boundless sea
> of clay and slush.

It is again the threat of formlessness; "evil wins." And Brueghel, incidentally, seems to me a good clue to Montale's minute realism, ever ready for surrealist outlets: those objects lovingly painted; those cold or intimate and brown tones; those warm homely interiors, so busy; those birds etched in flight . . . The reader is referred to the central part of this poem for telling details, keeping in mind that the Brueghelian reference can only strengthen the far weightier Dantesque one in throwing light on an inner quality of Montalean art: the accurate realism behind its metaphysical soarings. It isn't for nothing that our poet cultivates painting too.

Conversation with the dead, in itself a Dantesque stance, has inspired "To my Mother" and "Voce giunta con le folaghe" ("Voice Coming with the Moorhens"). To speak with his father, for Montale, is to speak with Dante, as the style of the following Purgatorial lines will show:

> L'ombra che mi accompagna
> alla tua tomba, vigile,

> . . . .

> l'ombra non ha più peso della tua
> da tanto seppellita, i primi raggi
> del giorno la trafiggono, farfalle
> vivaci l'attraversano, la sfiora
> la sensitiva e non si rattrappisce.

> L'ombra fidata e il muto che risorge,
> quella che scorporò l'interno fuoco
> e colui che lunghi anni d'oltretempo

(anni per me pesante) disincarnano,
si scambiano parole che interito
sul margine io non odo; l'una forse
ritroverà la forma in cui bruciava
amor di Chi la mosse e non di sé,
ma l'altro sbigottisce e teme che
la larva di memoria in cui si scalda
ai suoi figli si spenga al nuovo balzo.

The shadow that accompanies me,
watchful, to your grave,

. . . .

the shadow has no more weight than yours
now buried for so long, the first beams
of day transfix it, lively butterflies
cross it, the sensitive plant
skims it without crumpling.

The trusty shadow and the dumb man resurrected,
the one consumed by her internal fire
and he whom long years of trans-time
(years for me who weigh) are disembodying,
exchange words I cannot hear
stiffening on the bank; perhaps the former
will find again the form in which burned
love of her Mover and not of herself,
but the other is dismayed and fears
lest the ghost of memory in which he is warmed
for his children be extinguished at the new jump.

The *Purgatorio* reference is motivated by the very nature of memory: a fire assiduously purifying the image of our beloved ones when their presence is denied to us forever. And yet, in the context of this poem, memory as such provides no salvation or release. On the part of the persona, it appears as a force of fidelity which enacts the temporary resurrection of his father, who, on the other hand, is not helped by his own attachment to the children's remembrance of himself. The phantom father sounds very much like one of the *Purgatorio* shades who are burdened by earthbound concerns and have to be spurred on by Cato or some angel to do their purging.

In Montale's poem, the admonition has to come from Clizia, the angelic woman who visits so many of his lyrics and is here projected by the poet's imagination as "l'ombra fidata," "the trusty shadow":

> . . . Memoria
> non è peccato fin che giova. Dopo
> è letargo di talpe, abiezione
> che funghisce su sé . . .

> . . . Memory
> is no sin so long as it helps. Afterward
> it is a lethargy of moles, an abjection
> mildewing on itself . . .

Earthbound memory, then, is inertia and selfishness, something to be delivered from. It is subjected to entropy. The deliverance is pointed out by Clizia in her quest for "the form in which burned/ love of her Mover and not of herself," and this prospective "finding again" ("ritroverà") of the archetypal essence of heavenly love is another kind of memory: not the inertial memory of earthbound creatures, but the dynamic, emergent memory of their creative source, a Platonic anamnesis. It's entropy versus energy, respectively symbolized in the element of earth ("lethargy of moles") and that of fire ("the form in which burned. . ."). Here too, as in Dante's Purgatory, a tension is set up between memory and hope, hope being itself a higher memory. A kind of Lethe must be passed; Clizia is Virgil and Beatrice in one, for she embodies the spiritual force of transcendence in the midst of an opaque, terrene, inertial reality; as in Dante's vision, weight is equated with sin and weightlessness with purity.

But if the analogy with the Dantesque source is impressive, Montale is too much the modern spirit, beset by doubt and unbelief, to accept at face value even this demanding metaphysics which the poetical vision has conveyed to him, and so, unlike Dante, he shatters his own vision to reformulate it in the nihilist, Heideggerian terms presented by the conclusion:

> Così si svela prima di legarsi
> a immagini, a parole, oscuro senso
> reminescente, il vuoto inabitato
> che occupammo e che attende fin ch'è tempo
> di colmarsi di sé, di ritrovarci . . .

Thus is revealed before being tied up
to images and words, dark reminiscent sense,
the uninhabited void that we occupied
and that waits until it is time
to be filled with us, to find us again . . .

The ultimate reality looming behind "images" and "words" is an "uninhabited void," a nothingness waiting to re-engulf us. From it we came and
to it we shall return; it underlies our phenomenal existence; the poet mythi-
fies it as a transcendental womb endowed with "dark reminiscent sense,"
and thus postulates, beyond the different kinds of personal memory discussed before, an impersonal, cosmic, terrifying memory, a negative anamnesis.

Thus through the close analogy with Dante's style and Dante's Purgatorial situation (which extends to the details of the shades envisaged as
transparent and penetrable), this key poem tests the basic myths and the
basic doubts of Montale. By the same token, it configurates a precarious
metaphysics of memory and (since poetry is evocation) poetry. The pre-
cariousness of the whole searching vision finds a structural counterpart in
the changing posture of the persona. At first he addresses the dead father
("la tua tomba," "your tomb"); then he talks of him in the third person, to
let the dramatic exchange between father and Clizia do its objective work;
then, after their respective voices have been heard, broods on the meaning
of the self-evoked vision as a choral "we" that encompasses mankind in its
existential predicament. The modulations of the voice, from evocation to
brooding, are one and the same thing with the modulations of the vision.
And, throughout, the strength of Dantesque Purgatorial style counterbal-
ances the irrevocable crumbling of all things.

Indeed Montale can be considered a Dante without Dante's integrated
faith and without the ambition or power to write the encompassing epic of
salvation for his time. But this does not mean that the modern poet lacks a
Dantesque scope and depth of vision, with a corresponding strength of
style. Indeed, the demise of medieval cosmology and theology cannot pre-
vent Montale from cherishing his own myth. The harder his vision of barren reality, the more passionate his appeal to an unguaranteed source of

salvation personified as a woman: sunflower-like Clizia, the principle of love, wisdom, and creative power. In "Eastbourne" (from *Le Occasioni*) she is the cohesive force of Eros that keeps the world together, threatened by an impending victory of evil, and at the end of "L'orto" she takes shape as a prophet and creator.

All over, as we saw, she is the unworldly carrier of meaning in a hopeless world; tragic contrast arises from her incongruence to tangible, historical reality. She is the private residue of a once-shared myth, a personal faith of Manichaean type; we could say, taking our cue from the lines already discussed in "Voice Coming with the Moorhens," that the anachronistic hypostasis by which a disenchanted contemporary revives a medieval mystique is itself an example of the anamnestic process whereby Clizia is said to reapproximate the "form in which burned love of her Mover and not of herself." Poetry, for Montale, is the recovery, in new terms, of the unrationalizable vision long lost. Poetry is private, only because mass culture ignores its language. Poetry goes against the grain. Poetry is anamnesis. And just as the inspired few were often ostracized as heretics by the medieval organized church, the modern visionary is condemned to anachronism. He is not "of his time" and he can therefore best judge it.*

Montale does not always hypostatize his beloved in Gnostic terms. If in the Clizia poems the creative and redemptive force is only tangential to the world, because it is emphatically *not* of this world, the Eel of course embodies a different force, a triumph of the vital principle over the aridity of a desiccated reality, and the indomitable Fox of the sequel takes all the animal shapes to clinch this victory. The transcendent principle is usually incarnated in a migratory bird, to deny the world, while the immanent principle, which is also feminine, appears as a creature of land or water.

And yet, it is woman, throughout any apotheosis or animal embodiment; a person, rather than a disembodied force, though she is a center of magnetism. In this regard we may remember how intensely personal some of the

---

* A valuable additional clue to what I have come to call the Gnostic myth of Montale came from the poet himself when (1965) he recommended to me a book by the philosopher Piero Martinetti on *Gesù Cristo e il Cristianesimo* (Milan, 1964), which defends gnosis, Catharism, and other heresies as "the true Church."

feminine figures are in *Le Occasioni*, notably Dora Markus and Liuba. Liuba is caught, in a flash of piercing insight, as a defenseless creature of grace, surrounded by her womanly baubles — the hatbox, the cat — but it is these helpless things that become amulets of salvation in the "blind times" of horror. She is a Jewess fleeing Nazi persecution. The short poem's triumph is in the assurance of touch that converts the "occasional" detail into a biblical symbol of contemporary relevance — the lightness becomes apocalypse. Just as strongly individualized as Liuba is Dora, another Jewess, besieged not only by the dark times but by time itself, so that the singular destiny of her race comes to stand for human destiny as such — of those, that is, who refuse to "surrender voice, legend or destiny."

Poetical individualization, in these exemplary poems, is not a matter of descriptive portrayal: the essence of Liuba is grasped through her pathetic belongings; the essence of Dora through her feminine appurtenances (the lipstick, powder puff, and ivory mouse) and even more through her (outer and inner) gestures, an activity transcending any physiognomic description. In this connection it pays to recall how Dante gives a local habitation and a name to his Francescas and Pias and Piccardas, as well as to several of their male counterparts: not by describing their physique, but by making them talk or gesture. Even the bird similes so poignantly applied to the context of Francesca, the doomed lover, come to our mind when we read of Dora Markus, doomed by human perversity and by time, that her "restlessness makes [the poet] think/ of migratory birds crashing into a lighthouse/ in stormy evenings." Indeed (and this could be said of Francesca in a different register) Dora's "very sweetness is a storm."

Such a line ("è una tempesta anche la tua dolcezza") gives a cue to "La bufera" ("The Storm"), from which the later collection of 1956 takes its title. The more recent poem concentrates on a woman the gleam of lightning (her white forehead) and the black gloom of storm clouds (the "cloud" of her hair). Like a flash of lightning, that woman vanished "into darkness," whether death or home we do not know — and the ambiguity sounds intentional. Storm, apocalypse, black (or white) witchcraft of memory, transfiguration and passage (see "Il giglio rosso," "The Red Lily"), grief of the instant, ecstasy and pain of remembrance: from a thorough reading, there

emerges perhaps the best lyrical poet of the Italian twentieth century (with
the possible exception of Ungaretti), one belonging to the Western tradition which, with Proust, Joyce, Eliot, and Faulkner, has explored the para-
doxes of time, existence, finitude, and memory, outspokenly expressing the
impending disintegration of our civilization. History is thus experienced in
a deeper way:

> . . . ma una storia non dura che nella cenere
> e persistenza è solo l'estinzione.

> . . . but a history can only endure in ash
> and the only persistence is extinction.

That is what Montale says in "Piccolo Testamento," in keeping with his
vision of historical and cosmic entropy. And certainly we will not ask him
for the consolation of new gospels; it is enough that, in times of rhetoric
and confusion, he taught us to see with clarity the most disturbing realities.
Montale will never give us programs, only "occasions." Occasions of wonder, sorrow, and dream; unexpected colloquies with reality, lightnings of
revelation not to be reduced to a dogma; his limit is also his worth. What
else should we ask of a poet? Faith in our world, or rather in the possibility
of living in and improving it, is something we shall have to find in ourselves.
But it is well to keep in mind that Montale has been able to affect us so co-
gently as a modern voice because he has heeded the stylistic lesson of Dante,
and like him has pursued an uncompromising personal vision to the point
where it could possibly become a universal gnosis.*

* As my book was going to press, the first monograph in English on Eugenio Montale appeared in print, Arshi Pipa's *Montale and Dante* (Minneapolis, 1968). As the
title indicates, it has a special relevance to my subject.

Notes

NOTES

Introduction

1. Contini, "Un' interpretazione di Dante," *Paragone*, No. 188, October 1965, pp. 3–42.

Chapter I. Dante's *Convivio*: The Dialectic of Value

An earlier version of this chapter appeared in the Papers *of the Michigan Academy of Science, Arts, and Letters, XLVI (1961), 563–70.*

1. Domenico Vittorini, *High Points in the History of Italian Literature* (New York, 1958); G. A. Scartazzini, *Dantologia – Vita e Opere di Dante Alighieri* (Milan, 1894).

2. "Dico che pensai che da molti, di retro da me, forse sarei stato ripreso di levezza d'animo, udendo me essere dal primo amore mutato; per che, a torre via questa riprensione, nullo migliore argomento era che dire quale era quella donna che m'avea mutato." ("I say that I thought many people, behind my back, might have accused me of fickleness, once they heard that I had been changed from my first love; so that there was no better way to forestall such accusation than saying who the lady was that had so changed me.")

3. Karl Witte regarded the *Convivio* as evidence of Dante's temporary straying into heresy; see "Über Dante" (1831), reprinted in *Essays on Dante*, trans. and ed. C. Mabel Lawrence and Philip H. Wicksteed (London, 1898). In our century, Luigi Valli (*Il linguaggio segreto di Dante e dei "Fedeli d'Amore*," Rome, 1928) saw in the *Convivio* a confirmation of his bold esoteric reading of Dante's early verse as coded language meant for a heretical Albigensian sect. Valli claimed ancestry for his views in the unorthodox interpretations of Foscolo, Aroux, Rossetti, and Pascoli. See Werner Friederich, *Dante's Fame Abroad, 1350–1850* (Rome, 1950), and the bibliography in Bernard Stambler, *Dante's Other World* (New York, 1957). Even the very unbiased Karl Vossler (*Die philosophischen Grundlagen zum "suessen neuen Stils" des Guido*

Guinicelli, Guido Cavalcanti, und Dante Alighieri, Heidelberg, 1904), regarded the intellectualist leanings of the *Convivio* as proof of an Averroist influence. Finally, Denis de Rougemont (*Love in the Western World*, New York, 1940, 1955) accepts the "Albigensian" or Catharist theory with regard to troubadours and *Stilnovisti*, but makes Dante somehow overcome the religious schism; and others, like Stambler, Fergusson, and Singleton, consider it as a perfectly orthodox manifestation, consistent with the medieval *forma mentis*. Croce dismissed any esoteric allegory whatever in Dante.

4. *Conv.* iii, xi, 1: "Sì come l'ordine vuole ancora dal principio ritornando, dico che questa donna è quella donna de lo intelletto che Filosofia si chiama." ("Beginning from the start and principle once again, as order suggests, I say that this woman is that lady of the mind who is called Philosophy.")

5. See Benvenuto Terracini's sensitive observations in *Pagine e appunti di linguistica storica* (Florence, 1956), pp. 273–78.

6. See Vossler, *Die philosophischen Grundlagen.*

7. For instance, *Conv.* i, iii, 5: "Veramente io sono stato legno sanza vela e sanza governo, portato a diversi porti e foci e liti dal vento secco che vapora la dolorosa povertade" ("Truly I have been a boat with no sail or pilot, carried to different seaports and estuaries and shores by the dry wind rising from grievous poverty"); and again *Conv.* ii, i, 1: "Poi che proemialmente ragionando, me ministro, è lo mio pane ne lo precedente trattato con sufficienza preparato, lo tempo chiama e domanda la mia nave uscir di porto; per che, dirizzato l'artimone de la ragione a l'òra del mio desiderio, entro in pelago con isperanza di dolce cammino e di salutevole porto e laudabile ne la fine de la mia vena" ("Since by way of foreword, under my ministration my bread has been sufficiently prepared in the previous Treatise, it is high time that my ship should leave the harbor; therefore, having aimed the helm of reason toward the shore of my desire, I sail into the open sea with hope of smooth voyage and safe arrival at a goodly seaport at the end of my endeavor"); and the first tercet of *Purgatorio*: "Per correr migliori acque alza le vele/ omai la navicella del mio ingegno,/ che lascia dietro a sé mar sì crudele" ("To ply far better waters now sets sail/ the small ship of my genius,/ which leaves behind such a cruel sea"). It would be hard to deny the vital motivation of these images, or the counterpoint that they set up in the transition to and from the end of the first trattato of the *Convivio*.

8. Renucci, "Dantismo esoterico nel secolo presente," in *Atti del Congresso Internazionale di Studi Danteschi*, Vol. I (Florence, 1965).

9. Leo, Epilogue to *Vita Nuova, Das Neue Leben* (Hamburg, 1964); Contini, ed., *Le Rime di Dante* (Turin, 1939, 1946), and *Introduzione ai poeti del Duecento* (Milan, 1960); Singleton, *An Essay on the Vita Nuova* (Cambridge, Mass., 1958); Boyde, "Dante's Lyric Poetry," in U. Limentani, ed., *The Mind of Dante* (Cambridge, Eng., 1965).

Chapter II. Dante and the Drama of Language

This chapter, in slightly different form, appeared in S. B. Chandler and J. A. Molinaro, eds., The World of Dante *(University of Toronto Press, 1966).*

1. The contrast between Dante's epic ruggedness and Petrarch's lyrical smoothness, first acknowledged by Petrarch himself, is seldom overlooked by modern literary historians, but I hope I am not insisting on the obvious by pointing out how their differ-

ence in stylistic development implies a radically divergent philosophy of language. Dante's growth as a poet beyond the limited dreaminess of the *Vita Nuova* goes hand in hand with his growing vindication of the vernacular's literary worth as opposed to the Latin tradition to which Petrarch formally subscribed, to the point of writing most of his work in Latin (and that included the epic poem *Africa*) while looking with some condescension on his own vernacular lyrics. Petrarch's *Canzoniere* narrowed the boundaries of the Italian language in poetry by leading it to specialization; it was he who was the dominating influence on the whole European Renaissance to which Dante's steep peak remained inaccessible. Dante's effort was in the direction of linguistic experiment, variety, and inclusiveness, and he could absorb the folk poetry and language which Petrarch had to exclude from his formalizing style. It would seem, then, that of the two Dante was for centuries the far less imitable poet, contrary to T. S. Eliot's statement made in a changed context. It would also seem that the epic quality of Dante and the lyrical refinement of Petrarch cannot be dismissed as irrelevancies of genre classification when we try to define both artists in a common context. Furthermore, Dante's bold attitude in matters of language choice stands out as the forward-looking one especially when compared to Petrarch's coyness vis-à-vis the vernacular; one cannot help feeling that Petrarch, in this regard, had a regressive effect on Italian literature after Dante had done so much to advance the new linguistic cause.

2. For a telling assessment of these vicissitudes of Dante's poetry in the English-speaking world, see William De Sua's *Dante into English* (Chapel Hill, N.C., 1964). For valuable documentation to the same effect in a far broader geographic and historical context, see Friederich, *Dante's Fame Abroad*.

3. Marzot, *Il linguaggio biblico nella Divina Commedia* (Pisa, 1956). The value of this study lies in its treatment of the impact of biblical language on Dante as an inner affinity and not an external influence. Apart from this, its introductory chapter has some relevance to the *Comedy*'s stylistic pluralism.

4. Malagoli, *Linguaggio e poesia nella Divina Commedia* (Genoa, 1949); *Saggio sulla Divina Commedia* (Florence, 1962). Malagoli is sensitive to the range, variety, and tensions of Dante's style.

5. Spoerri, *Dante und die europäische Literatur – Das Bild des Menschen in der Struktur der Sprache* (Stuttgart, 1963). This is a memorable interpretation along existentialist lines; the emphasis it places on language can be sampled from the statement that Dante's poetical word is "Geschichtsbildend und Gemeinschaftsstiftend."

6. For an evaluation of the metaphoric function in the *Convivio*, see Benvenuto Terracini, "La forma interna del Convivio," in *Pagine e appunti di linguistica storica*; and Chapter I, above.

7. Nardi, *Dante e la cultura medievale* (Bari, 1949), pp. 217–47.

8. *Ibid.*, pp. 244–47.

9. Palgen, *Werden und Wesen der Komödie Dantes* (Graz, 1955). Palgen seems more preoccupied with refuting any possible relevance of Dante's vision to a humanism in gestation than with doing justice to the actual poetry and thought of the epic singer. His array of medieval sources is impressive, and he certainly brings out the extent to which Dante relied on a specifically medieval folkloristic tradition that had obliterated or seriously distorted its classical sources. But he makes it a matter of servile dependence and literal transposition, thereby disregarding those aspects in which Dante reshaped his sources for his own purposes.

10. Brandeis, *The Ladder of Vision* (Garden City, N. Y., 1960).

11. Dante, *The Inferno*, tr. John Ciardi (New York, 1954), p. 42. Though Ciardi's version sometimes distorts or cheapens Dante's text (as in the Ulysses episode), it often brings out relevant implications, as here.

12. T. S. Eliot, *Dante* (London, 1929); *Selected Essays* (New York, 1950).

13. Vossler, *Die göttliche Komödie. Entwickelungsgeschichte und Erklärung* (Heidelberg, 1907–10; 2d. ed., 1925; tr. W. C. Lawson, *Medieval Culture – An Introduction to Dante and his Times*, London and New York, 1929). The introductory chapter compares Dante and Goethe as outstanding examples of the *Naïver Dichter*, the artist of the native, spontaneous, and whole, as opposed to the *Sentimentalischer Dichter*, who is intellectually split by the effort to regain the lost source of native vision.

14. My idea of that chronological sequence follows Bruno Nardi's position rather than Bruno Migliorini's thesis as set forth in *Questioni e correnti di storia letteraria* (Milan, 1949), pp. 1–75, for I see the *De Vulg. El.* as subsequent to the *Convivio* and not simultaneous. This much I gather from internal evidence in *Conv.* i, v, 10: "Di questo si parlerà altrove più compiutamente in uno libello ch'io intendo di fare, Dio concedente, di Volgare Eloquenza" ("Of this, more will be said, in fuller scope, in a booklet I plan to write, with God's help, on Vernacular Eloquence"). And if we keep in mind the dialectical movement of Dante's linguistic thought from *Convivio* i to *De Vulg. El.*, we cannot escape the inference that the Latin treatise came after *Convivio* i, even if its composition may have overlapped that of the remaining chapters or trattati.

15. For reasons of artistic expediency, Dante, in the *Comedy*, often makes the devils talk, as in Malebolge, or in the case of Plutus, whose cryptic outburst, "Pape Satàn, aleppe," has busied ambitious commentators as much as Nimrod's has. Thus it cannot be said that in this regard the major poem always confirms the interesting myth of *De Vulg. El.* It remains true that Dante feels the articulate word is the essentially human endowment; and he feels this philosophically as well as poetically.

16. The multilingual situation was common to many a medieval writer, and we can find several instances of medieval polyglot poetry in the English area, as the *Oxford Book of English Verse* shows. German literature was also affected by linguistic pluralism in early medieval devotional writing (which included glossaries and translations of the interlinear kind) and in the early humanist phase. That was due to the existence of Church Latin (sometimes supplemented by Greek) as a ritual and scholarly language, and to the concomitant availability to the budding poet of more than one competing vernacular. In this connection, Italian Sordello's use of Provençal readily comes to mind, along with the fact that one poem of doubtful Dantean attribution (though certainly coming from his time and school), namely the canzone numbered v among the "Rime Dubbie" in *Le opere di Dante* (Società dantesca italiana, Florence, 1960), runs in a Franco-Latin-Italian trilingual pattern (one language to the line). One can also refer to the Franco-Italian contamination which resulted in the *cantores francigenarum* tradition. The testimonial of *De Vulg. El.*, along with Dante's poetic practice, shows that he did not feel Provençal (or even French) to be a really alien language, though he did not like to see it preferred to the Italian vernacular; and, while capable himself of writing beautiful verse in *langue d'oc*, he shrank from contamination. Teofilo Folengo's invention of Macaronic Latin would have puzzled him; his own experiment

with linguistic coinages (of the possibly contaminating kind) was restricted to the focally babelic utterances of Plutus and Nimrod, as examples of perverted language.
Dante's linguistic axis is the Italian vernacular, but he is conscious of functioning in a
multilingual context, and his discriminating amity to Provençal and Latin may remind
us of the "multi-dialect" approach which led classical Greek writers to stabilize Doric
as the language of the tragic chorus, Ionic as the language of tragedy and epic, and At-
tic as the language of prose. Dante's use of frequent Latin inserts from Church ritual in
the *Divine Comedy* certainly adds to the epic's linguistic dimensions, though these dimensions avoid the confusion of hybridism because they function separately within
the main framework as perspectival devices. For a provocatively succinct treatment of
medieval complexities of language and their modern counterparts, see Gianfranco Contini's preface to C. E. Gadda's *La cognizione del dolore* (Milan, 1962), and also references in S. Avalle d'Arco, "Lingua, stile e scrittura," in *Questo e altro*, Vol. VIII (Milan, 1964).

17. My point is that linguistic pluralism was one of the cultural experiences Dante
used to dramatic advantage in his poem, and it could become babelic in its infernal
aspect, polyphonic instead in its purgatorial or paradisal one. Structurally, that is a
conversion of the unrelated to the harmonized multiplicity, of history as Fall to history
as Redemption. I speak of polyphony because I think of the individuality each poetical
voice (and each soul) retains in the ascending chorus. And I would like to add that
the polyglot trait of medieval writing constitutes a generally overlooked precedent for
Dante-inspired moderns like Ezra Pound, T. S. Eliot, and James Joyce. In *De Vulg. El.*
II, vii, Dante approaches a purist position in matters of word choice for the lofty
("tragic") style in poetry; he eliminates "childish" (*puerilia*), "womanish" (*muliebria*),
and "virile, but uncouth" (*virilia . . . silvestria*) vocables, and concentrates on two varieties of "virile-urban" words, the "smooth-combed" (*pexa*) and the "tough" or
"rugged" (*irsuta*), which qualify as "grandiose" (*grandiosa*), to the exclusion of the
"slippery" and "coarse" ones (*lubrica et reburra*). The "tragic" poets in the vernacular
must use only *vocabula nobilissima*; examples of the rejected word types are, among
others, *mamma e babbo, placevole, greggia, cetra, femina, corpo*. This flies in the face
of stylistic procedure in all of the *Inferno* and noteworthy parts of the other two canticles, whose lexical range is far broader than the precepts of the *De Vulg. El.* would
allow. Once again, we notice a dialectical movement, rather than a smooth progression,
in his thought and practice; for here the *Comedy* inverts a basic point of the previous
book by incorporating in its style the harsh, the horrid, and the disgusting, as a phase
of language to be purged within the actual progress of the poem, and not to be left out
a priori. Concessions to the requirements of mimetic style are limited in *De Vulg. El.*
to admitting *vocabula irsuta* (blunt monosyllables and heavy polysyllables) in the en-
nobling company of the preferably trisyllabic, melodious *pexa*; likewise, *rime aspre*
(*rithimorum asperitas*), harsh rhymes, are to be avoided unless in proper combination
with the sweet ones (*rithimi lenes*) or *rime dolci*, for "lenium asperorumque rithimorum mixtura ipsa tragedia nitescit." It is also remarkable that *tragedia* denotes the
lofty style in *De Vulg. El.*, while *Commedia* is the title Dante chose for his epic poem,
which moves from the "low" to the "lofty."

18. For a recent and valuable article on this subject, see J. Cremona, "Dante's Views
on Language," in U. Limentani, ed., *The Mind of Dante*.

Chapter III. Francesca and the Tactics of Language

This chapter, in slightly different form, appeared in Modern Language Quarterly, *Vol. 22, No. 1 (March 1961).*

1. I have omitted passage reference numbers when quoting further from the canto of Francesca.

2. Other versions of the text make the verb intransitive, "si tace"; but Vandelli's critical edition affords a subtler range of overtones. If we take "ci" as a dative form, it means that "the wind is silent for us," but not in itself; the lull in the storm does not involve other spirits, only Paolo and his lady. But the attractiveness of stress is such that the verb may acquire a stronger meaning and function, with a bold twist of syntax; and then the "ci" becomes a direct object of it, in a transitive nexus which brings out the animistic action of the wind as an agent. "Tacere" in Italian can be transitive, and then it means "to omit any mention of." This would not be the emergent meaning in the context at hand, where "ci tace" might be adequately interpreted, transitively, as "by being silent leaves us alone." While obviously including the intransitive reading as above given, the transitive interpretation of "ci tace" may be expanded to extreme poignancy if we keep in mind the whole tercet where it occurs: "of whatever you like to talk and hear, we will talk and hear you talk while the wind, as it is doing now, keeps silent for us and thus leaves us alone." Clearly the word "tacere" ("to be silent") is here contrasted only indirectly with the previous roar of the gale, and directly instead with the actual and intended conversation of the focused foursome. When the wind of unchecked passion subsides, speech can arise in its higher form and clarity, as it does here; the word of poetry takes shape above, and from, the silence of passion. At the same time, the wind's roar is a ghastly distortion of sound, and even more of human discourse which is articulate sound; but in a metaphor based on ironic antithesis, it can be called a kind of talk. Here, for instance, the talk of human beings briefly supersedes the "talk" of the wind, and this emphasizes the difference along with the elemental affinity. Now that the wind keeps silent, we can do our talking; obviously, he (the wind) has done all the talking so far, and it was a language which did not admit of dialogue (listening and discoursing), but was in fact a ceaseless, senseless monologue, "full of sound and fury, signifying nothing," which engulfed Paolo and Francesca. The minute they step out of it to approach the two compassionate visitors, therefore, Paolo and Francesca cease to be part of that frantic "talk" (really a howl) and reemerge into human individualization. It could be said that the mere fact of being able to speak with Dante is for them a temporary resurrection; it is certainly a return from the world of meaninglessness and chaos to the world of discourse and meaning. If so, the intense verb "ci tace" gains a further dimension, closely related, as will be seen, to the total meaning of the episode: "the [inarticulate] talk of the wind omits us, leaves us out [of its frenzy]." This semantic dimension suggests itself even if we follow a majority of the commentators in reading "ci" adverbially as the equivalent of "here": "while the wind . . . is silent here."

3. See *De Sanctis on Dante,* ed. and trans. Joseph Rossi and Alfred Galpin (Madison, Wis., 1957), pp. 33–52; Francesco de Sanctis, *Lezioni sulla Divina Commedia,* ed. Michele Manfredi (Bari, 1955), pp. 137–47 and *passim.* These essays, which represent lecture drafts or notes from his Dante courses as given first in Turin and then in Zurich from 1854 to 1857, contain valuable elements for our understanding of De Sanctis and Dante, and are actually the headwaters of his 1866 *Saggi critici,* including the one on

Francesca da Rimini in its final form. See also his *Storia della letteratura italiana* (1870–71). As for Benedetto Croce, I refer here to his *La poesia di Dante* (Bari, 1921). Finally, Maud Bodkin, in *Archetypal Patterns in Poetry* (New York, 1934, 1958), concurs with De Sanctis' vindication of earthly love in connection with Francesca. See especially Chapter IV, "The Image of Woman."

4. As everybody remembers, Dante is lost in a dark wood at the outset, and shortly after (*Inf.* ii, 141) describes his decision to follow Virgil's guide through the wilderness of Hell as an entering "per lo cammino alto e silvestro." He can be said to find himself in a situation of poetically literal and allegorically moral "bewilderment."

5. Erich Auerbach, *Mimesis* (Bern, 1946; New York, 1957), particularly the chapter on Farinata. Among Leo Spitzer's well-known studies in Romance literatures, particularly relevant is his "Il Canto xiii dell'Inferno," *Lettura di Leo Spitzer*, in Giovanni Getto, ed., *Letture dantesche* (Florence, 1964).

6. It will be noticed that Dante here makes Love a fatal power, and his line anticipates (grammatically and semantically) Francesca's first speech.

7. Erich von Richthofen, *Veltro und Diana* (Tübingen, 1956).

8. Singleton, *An Essay on the Vita Nuova*. See also his later *Dante Studies* volumes; the second of these discusses the allegorical structure of the *Inferno*, and the third, published in 1958 by Harvard University Press with the title *Journey to Beatrice*, dwells on the same aspect of the *Purgatorio*. Apart from this, I find of particular interest his explication of the first two cantos of the *Inferno*, published in the Dante issue of *Kenyon Review* (Vol. xiv, Spring 1952), along with remarkable contributions by T. S. Eliot, Allen Tate, Francis Fergusson, R. P. Blackmur, Erich Auerbach, and Robert Fitzgerald.

9. Valency, *In Praise of Love* (New York, 1959).

10. De Rougemont, *Love in the Western World* (New York, 1940, 1958).

11. A problem of interpretation is involved in Francesca's expression "la prima radice/ del nostro amor." Dante had asked her to tell him the manner and occasion of secret love's mutual revelation between herself and Paolo, but she declares herself ready to let him know the "first root" of their love. Actually, she has already told him in her first speech how "Love . . . possessed this man for the beautiful body" because he had a "gentle heart"; now, her confidential words will describe the manifestation of that love, its rise ("radice") as an acknowledged and consciously shared rapport in the heart and (as we believe) in the flesh. For, despite Dante's awareness of a spurious literary element in Francesca's sin, it would be naïve to interpret her words literally and imply that the reading of *Lancelot du Lac* marked, of itself, the beginning of love in the two siblings-in-law. The irony of their situation is included in the tragedy and does not obliterate it; passion, not only literature, plays a fundamental role in it, as Dante very well knew, for it was common knowledge that Paolo had been employed by his wily brother Gianciotto to woo Francesca for him. Thus Paolo's fiction became reality (in a fatal way), and the other fiction, the story of Lancelot and Guinevere, could act so powerfully on the two unhappy lovers only because of the initial situation — the parallelism is multiple. Still, "prima radice" is a strong expression and does reverberate on the part played by literature as a seducer. It also contains, however, elements of nontemporal quality, as if Francesca in her reply expanded Dante's words to imply a curiosity about more than the extrinsic occasion of love's reciprocal unveiling; about, in fact, the very nature and essence of that love as borne out by its sudden outburst in the given circumstances. She understands Dante's interest is pas-

sionate and far from shallow; he has *affetto*, and he wants to get at the root of things. To reward his tact and concern, she gives him the intimate confession after the initial epitaph, which though beautifully poetical is a bit more official than what follows. In view of this, I would not overplay the "parody" aspect of this episode, as Poggioli does in his remarkable analysis; it would be just as much an oversimplification as the romantic reading that ignores it.

12. It is interesting to observe that even the best modern translators (Binyon, Ciardi) are either unaware of this "muovere-menare" dichotomy or are unable to render in English its subtle gradations.

Chapter IV. Dante's Noble Sinners: Abstract Examples or Living Characters?

This chapter, in slightly different form, appeared in G. L. Rizzo and William De Sua, eds., Dante Symposium *(University of North Carolina Press, 1965).*

1. Montano, *Storia della poesia di Dante*, 2 vols. (Naples, 1962), *passim.*
2. Spoerri, *Dante und die europäische Literatur.*
3. For a recent vindication of Farinata's tragic stature, not unmindful of De Sanctis' nineteenth-century essay, see Kalikst Morawski, "The Tragic Aspect of the Farinata Episode in the *Inferno*," *Books Abroad*, May 1965 (Dante issue), pp. 58–68.
4. Brandeis, *The Ladder of Vision*, pp. 41–52.
5. G. A. Borgese, "The Wrath of Dante," in Mark Musa, ed., *Essays on Dante* (Bloomington, Ind., 1964), pp. 94–109.
6. In this connection, see the brilliant alternative reading of this episode that Irma Brandeis gives in her essay "Glimpses of the Master's Hand: Dante's Ulysses" (*Cesare Barbieri Courier*, Special Issue, 1965). Miss Brandeis sees an element of deception in Ulysses' famous speech to his shipmates, but she senses the Faustian greatness of the Dantesque figure.
7. Nist, "The Impurities in Dante's *Commedia*," *Books Abroad*, May 1965, pp. 49–57.
8. Ciardi, trans. *The Inferno*, p. 224. I also take exception to Ciardi's rendering of "virtute e conoscenza" as "manhood and recognition," which distorts Dante pitifully. This proves how a gifted translator of poetry can succumb to narrow-mindedness.

Chapter V. Patterns of Movement in the *Divine Comedy*

This chapter, in slightly different form, appeared in Italica, XL, No. 2, 1963.

1. Paul R. Olson's "Theme and Structure in the Exordium of the *Paradiso* (*Italica*, XXXIX, No. 2, 89–104), which appeared after my own essay had been completed, exhibits certain analogies in method.

Chapter VI. *Purgatorio*, Canto v: The Modulations of Solicitude

This chapter, in slightly different form, appeared in Books Abroad, May 1965 (Dante issue).

Chapter VII. Dante's Presence in American Literature

This chapter, in slightly different form, appeared in Dante Studies, LXXXIV (1966).

1. As William De Sua shows in his perceptive book, *Dante into English, 1750–1950*

(Chapel Hill, N.C., 1964), Henry Cary's English translation of the *Divine Comedy* was the standard one for generations of Romantic and Victorian readers on both sides of the ocean, but American translators soon arose to compete with him, and not a few American men of letters read Dante in Italian. Lorenzo da Ponte's teaching at Columbia, and Longfellow's at Harvard, fostered this trend. See also Friederich, *Dante's Fame Abroad.*

2. J. Chesley Mathews, "The Interest in Dante Shown by Nineteenth-Century American Men of Letters," in *Dante Alighieri — Three Lectures* (Washington, D.C., 1965), pp. 1–22.

3. Angelina La Piana, *Dante's American Pilgrimage* (New Haven, Conn., 1948).

4. One such reference is in poem No. 371, in *The Poems of Emily Dickinson*, ed. Thomas H. Johnson (Cambridge, Mass., 1955), dealing with antique books:

> A precious — mouldering pleasure — 'tis
> . . . .
> When Sappho — was a living girl —
> And Beatrice wore
> The Gown that Dante — deified — (st. 5).

The other reference is to Dante's great love, in Letter No. 393 (Summer 1873) to Susan Gilbert Dickinson, where Dante is mentioned in this respect along with Swift and Mirabeau (*The Letters of Emily Dickinson*, ed. Thomas H. Johnson, Cambridge, Mass., 1958). No direct reference, except for a mention of Dante's portrait as published by a local newspaper, is to be found in Jay Leyda, *The Years and Hours of Emily Dickinson* (New Haven, Conn., 1960).

5. See *De Sanctis on Dante*, ed. and tr. Rossi and Galpin, as well as De Sanctis' *Saggi critici* and *Storia della letteratura italiana.*

6. See Chapter IX, below, and Toni Comello, "Dante e Montale," *Dimensioni*, Nos. 5–6 (Sept.–Oct. 1961), pp. 13–19.

7. For the Shakespearian aspect of mid-nineteenth-century American classics, see F. O. Matthiessen, *American Renaissance* (New York, 1941).

8. See Melville's poem, "Greek Architecture."

9. For a balanced assessment of Pound's literary career and poetical achievement, with useful bio-bibliographical data, see G. S. Fraser, *Ezra Pound* (New York, 1960), and Donald Davie, *Ezra Pound, Poet and Sculptor* (New York, 1964).

10. For the debate between Pound and Harriet Monroe *re* Eliot, see *The Letters of Ezra Pound, 1907–1941*, ed. D. D. Paige (New York, 1950).

11. See Frederick W. Locke, "Dante and T. S. Eliot's *Prufrock*," *Modern Language Notes*, LXXVIII (Jan. 1963), 51–59.

12. The Italian lines from Dante are slightly altered in the long-current Faber and Faber edition of Eliot's collected poems: ". . . la quantitate/ *Puote veder* de l'amor . . ." perhaps to fit a personal situation, since the 1917 volume, *Prufrock and Other Observations*, is dedicated to the memory of a French friend of Eliot's who died in battle at the Dardanelles.

13. Eliot's attraction to modern French poetry went as far as his writing French verse himself (see the *Collected Poems, 1909–1935*), but, as he said in an interview with Donald Hall, this was a temporary phase, and Eliot did not feel he could become a French symbolist poet like the earlier American expatriates, Stuart Merrill and Francis Vielé-Griffin.

14. See his translations from Arnaut Daniel, Guido Cavalcanti, and many other poets in Ezra Pound, *Translations*, ed. Hugh Kenner (Norfolk, Conn., [1954], 1963). Another source for understanding Pound's literary predilections in world poetry is *Confucius to Cummings: An Anthology of Poetry*, ed. Ezra Pound and Marcella Spann (New York, 1964).

15. The literary essays he published in 1918, 1920, 1931, and 1934 under titles like *Pavannes and Divisions, Instigations, ABC of Reading*, and *Make It New*, are well sampled in *Literary Essays of Ezra Pound*, ed. T. S. Eliot (London, 1954).

16. See the volume, *Translations*, cited in note 14 above.

17. Pound told Donald Hall that he had been working at the *Cantos* since 1904. The first three *Cantos*, however, were published in 1919, in the volume *Quia pauper amavi* (London), and they represented only very rough drafts for the later version. Then in 1921 the volume *Poems, 1918–1921* (New York) included four drafts of early *Cantos*. See also *The Cantos of Ezra Pound* (New York, 1949), containing all the prewar *Cantos* plus the *Pisan Cantos* (LXXIV–LXXXIII); *Section: Rock-Drill: 85–95 de los cantares* (Milan, 1956), and *Thrones: 96–109 de los cantares* (London, 1960).

18. Originally published by the *Paris Review* and then reprinted in *Writers at Work*, Second Series, ed. Van Wyck Brooks (New York, 1965), pp. 37–59.

19. Thomas Clark, "The Formal Structure of Pound's *Cantos*," in *East-West Review* (Kyoto, Japan), I, No. 2 (Autumn 1964), 97–144.

20. From the quoted interview with Donald Hall, now in *Writers at Work*, Second Series, *passim*.

21. *Canto* LXXXI, *passim*.

22. *Canto* LXXVI.

23. Hugh Kenner, *The Poetry of Ezra Pound* (Norfolk, Conn., 1951).

24. I heard the interview as tape-recorded in 1958; it is now reprinted in *Writers at Work*, Second Series, pp. 91–110.

25. The same Bradleyan theme suggested to the poet by the Ugolino episode was to be later descried in the first of the quotations from Herakleitos that he prefixed to the *Four Quartets*; for the "idìan phrònesin" therein lamented is the choice of idiosyncrasy over communication.

26. The last three items may be found in T. S. Eliot, *On Poetry and Poets* (New York, 1957). Useful selections and excerpts from much of his earlier criticism are included in *T. S. Eliot, Selected Prose* (London and Baltimore, Penguin Books, [1953], 1955).

27. *Four Quartets* (London, 1944, 1955), pp. 38–40. In his contribution to the volume *Letterature Comparate* (Milan, 1948), Mario Praz observed that this section of *Little Gidding* is the most felicitous adaptation of Dante's meter to English verse, and as early as 1942, in his book *Machiavelli in Inghilterra e altri saggi* (Rome), he had commented on Eliot's indebtedness to Dante. That chapter, "T. S. Eliot e Dante," is now available in English translation in Praz's *The Flaming Heart* (Garden City, N.Y., 1958). See also Praz's "Dante in Inghilterra (e in America)," in *Maestro Dante*, ed. V. Vettori (Milan, 1962), pp. 63–94, now translated in *Forum for Modern Language Studies*, I, No. 2 (April 1965), 99–116. Praz has been the first to emphasize the connection in question. I myself briefly treated some aspects of the present theme in my article, "Dante nella letteratura americana," in *Il Veltro*, IV, No. 1–2 (Jan.–Feb. 1960), 37–43.

28. *The Letters of Hart Crane, 1916–1932*, ed. Brom Weber (New York, 1952; Berke-

ley, Calif., 1965); *The Complete Poems of Hart Crane*, ed. Waldo Frank (Garden City, N.Y., 1958).

29. In my *The Inclusive Flame: Studies in American Poetry* (Bloomington, Ind., 1963, 1965).

30. See Tate's essay on "The Symbolic Imagination: A Meditation on Dante's Mirrors," in the Dante issue of *Kenyon Review*, XIV (Spring 1952), 256–77.

31. Robert Duncan, *The Sweetness and Greatness of Dante's Divine Comedy, 1265–1965* (San Francisco, 1965).

Chapter VIII. Vico and Dante

This chapter, in slightly different form, appeared in Giambattista Vico: An International Symposium, *edited by Giorgio Tagliacozzo, co-editor Hayden V. White (Johns Hopkins Press, 1969).*

1. As Fausto Nicolini shows in a note on p. 953 of his edition of *Giambattista Vico, opere* (Milan and Naples, 1953), references to Dante are scattered throughout Vico's writings, from the *Fourth Academic Oration*, dating from 1703, down to the third edition of *The New Science*. Of particular importance are the references contained in the *Autobiography* (1728–29) and in the three editions of *The New Science* (1725, 1730, 1744). Two sustained statements on Dante having the importance of independent essays are the Letter to Gherardo degli Angioli of December 26, 1725, and the review-article called "Discoverta del vero Dante" ("Discovery of the True Dante") written between 1728 and 1730. The latter essay has been translated by Irma Brandeis in *Discussions of the Divine Comedy* (Boston, 1961), pp. 11–12.

2. Though Foscolo's greatest achievement is his poetry, his vigorous criticism merits consideration as a fruitful contribution, especially to Dante studies, in the early-nineteenth-century context of Italian and English culture. René Wellek throws generous light on Foscolo as critic (*A History of Modern Criticism, 1750–1950*, Vol. II, New Haven, Conn., 1955), but fails to mention the connection with Vico's thought. Foscolo's "Parallel between Dante and Petrarch" (*Essays on Petrarch*, London, 1823; reprinted in Brandeis, *Discussions of the Divine Comedy*), in part develops Vico's ideas, as the following excerpt shows: "Dante, like all primitive poets, is the historian of the manners of his age, the prophet of his country, and the painter of mankind . . ." Vichian ideas, colored by his own sense of personal self-assertion and patriotic engagement, likewise inform his academic address of 1809 at Pavia University, "On the Origins and Function of Literature." Even more strikingly, *The New Science*'s epic sense of human history suffuses Foscolo's best known poem, *Of Sepulchers* (1807): "Since nuptial ceremonies, tribunals and altars/ Managed to civilize the human beasts . . ." With classical polish, the Vichian epic of civilization also makes itself heard in Foscolo's last verse composition, *The Graces*. Dante and Vico were both supreme exemplars of moral and intellectual achievement to Foscolo, whose poetic persona, in the *Sepulchers*, carries strong connotations of a Dante-like exile, and rightly so, because Foscolo did prefer exile to political compromise.

De Sanctis' memorable studies on Dante appeared in 1866 in a collection of critical essays and in 1870 with the publication of his *History of Italian Literature*. They are available in Rossi and Galpin, eds. *De Sanctis on Dante*. Though his philosophical approach, based on Hegel, differs from Foscolo's, De Sanctis resembled his older compatriot in many respects. Like him he was politically engaged on the liberal side and suffered exile, and like him he joined a love for Dante with a love for Vico, whose thought has always appealed to Italian Hegelians. De Sanctis' stature as a critic has been vindicated by René Wellek in his *History of Modern Criticism*, Vol. IV (1965). Useful outlines of Vico's fortune as a thinker are to be found in the preface to Max Harold Fisch and Thomas Bergin, trans., *Autobiography of Giambattista Vico* (Ithaca, N.Y., 1944; paperback ed. 1963), and in Nicolini's introduction to *Giambattista Vico, opere*.

3. Werner, *Giambattista Vico als Philosoph und gelehrter Forscher* (Vienna, 1879), pp. 301–2. Translation mine.

4. Spoerri, *Dante und die europäische Literatur* (Stuttgart, 1963).

5. Fubini, *Stile e umanità di Giambattista Vico* (Bari, 1946), pp. 173–205. See also pp. 97–158 for a discussion of Vico's language.

6. Benedetto Croce, *La filosofia di Giambattista Vico* (Bari, 1911); tr. R. G. Collingwood, *The Philosophy of Giambattista Vico* (London, 1913).

7. Brandeis, *Discussions of the Divine Comedy*, pp. 11–12.

8. This poem is to be found on pp. 352–55 of Vico's *L'Autobiografia, il carteggio e le poesie varie*, ed. Croce and Nicolini (Bari, 1929).

9. Brandeis, *Discussions of the Divine Comedy*, p. 12.

10. With the exception of Alfieri, these writers were all variously affected by Vico. While Foscolo and Leopardi responded to Vico's ideas on myth and history in a starkly irreligious way, Manzoni was drawn as a liberal Catholic to Vico's conception of Providence, which operates, with certain modifications, in the world of *The Betrothed* and of the tragedy *Adelchi*.

11. Croce and Nicolini, eds., *L'Autobiografia*, pp. 154–56.

12. See Nicolini, ed., *Vico, opere*, p. 367: "The somber pessimism of this poem is perhaps to be related to the religious weaknesses and errors that worried Vico's youth, and also to his poor health . . ." The poem was written in 1692 and published in 1693, and, while it harks back to Petrarch, it has a strength of its own, surprisingly anticipating Leopardi. Toward the end, it envisages the Vatolla groves as a Dantesque harsh wood. The despondent mood reappears in much of Vico's verse, but the sonnet to Filippo Pirelli counteracts it with the prophecy of glory to come, after death, to the thinker who was led by Providence to discover the purposive order of human history and thereby to overcome his own misery. (Croce and Nicolini, eds., *L'Autobiografia*, p. 363; Nicolini, ed., *Opere*, p. 164.)

13. See their introduction to *Autobiography of Vico*.

14. For Vico's connections with this school, as well as with other contemporary and earlier philosophical sects, see Nicola Badaloni, *Introduzione a G. B. Vico* (Milan, 1961), a work which, however, limits the scope of Vico's originality and makes him sound more time-bound than he actually was.

15. Fisch and Bergin, eds., *Autobiography*, pp. 132, 134. To these statements add the remarks in the concluding paragraph of the book, where Vico says that many fellow citizens shunned or mocked him as a lunatic and that he took advantage of these aggravations to withdraw to his desk, where, as in a "high, unbreachable fortress," he meditated further works, thus eventually achieving his masterpiece.

16. Fergusson, *The Idea of a Theater* (Princeton, N.J., 1949), *Dante's Drama of the Mind* (Princeton, 1953), *Dante* (New York, 1966).

17. From Hölderlin's "Patmos," lines 3–4.

18. See Chapter II, above.

19. Fisch and Bergin, eds., *Autobiography*, pp. 133–34.

20. *The New Science of Giambattista Vico*, tr. Thomas Bergin and Max Harold Fisch (Ithaca, N.Y., 1948, 1961), Section VII, par. 688, Conclusion, par. 1099. In the unabridged edition of 1948 see par. 369 of Book II, "On Poetic Wisdom," where the unattended children of fallen mankind roaming the worldwide forest after the Flood are left to their own devices and roll in their excrement, which is supposed to bring about an abnormal growth of the body, thus making them giants. This is one of the strongest passages, stylistically speaking. On a different level, take par. 1108 from the conclusion of the work for a masterly treatment of the idea of historical Providence as mankind's propelling mind working against and beyond each particular purpose of human action to bring about courses and recourses of civilization. Cogency of thought is here allied to poetical strength of style, with a concision worthy of Dante.

21. Bergin and Fisch, eds., *New Science*, Book II, par. 457, p. 111.

22. I like to stress the problematic versus the systematic aspect of Vico's thought, because it brings him closer to our own difficult age. But already Leopardi's dilemma of fiction and truth could be said to resume certain emphases of Vico's. In any case, Vico's revaluation of Dante was a prophecy of Romanticism, and both writers were to share a revival in Romantic times.

Chapter IX. Eugenio Montale's Dantesque Style

An earlier version of this chapter was published in the Milan magazine Aut Aut *(No. 35, 1956) and in* La lotta con Proteo *(Milan, 1963). The English translation first appeared in* Sewanee Review, *LXVI (Winter 1958), 1–32.*

1. In *T. S. Eliot, a Symposium*, ed. R. March and M. J. Tambimuttu (London, 1948; Chicago, 1949). More recently, Sergio Pannella examined the affinities between Montale and Eliot under a different aspect (*Galleria*, December 1954).

2. Since the original writing of this essay, Montale has fully acknowledged his interest in Dante; see his revelatory contribution to *Atti del Convegno Dantesco*, Vol. II (Florence, 1966).

3. This "Motet," which I have discussed in "Montale's 'Motets,' the Occasions of Epiphany," *PMLA*, LXXXII (December 1967), 471–84, starts with an obvious echo of the Dantesque lizard that "under the great flail/ of dog days' heat, moving from hedge to hedge,/ flits lightning-like across the path," to end on a note from Shakespeare's *The Tempest*.

4. It is, however, interesting to note that Montale translated a poem by Emily Dickinson (see his *Quaderno di traduzioni*, Milan, 1948), as well as Melville's *Billy Budd* (Milan, 1942). Montale's own preface to the latter translation was eventually published in *Sewanee Review*, LXVIII (Summer 1960), 419–22.

5. Detailed studies of this complex poem have appeared since the original publication of the present essay; see especially Silvio Avalle d'Arco, *Gli orecchini di Montale* (Milan, 1966), and Oreste Macrì's essay in *Realtà del simbolo* (Florence, 1968; first published in *Letteratura*, 1966, Montale issue). See also Silvio Ramat, *Montale* (Florence, 1965).

6. See Williamson's articles on contemporary Italian poetry in *Poetry* (Chicago), December 1951 and January 1952. But since 1966 Macrì's study of this poem (now available in *Realtà del simbolo*) has become indispensable; it shows how some of the ambiguities are expressively functional and others only apparent.

7. Originally published in *Rassegna d'Italia* (January 1946) and reprinted in G. Spagnoletti, ed. *Poesia italiana contemporanea* (Parma, 1949, 1959).

Index

INDEX

Adam, 29, 31, 32, 40, 61

Ahab, Captain, 77, 120–22

Alfieri, Vittorio, 152

Allegory: used in *Conv.*, 9–11, 16, 35–36, 184; problem of, in Dante's lyrics and prose, 16, 36; Geryon as figure of, 81; in Hawthorne and Melville, 124; of poets and of theologians, 132; of civilization in *Comedy*, 156; dismissed by Croce, 196n3

Anachronism: of Dante's philosophy, 4–6; as hypostasis in Montale's poetry, 184, 190

Anamnesis, Platonic, in Montale's poetry, 188, 189, 190

Anceschi, Luciano, 164

Angioli, Gherardo degli, 148–49, 152, 153

Apocalyptic attitude: in Dante, 1, 6, 7, 24; in Pound, 133; in Montale, 162, 163, 177, 182, 183, 191, 192

Aquinas, Saint Thomas, 12, 59

Archetypal imagery: in *Comedy*, 4; in *Conv.*, 15, 25–26, 29; of parenthood and childhood in *Comedy*, 31; of City and Forest, 33–34, 124–25, 157; of whirlwind, 51; of Love as fatal power, 57–58; of birds as instinct-driven, 64; of sea as peace, 65; of whirlwind and whirlpool in Dante and Melville, 77, 122; of flight, 86–87; of navigation and submersion, 87–88; of winged and marine-reptilian creatures in counterpoint, 88–89, 90; of arrows and lightning, 90, 100, 101, 104; of winged boats, in Dante and modern writers, 96–97, 140, 185; of light, 97–99, 102, 111; of darkness and light in Hawthorne, 124; as "imaginative universal" in Vico's conception, 147; of Dark Wood in Dante and Vico, 147, 156; of Wood of Suicides in Montale, 167–68; of abyss monsters, 172; of Karma-like wheel in Montale, 176; of winged or birdlike woman, 178, 180, 182, 183; of woman as Christ-bearer, 184; of eel as vital force, 180–81; of migratory birds and storm in Montale and Dante, 191. *See also* Myth

Aristotle, 13, 53, 59, 61, 155

Auerbach, Berthold, 2, 54, 70

Babel, Tower of, 34, 39, 40, 157

Bacon, Sir Francis, 155

Badaloni, Nicola, 206n14

Baudelaire, Charles Pierre, 128

Bergin, Thomas, 153

Bernard, Saint, 59, 61

Binyon, Laurence, 135, 202n12

Bodkin, Maud, 53